Human Memory

McGraw-Hill Series in Psychology

Consulting Editors: Norman Garmezy, Harry F. Harlow, Lyle V. Jones, and Harold W. Stevenson

ADAMS, Human Memory

BEACH, HEBB, MORGAN, AND NISSEN, The Neuropsychology of Lashley

VON BÉKÉSY, Experiments in Hearing

BERKOWITZ, Aggression: A Social Psychological Analysis

BERLYNE, Conflict, Arousal, and Curiosity

BLUM, Psychoanalytic Theories of Personality

BROWN, The Motivation of Behavior

BROWN AND GHISELLI, Scientific Method in Psychology

BUCKNER AND MCGRATH, Vigilance: A Symposium

COFER, Verbal Learning and Verbal Behavior

COFER AND MUSGRAVE, Verbal Behavior and Learning: Problems and Processes

CRAFTS, SCHNEIRLA, ROBINSON, AND GILBERT, Recent Experiments in Psychology

DAVITZ, The Communication of Emotional Meaning

DEESE AND HULSE, The Psychology of Learning

DOLLARD AND MILLER, Personality and Psychotherapy

ELLIS, Handbook of Mental Deficiency

EPSTEIN, Varieties of Perceptual Learning

FERGUSON, Statistical Analysis in Psychology and Education

FORGUS, Perception: The Basic Process in Cognitive Development

GHISELLI, Theory of Psychological Measurement

GHISELLI AND BROWN, Personnel and Industrial Psychology

GILMER, Industrial Psychology

GRAY, Psychology Applied to Human Affairs

GUILFORD, Fundamental Statistics in Psychology and Education

GUILFORD, The Nature of Human Intelligence

GUILFORD, Personality

GUILFORD, Psychometric Methods

GUION, Personnel Testing

HAIRE, Psychology in Management

HIRSCH, Behavior-genetic Analysis

HIRSH, The Measurement of Hearing

HURLOCK, Adolescent Development

HURLOCK, Child Development

HURLOCK, Developmental Psychology

JACKSON AND MESSICK, Problems in Human Assessment

KARN AND GILMER, Readings in Industrial and Business Psychology

KRECH, CRUTCHFIELD, AND BALLACHEY, Individual in Society

Human Memory

JACK A. ADAMS
Professor of Psychology
University of Illinois

McGRAW-HILL BOOK COMPANY
New York ● *St. Louis*
San Francisco ● *Toronto*
London ● *Sydney*

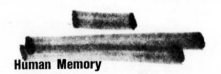

Human Memory

Preface

There has never been a book on memory that gives the solid empirical data of the psychological laboratory and the theories that have sprung from them. If we ignore popular tracts for the layman, there are only two books on memory of any scientific substance. Both are old and both have been reports of an investigator's personal research program. One is the work of Ebbinghaus entitled *Memory: A Contribution to Experimental Psychology*, written in 1885. It is a giant in the field of memory because it opened the topic as an experimental science and, for that reason, towers high in the history of psychology. The other is Bartlett's book *Remembering: A Study in Experimental and Social Psychology*, written in 1932, which attempted an experimental understanding of the retention of behavior far more complex than the comparatively simple rote verbal responses which Ebbinghaus sought to understand. In contrast, this book reports only occasional experiments of the author's. Instead, it seeks to cover the research and theories of memory as they are found in contemporary experimental psychology. It is hoped that this is accomplished with fairness and some completeness, although critics tell us that no book can completely transcend the biases of the writer and the scientific directions that his background leads him to consider as important.

I am especially grateful to Mrs. Genevieve Baker, Mrs. Carol Marsh, and Mrs. Edith Terwilliger, who bore with patience the long hours of typing and editorial work that went into the preparation of the manuscript. My colleague, William E. Montague, reviewed the manuscript and is responsible for a number of refinements in the final version. I am indebted to him.

Jack A. Adams

Contents

Preface, vii

1. Introduction, 1

2. Definition of Memory and Some Distinctions, 7

3. Theories of Memory, 21

4. The Laws of Verbal Interference, 49

5. Serial Recall of Verbal Responses in Short-term Memory, 103

6. Free Recall of Verbal Responses, 151

7. Recall of Verbal Responses in Long-term Memory, 179

8. Recall of Motor Responses, 213

9. Recognition Memory, 243

10. Some Theory and Concluding Remarks, 277

Index, 321

Introduction 1

This book will make no pretense of being an historical treatise that examines the speculations about memory since early Greek philosophy. Nor will it try to be a scholarly tour de force that reviews all empirical research on memory since Ebbinghaus (1913), although modern work, which is the bulk of the subject matter, will be given thorough treatment. The avoidance of full coverage does not suggest that the older writings and empirical findings are without interest, for all students of memory should know on whose shoulders they stand. Philosophical speculation will be avoided because it is outside the scientific concern of the author and because a considerable portion of it has been given a competent treatment by Gomulicki (1953). The early empirical findings have also been given some coverage by Gomulicki, but a more compelling reason for sidestepping them is that early laboratory studies are inadequate by modern standards of experimental design and controls. Inevitably as any science advances, it leaves in its wake much of the early research that lacked the tools, techniques, and variables that later investigators find necessary for the controlled collection and the interpretation of their data, although a core of empirical truth is passed on to later generations. That the relatively recent studies presented in this book will experience the same demise is sure, and this is an argument for pausing and asking about the state of the art and the durable truths that are emerging. Research on memory has taken large steps in recent years, and our present understanding has reached heights beyond all expectation that a prophet of, say, 1950 might have had. Any author risks overselling a topic that drives him strongly enough to write a book, but the dramatic growth of research on memory is an inescapable fact of modern experimental psychology, and our scientific understanding has taken on new and respectable dimensions. The intent of this book is to draw these dimensions and see which ones are

developing with strength and which are diminishing in significance.

This book is mostly about laboratory investigations of the
memory of the normal human subject and, being a book on experimental psychology, mainly sidesteps clinical, nonexperimen-
tal observations on the psychopathology of memory (Freud,
1943). The emphasis on human behavior is less a biased selection of subject matter than a reflection of the arena where research on memory has primarily taken place. Investigators who
use animals, or who study isolated and comparatively simple
human response systems like the eye blink, have given a disproportionate emphasis to learning and motivation variables and
have played down forgetting. Because the directions of a science
evolve out of the free interests of investigators, one can only
speculate why these interests have historically patterned themselves this way. An obvious reason is the great importance of
learning and motivation for behavior theory. Scientists who are
interested in basic laws and theory have often chosen to work
with animals and simple human response classes in the belief
that closer control of relevant variables is more likely and that
goals of law and theory are more readily achieved. But is not
forgetting equally important for behavior theory? Undoubtedly
it is because even routine and unavoidable variables like time
between practice trials in a learning experiment can result in
forgetting over the interval. Nevertheless, the historical fact is
that investigators who use animals and simple response classes
have never dwelt on memory very long. Physiological psychologists, in their search for the brain locus of memory, use animals
in their work and have been minor exceptions to this trend (e.g.,
Lashley, 1950; Thompson, 1965), although their work is yet to
have an impact on behavior theory.

It is wrong to say that research on memory was undertaken
by investigators of human behavior by default because so many

other experimental psychologists were not interested. Perhaps it is better to say that the investigator of human behavior, basic and fundamental though his interests be, is never entirely uninfluenced by the practical problems of his fellowman, and memory has always been a pervasive factor in the conduct of human affairs. Man's concern with memory since early history has not been a detached interest like the study of Aztec pottery but has been driven by a concern rooted in a myriad of everyday problems. This does not mean that all work on memory has been narrow and applied, but it does suggest that the pressure of human affairs has been a stimulus for research on memory and has settled it at the human level. Whether focus on the human being has been an optimum scientific strategy, or even a good one, is debatable, but certainly it is understandable in terms of the motives that impel scientists to take the courses that they do. For better or worse then, this book has human beings and their relatively complex patterns of responding as its emphasis.

This book is at an intermediate level of difficulty, and the reader will benefit from background in general experimental psychology that includes human learning and retention. The reader will have an easier task if he knows the nature of materials, methods, and devices used in verbal and motor research, as well as some of the basic findings and prominent issues in modern theories of learning and perception (Osgood, 1953; Kimble, 1961; Melton, 1964; Hall, 1966; Hilgard & Bower, 1966; Underwood, 1966). Despite these hopes for the reader's background, an effort has been made to make the book readable in its own right, with minimal assumptions about training in experimental psychology.

REFERENCES

Ebbinghaus, H. *Memory: A contribution to experimental psychology.* (Trans. by Ruger & Bussenius.) New York: Teachers College Press, Columbia Univer., 1913.

Freud, S. *A general introduction to psychoanalysis.* New York: Garden City, 1943.

Gomulicki, B. R. The development and present status of the trace theory of memory. *Brit. J. Psychol. monogr. Suppl.,* 1953, No. 29.

Hall, J. F. *The psychology of learning.* New York: Lippincott, 1966.

Hilgard, E. R., & Bower, G. H. *Theories of learning.* (3d ed.) New York: Appleton-Century-Crofts, 1966.

Kimble, G. A. *Conditioning and learning.* New York: Appleton-Century-Crofts, 1961.

Lashley, K. S. In search of the engram. *Symp. Soc. exp. Biol.,* 1950, 4, 454–482.

Melton, A. W. (Ed.) *Categories of human learning.* New York: Academic, 1964.

Osgood, C. E. *Method and theory in experimental psychology.* New York: Oxford, 1953.

Thompson, R. Centrencephalic theory and interhemispheric transfer of visual habits. *Psychol. Rev.,* 1965, 72, 385–398.

Underwood, B. J. *Experimental psychology.* (2d ed.) New York: Appleton-Century-Crofts, 1966.

Definitions of Memory and Some Distinctions 2

Memory is a learned capability for responding, and its persistence over time is measured by the retention test. Loss of memory strength over time is called "forgetting." The layman, and too many psychologists, believes that a change in memory is revealed whenever retention is less than perfect. If an adult is unable to recall the capital of Illinois, which he learned in primary school, he may assume that something has happened to his memory state over the retention interval. Something *could* have happened to it, but nothing *may* have happened because a retention loss is not the same as a memory loss. Indeed, the memory state may be perfectly intact, but performance could have been lacking at the test because any of a host of other variables might have changed to produce the retention decrement. Motivation might have lessened, fatigue might have been present, or insufficient stimulus cues might have been operative to arouse the memory state to its full expression. Any of a number of nonmemory states could have lowered performance at the retention test.

A commonsense view would say that the study of memory is the investigation of all these variables that are determinants of behavior at the retention test. Instead, this book takes the point of view that the proper and very particular domain of memory research is not performance at the retention test but rather retention performance as it reveals something about the memory states which have survived over the retention interval and which underlie the fundamental capability to respond. More specifically, it is assumed as a fundamental premise that *habit is the persistent state of the subject that is memory, and memory research has as its battlefront habit and the variables which affect it over the retention interval.* Lest there be misunderstanding, let this thesis be formalized as a *definition of memory and forgetting:* Memory is the habit states of a subject that give the capability for correct occurrences of a criterion response. There is an initial acquisition session in which the subject makes a discriminative response to a stimulus, followed by a period of time called the "retention interval" when the criterion response does not occur. After the interval there is a retention test in which the subject is asked to *recall* the criterion response in its original form when a stimulus is presented or, in the case of *recognition,* to indicate with an identification response whether he has experienced the stimulus or the criterion response before.

The study of forgetting is a search for variables and their functions that influence change in memory over the retention interval and cause a decrement in correct responding, and for the inferences that these relationships allow for mechanisms of memory and forgetting. Nothing in this definition should be construed as limiting the response at the retention test to the action of a single memory state. Chains and networks of covert events, as in a problem-solving situation, may intervene between the stimulus and occurrence of the criterion response and require activation of several habit states. Moreover, recall and recognition may be based on different habit states.

There are several aspects of this definition which deserve comment. First, recall and recognition are distinguished as two basic ways in which retention is observed objectively. Recall requires the subject to remember the response in its original form, and the degree to which this is not done is an index of forgetting. Recall is the capability for repeating a response, and it is assumed that this capability is dependent importantly upon habit and its strength. In the interest of consistent terminology, habit and memory trace will be used interchangeably when recall is being discussed. Recognition, on the other hand, requires a recognition test of retention in which the subject is asked to identify the criterion events from among alternative, new events. Here the observable response at the retention test is not an attempt to repeat an earlier response but, instead, is an identifying response.

The recognition paradigm can be applied to either stimuli or responses. The subject can identify stimuli which he has experienced before or responses that he has made before. There is some confusion in the use of the term "recognition" as it applies to stimuli, and it should be clear that it will be used only in the sense of an identifying act. The use to which the term will *not* be put is that of correctly naming a stimulus when it is presented (e.g., Binder, 1955; Binder & Feldman, 1960). Examples of the latter use are a musician properly naming G sharp when he hears it or a subject saying "Apple" when he is tachistoscopically presented the picture of an apple for 50 milliseconds. This type of recognition is actually a kind of recall, in which the subject is asked to give a learned response to a stimulus.

A primary theoretical question is whether recall and recognition are measures of the same or different habit states. Recall has been the side of retention research identified with the psychology of learning, and recognition has had close alliance with perception psychology. Therefore in some respects the classical divisions between perception and learning come into play (Postman, 1963). Ideally, we would like to embrace parsimony and have only one mechanism for memory, but the facts may eventually dictate otherwise. If recall and recognition have different variables and different functions associated with each of them, two basic memory states become scientifically defensible. That there may be two states does not necessarily imply that one is learned (our conventional meaning of habit) and one is not. In fact, as a working premise, it is useful to consider them as two kinds of habits, and the heart of the foregoing definition of memory and forgetting is that research on memory is fundamentally a concern with habits and their fate over the retention interval.

Later, in Chapters 9 and 10, perceptual trace as a mechanism for recognition will be distinguished from the memory trace which underlies recall, and an attempt will be made to decide about their independent status. For the most part, however, the discussion will be about memory trace. Whether there are one or two states does not influence the definition of memory and forgetting that has been given—only the eventual complexity of the laws of memory. In the meantime, it is sufficient to remember that there may be two basic memory states to worry about.

At the peril of being obvious, it seems worthwhile to distinguish between stimulus trace and memory trace as it has been defined. Stimulus trace is the internal trace of the environmental stimulus that can persist for some time after the external stimulus has ceased. Stimulus trace can serve as a signal for response, or as a carrier of perceptual data from which information is extracted and reported. This distinction between stimulus trace and memory trace may not always be fully appreciated. Because both kinds of trace have an internal persistence over time, it is easy to slip into an uncritical attitude that accepts both traces as aspects of memory. No one has made a formal position of this view, but let it be clear that habit traces are the emphasis of this book. This is not to deny the importance of stimulus trace for behavior. Physiological evidence for stimulus trace is documented by Lorente De Nó (1938), Burns (1951), and Evans and Robertson (1965). Stimulus trace as a behavioral construct has been used by Pavlov (1927, pp. 42–43), Hull et al. (1940), Hull (1943, 1951, 1952), Spence (1956, pp. 94–95), Konorski (1961), and Adams (1964, p. 185).

THE LEARNING–PERFORMANCE DISTINCTION

The contention that the scientific investigation of memory is the study of habits and their fate over the retention interval, and not the uncritical study of any retention measure, is casting lot with the distinction between learning (habit) and performance

(Brown, 1961, p. 99; Kimble, 1961, p. 5). To make this distinction, it is necessary to accept for working research purposes a learning theory that specifies how habit and other state variables are defined and related to performance. The learning-performance distinction says that all relevant variables determine momentary performance, but only a subset of them defines habit or learning states. There are about as many operational definitions of learning as there are theories of learning (Kimble, 1961, Ch. 1), but there is general agreement that learning is a reasonably stable state of the organism produced by the systematic association of reinforcing events, the criterion response, and the stimulus. In order to study forgetting, or the conditions under which habit loses some or all of its capability over the retention interval for activating the response, it is necessary that habit and non-habit operations be specified in the theory so that it is clear that habit is under scrutiny. The learning theory of Hull (1943, 1951, 1952) is a good example of distinguishing clearly between learning and nonlearning variables. His theory consists of a network of hypothetical constructs which are anchored operationally to manipulable independent variables on the one hand and dependent behavioral measures on the other. To avoid the tedium of discussing the operational definitions of all Hull's constructs, only the main constructs themselves and their interrelations will be briefly sketched. Habit, or $_sH_R$, is defined as the associative bond between a stimulus and a criterion response, and it is independent of a general drive state D which is a nonhabit variable. Habit and drive combine to produce a higher-order concept called "excitatory potential" $_sE_R$. From $_sE_R$ is subtracted $\dot{I}_R$, an inhibitory or fatigue-like state, and the resultant is effective excitatory potential called $_s\bar{E}_R$. Hull then imposes an inhibitory oscillatory construct $_sO_R$ to account for the ubiquitous, seemingly random variability of behavior, and the final outcome is predicted functions for response measures.

All of this is an inadequate condensation of the life's work of an imaginative theorist, but it illustrates the kinds of theoretical distinctions that are important for focusing on habit and examining influences on it over the retention interval. A memory investigator working within Hull's theory would know which variables define habit states and which do not, and he would be able to design experiments that bear on the retention of habit as Hull defined it. Hull's theory is used here only for the learning-performance example it provides, and there is no intent to imply that a mathematical model like Hull's is necessary for memory work. What it does mean is that a scientific approach to memory must be based on some kind of theory that makes a learning-performance distinction as Hull does, even though the theory is crude, preliminary, and qualitative.

There must be a basis for believing that habits are being studied. The belief may be wrong, in the sense that a definition of habit may be wrong at any given time, but this is a matter of empirical fact that will be corrected in the normal development of psychology as a science. The point is that an experimenter must have ideas about the variables which define habit, and a knowledge of how these variables differ from those defining other conceptual states, in order to exert experimental control and design experiments which bear on habit and its retention. He must be assured that in observing *performance* he can infer about *learning*.

The Problem of Motivation and Memory

The learning-performance distinction is straightforward enough and ordinarily should not trouble anyone, but sometimes just the opposite has been true. Consider the topic of motivation and its effect on memory (see Weiner, 1966, for a literature survey and discussion). The workers in this area have concerned themselves primarily with performance differences at the retention test that are related to motivational level in original learning. They have not attended to the more basic learning-performance distinction and asked whether motivation produces greater survival for responses over the retention interval by its effect on habit strength. Influenced importantly by Hull's thinking, many think that motivation is a nonhabit, performance variable (Brown, 1961), but it is recognized that the independence of habit and motivation is a hypothesis which must be proved empirically. To prove a dependency between motivation and habit would not necessarily mean that motivation *is* habit and that motivation is not a useful construct in its own right (for a discussion of this possibility, see Brown, 1961, Ch. 4).

Although not within a context of memory per se, animal-learning psychologists have been concerned with the effect of motivation on learning for some time (Kimble, 1961, pp. 411–416; Spence, 1956, p. 168), and a clear answer is yet to come. With all its problems, the animal-learning domain seems simple when compared to the corresponding topic for human learning and retention. A typical human experiment in this area (e.g., Heyer & O'Kelly, 1949; Weiner & Walker, 1966; Kernoff, Weiner, & Morrison, 1966) uses different levels of incentive motivation in original learning, like highly motivating instructions or money reward, and then uses standard recall procedures after the retention interval. Beneficial differences in behalf of motivation have often been found for recall in experiments of this sort, but the blunt truth is that nothing decisive can be said about motivation and its effect on habit. Differences at the retention test cannot be unequivocally interpreted because they are performance differences that do not allow straightforward inferences about learning.

There are at least three possibilities for these positive influences of motivation on retention. First, motivation in original learning could have produced habit increments that persisted to the retention test, but this might have been true even if no differences in retention had been found. On the assumption that motivation produces stimuli which are part of the cue complex to which the response is learned (Hull, 1943), a change from high incentive in original learning to a lower level at retention could produce a generalized, reduced amount of habit strength essentially equivalent to the habit strength for subjects who originally had less incentive. Second, motivation probably has some decay period after arousal and continues a short while into the retention interval, which means that original motivation could affect recall when retention intervals are quite short and create effects which are independent of habit changes (for experiments that may have this problem see Weiner & Walker, 1966; Kernoff, Weiner, & Morrison, 1966). Third, and most complex, is the possibility that in the retention test the verbally adroit human subject could activate a covert reminder of the consequences of good performance that the conditions of motivation established for him, and this response could provide cues for heightened motivation to benefit recollection of the criterion response. Here we have a chain of responses, all of which are learned and must be recalled, and part of the chain bears on the motivational state. Conceptually, this motivational state could be independent of habit strength, although it is dependent on the habit strength of the responses which provide the cues that arouse it.

This brief methodological examination of motivation is aimed at highlighting the difficulties that can surround the learning-performance distinction and the theoretical emptiness in dwelling uncritically on the determinants of performance at the retention test. A teacher may find it useful to know that originally motivated pupils recall more, but this pragmatic fact has a long research struggle facing it before the specific variables and the states they define are sufficiently untangled to please theoretical psychologists who are interested in precise knowledge about memory. Scientific psychology has matured enough to be impatient with workaday if-then laws (if the subject is motivated in original learning, then he recalls more), and the impatience is directed toward the low-order quality of these laws, not toward practicality. Scientific psychology is tolerant of the practical world's need for behavioral laws, but it cannot be content with low-order principles that are of minor value for both science and the practical world.

Work Inhibition

It is not the intent to review all performance variables and show how improper experimental design or analysis results in wrong estimations of the determinants of habit retention. However, the variables defining work inhibition have not always been properly controlled in forgetting experiments, with the result that estimates of retention have often been distorted.

By work inhibition is meant the negative aftereffects of response occurrences which depress performance. It is a concept that roughly conforms to the layman's notion of fatigue, although fatigue for the experimental psychologist is a term that has fallen from favor because of vagueness. The most intensive and worthwhile research on this topic was done under the rubric of Hull's I_R concept (Hull, 1943), which was called "work inhibition" and had a negative relationship to performance.

Work inhibition increased as number of responses and amount of physical work involved in making the response increased and decreased as a function of rest time between responses. The resultant of these variables defined the amount of work inhibition which Hull defined as a performance depressant subtracted from excitatory potential $_sE_R$. Although Hull defined motivation D as solely a nonhabit variable, total work inhibition

$\dot{I}_R$ had the dual theoretical status of nonhabit I_R and habit $_sI_R$ components. The ramifications of this duality are considerable, and it stimulated a great deal of research. But let it suffice to say that $_sI_R$ did not withstand a concerted experimental attack (e.g., Adams & Reynolds, 1954). This left I_R as the viable element of Hull's work inhibition, and it was a formal way of stating much of what the layman means by fatigue—performance is depressed with work and recovers with rest. Although undoubtedly wrong in some of its details, there is no doubt that psychology needs a concept of temporary work inhibition in its theoretical arsenal.

For forgetting research, the principal methodological difficulty with temporary work inhibition is that its recovery over rest operates counter to forgetting decrement for habit and obscures its course. Decay of work inhibition in the retention interval produces a performance gain that opposes evidences of forgetting in the retention test and, in some cases, eliminates them. This problem is particularly evident for many motor tasks where work inhibition is prominent, and it is a factor which has caused some to underestimate the forgetting of motor responses (Adams, 1964, pp. 189–191). Obviously, a performance variable of this potency must be controlled so that changes in habit over the retention interval are unequivocally revealed, and the easiest way to do this is to widely distribute training trials; thus minimizing the accrual of temporary work inhibition.

An influential paper by McGeoch (1932) is a good example of the failure to appreciate the learning-performance distinction and the need to control for the spontaneous gain over rest which works counter to forgetting loss. McGeoch argued against the trace decay hypothesis of forgetting (spontaneous degeneration of the memory trace—see the next chapter) because gain sometimes occurs. According to McGeoch, the trace decay hypothesis must be invalid because it predicts loss, not improvement, over the retention interval. McGeoch may be right about trace decay as inadequate for an explanation of forgetting, but his line of reasoning is wrong. Inferences cannot be made about spontaneous change in the memory trace when a counteracting variable clouds it. McGeoch, for all his contributions, lived at a time before the learning-performance distinction was clear. As a result he failed to see how changes in learning could be obscured by performance variables.

The learning-performance distinction in its operational details is dynamic and in a state of change, and it may always be because it is no better than the state of learning theory at any particular time. Nevertheless, it is a distinction whose importance is now understood, and we are conceptually equipped to define retention experiments that show changes in habit by a current definition. Without such a frame of reference we will reveal little about the change in memory that is called forgetting and which has fascinated man since the beginning of his intellectual history.

REFERENCES

Adams, J. A. Motor skills. *Annu. Rev. Psychol.*, 1964, **15**, 181–202.

Adams, J. A., & Reynolds, B. Effect of shift in distribution of practice conditions following interpolated rest. *J. exp. Psychol.*, 1954, **47**, 32–36.

Binder, A. A statistical model for the process of visual recognition. *Psychol. Rev.*, 1955, **62**, 119–129.

Binder, A., & Feldman, S. E. The effects of experimentally controlled experience upon recognition responses. *Psychol. Monogr.*, 1960, **74** (Whole No. 496).

Brown, J. *The motivation of behavior.* New York: McGraw-Hill, 1961.

Burns, B. D. Some properties of the isolated cerebral cortex of the unanesthetized cat. *J. Physiol., London*, 1951, **112**, 156–175.

Evans, C. R., & Robertson, A. D. J. Prolonged excitation in the visual cortex of the cat. *Science*, 1965, **150**, 913–915.

Heyer, A. W., Jr., & O'Kelly, L. I. Studies in motivation and retention:

II. Retention of nonsense syllables learned under different degrees of motivation. *J. Psychol.*, 1949, 27, 143–152.

Hull, C. L. *Principles of behavior.* New York: Appleton-Century, 1943.

Hull, C. L. *Essentials of behavior.* New Haven: Yale Univer. Press, 1951.

Hull, C. L. *A behavior system.* New Haven: Yale Univer. Press, 1952.

Hull, C. L., Hovland, C. I., Ross, R. T., Hall, M., Perkins, D. T., & Fitch, F. B. *Mathematico-deductive theory of rote learning.* New Haven: Yale Univer. Press, 1940.

Kernoff, Phyllis, Weiner, B., & Morrison, M. Affect and short-term retention. *Psychon. Sci.*, 1966, 4, 75–76.

Kimble, G. A. *Conditioning and learning.* New York: Appleton-Century-Crofts, 1961.

Konorski, J. The physiological approach to the problem of recent memory. In J. F. Delafresnaye (Ed.), *Brain mechanisms and learning: A symposium.* Springfield, Ill.: Charles C Thomas, 1961. Pp. 115–132.

Lorente De Nó, R. Analysis of the activity of the chains of internuncial neurons. *J. Neurophysiol.*, 1938, 1, 207–244.

McGeoch, J. A. Forgetting and the law of disuse. *Psychol. Rev.*, 1932, 39, 352–370.

Pavlov, I. P. *Conditioned reflexes.* London: Oxford Univer. Press, 1927.

Postman, L. Perception and learning. In S. Koch (Ed.), *Psychology: A study of a science.* Vol. 5. New York: McGraw-Hill, 1963. Pp. 30–113.

Spence, K. W. *Behavior theory and conditioning.* New Haven: Yale Univer. Press, 1956.

Weiner, B. Effects of motivation on the availability and retrieval of memory traces. *Psychol. Bull.*, 1966, 65, 24–37.

Weiner, B., & Walker, E. L. Motivational factors in short-term retention. *J. exp. Psychol.*, 1966, 71, 190–193.

Deliberately omitted from the last chapter was any mention of the nature of the forgetting process or the mechanisms by which habit strength is weakened over the retention interval. This chapter will examine theories of the forgetting process, as well as the distinction between short-term and long-term memory. No effort will be made to choose among the viewpoints on the basis of empirical evidence. Later chapters will discuss data and their power for distinguishing the theories.

FATE OF THE STORED TRACE—THREE MAIN THEORIES

Trace Decay

The basic assumption of trace decay theory is that habit spontaneously decays over the retention interval and that forgetting is a result of a weakened trace at the retention test. Trace decay is an old hypothesis (Gomulicki, 1953), with a long history of intuitive appeal for students of memory. Over the retention interval, a subject has seemingly innocuous and neutral experiences as far as the criterion material being remembered is concerned, and yet he customarily shows forgetting in the laboratory retention test. What could seem more reasonable than an assumption of spontaneous deterioration of the trace? Obviously, however, intuitive attractiveness is insufficient for scientific theory. Trace decay *may* be the reason for forgetting, but activity in the retention interval must be proved as truly neutral and not an agent that works to reduce the strength of the trace by interference with it. Ideally, empty time is needed for the retention interval, but realistically, events occur in time and always exist as potentially confounding for tests of trace decay theory. Experimental tests of trace decay theory have attempted to minimize the action of interfering events in the hope of revealing the effects of trace decay directly, if they are there at all.

The trace decay theory has had its modern adherents (Tolman, 1949, p. 152; Conrad & Hille, 1958; Brown, 1958; Broadbent, 1958, pp. 226–228), but it never really flourished after the massive assault launched by McGeoch (1932). McGeoch reacted against Thorndike's law of disuse (Thorndike, 1913, p. 4), which is another label for the trace decay theory. In his classic criticism of Thorndike's view, which was reemphasized some years later in a widely used textbook by Osgood (1953, p. 549), McGeoch wrote:

> Even were disuse and forgetting perfectly correlated, it would be fruitless to refer the forgetting to the disuse as such. Such reference is equivalent to the statement that the passage of time, in and of itself, produces loss, for disuse, literally interpreted, means only passivity during time. In scientific descriptions of nature time itself is not employed as a causative factor nor is passive decay with time ever found. In time iron, when unused, may rust, but oxidation, not time, is responsible. In time organisms grow old, but time enters only as a logical framework in which complex biochemical processes go their ways. In time all events occur, but to use time as an explanation would be to explain in terms so perfectly general as to be meaningless (McGeoch, 1932, p. 359).

McGeoch went on to develop his main position that interference is more compelling as an explanation of forgetting and deserves primary theoretical status.

McGeoch is sound in his argument that interference can be a worthy explanation of forgetting. McGeoch and his associates did much to develop our early understanding of interference, and they gave impetus to the interference theory of forgetting. But to demonstrate that interference can be a variable for forgetting does not prove the trace decay view wrong. Interference can induce a forgetting decrement, but this does not mean it is the sole explanation of forgetting. Trace decay can occur, too;

and it will take perceptive, discriminating experimental designs to untangle these two possible influences.

McGeoch was wrong in discounting trace decay because time is the independent variable. A measure of time is a perfectly respectable independent variable and has been throughout the history of science. Certainly it is unnecessary for a scientific law to say *why* time has the effects it does. In general terms, lawfulness only requires that (1) a dependent variable be a specifiable function of one or more independent variables and (2) the variables be defined objectively so that any scientist can manipulate them. Time, in this general sense, is as defensible an independent variable as one could name. The law of falling bodies or the laws of planetary motion have time as an independent variable even though physics does not have the foggiest notion of what gravity as the force working in time *really* is. No one would deny the usefulness and precision of these laws. Time deserves an unquestioned role in a science as long as it can be shown to be a reliable determinant of dependent variables. Other processes working in time may be uncovered eventually and lead to new laws, and a science may come to regard these new laws as more fundamental for explanation. But even such fundamental laws could involve processes that operate in time, and so it would seem that time can appear as an independent variable even when laws assume the mature state that McGeoch prefers. Nagel (1961, pp. 73–78), in his book on the philosophy of science, makes a distinction between causal laws and "dynamical" (time function) laws that would have pleased McGeoch, but the making of the distinction does not cause Nagel to reject dynamical laws.

In summary, there is no intrinsic reason why trace decay cannot be a valid explanation of forgetting. But that it is logically possible for the theory to be valid does not mean that predictions from it are in accord with empirical facts. Whether the predictions coincide with empirical facts is a problem for research.

Trace Transformation

The trace decay theory must be distinguished from the trace transformation view that was held by gestalt psychologists. Koffka (1935, p. 523), for example, admitted the possibility of spontaneous decay of the trace, but he felt that a *change* in the configuration of the trace, not weakening, was more probable. Koffka (1935) and Köhler (1947) are primary sources for this point of view, but Osgood (1953, pp. 551–554) has a very satisfying summary. Gestalt psychologists were perception theorists and stimulus recognition was their overwhelming interest. Recall, from the transformation point of view, was given more emphasis by Bartlett (1932).

The gestalt psychologists contended that traces of perceptual experience, like seeing a geometric form, are subject to two sources of change over the retention interval: (1) spontaneous internal influences inherent in perceptual mechanisms of the brain which transform the trace toward an "ideal" prototype figure for its class and (2) external influences from similar experiences which have traces that interact with those of acquisition. Consider a circle with a small gap in it which is shown to the subject in acquisition. In the absence of external experience the circle should change spontaneously in the direction of a "good," geometrically ideal figure like a perfect, closed circle. External influences could also alter the trace of the partial circle to the extent that they are similar. A prediction about retention of the original trace is somewhat vague, mainly because external and internal influences may or may not be complementary. And, the central notion that dynamic brain forces urge a figure toward an ideal configuration was a doubtful hypothesis attractive only to the ingroup of the gestalt movement. Whatever merit the notion might have had, it fell decisively under a strong experimental attack by Hebb and Foord (1945). No one bothers much with the old-line gestalt views any more, and they are presented briefly only to ensure that trace decay and trace transformation are clearly distinguished.

Interference

The contemporary interference theory of forgetting holds that competing responses learned before acquisition of criterion responses (proactive inhibition), or in the retention interval (retroactive inhibition), induce the decrement in criterion performance that we call forgetting. The evidence for this theory is largely empirical and pretheoretical; therefore the term "theory" may be mildly inappropriate. The reason it is called "pretheoretical" is that the theory specifies little in the way of mechanisms that say why interfering responses function as they do.

One possible explanation is the *erosion hypothesis* which is unashamedly offered without a whit of empirical support. The hypothesis assumes that the trace is intrinsically eroded, in a manner corresponding to trace decay, by the action of interfering activities. The end product at the retention test could be the same as trace decay, but the implications of the two points of view are quite different. Trace decay theory predicts that forgetting *must* occur because the trace spontaneously weakens no matter what the experiences of the subject, but the erosion view would hold that forgetting *may* occur, depending upon the nature and amount of interference.

The *inhibition hypothesis* is another possibility, and its implications are discussed in more detail in the next section on the permanence of memory. The assumption is that interference leaves the trace completely intact but builds an inhibitory barrier that prevents activation of memory by a stimulus, thereby preventing the response from occurring. Or, alternatively, the memory could be activated by the stimulus but inhibition would somehow prevent the firing of the response effector system.

The absence of data for these two hypotheses, or even likely ways that they might be tested, reduces their attractiveness. Nevertheless, the basic mechanisms of interference deserve ideas, even unattractive ones, because they involve issues about memory that are powerful in their ultimate implications; and it is to these issues that we turn next.

HYPOTHESIS THAT MEMORY IS PERMANENT

In the previous section, the possibility was raised that interference *could* be a matter of erosion of traces, but that inhibition of traces was equally plausible. A special implication of the inhibition hypothesis is that memory is permanent—forgetting is only a matter of building inhibition, and the traces themselves are left completely intact. This is an exciting idea with vast implications. If forgetting, in the sense of an irretrievable deterioration of the trace, does not occur, the memory agent is potentially available in the central nervous system even though no overt response can be elicited from the subject. The inhibition barrier may be impenetrable, and if so, the practical consequences of trace decay and inhibition would seem about the same because nothing could be done to reverse the effects of forgetting variables. But, if somehow the inhibition barrier could be pierced, we are confronted with the fascinating possibility that ways may be devised to stimulate responses that normally would be considered forgotten. A big issue for memory is the fate of the trace over time, and if the trace were shown to be permanent, the focus would shift to the problems of retrieval from memory storage.

It is hard to imagine the practical implications of this hypothesis, even if only partly true. Consider the inefficiency from which society suffers because of forgetting and the inadequate behavior which it produces. Consider that education is less effective because of a student's forgetting from one lesson to the next. What of the refresher reading and the library searches we all undertake because knowledge has been forgotten? Think of the refresher courses and schools which people attend to regain the useful knowledge they once had. How about the airplane crash because the pilot forgot the required sequence of responses to remedy an emergency? There is no doubt that forgetting gives society a heavy burden. One must regret that the hypothesis of permanent memory has not received serious research attention, perhaps via the route of efficient methods of retrieval to tap stored material that would otherwise be unrecalled and considered forgotten. Actually, the hypothesis has been a minor theme, and sometimes an obscure one, in the psychological literature for a long time.

William James's Hypothesis

William James believed that some individuals had permanent memory:

> The persistence or permanence of the paths is a physiological property of the brain-tissue of the individual, whilst their number is altogether due to the facts of his mental experience. Let the quality of permanence in the paths be called the native tenacity, or physiological retentiveness. This tenacity differs enormously from infancy to old age, and from one person to another. Some minds are like wax under a seal—no impression, however disconnected with others, is wiped out. Others, like a jelly, vibrate to every touch, but under usual conditions retain no permanent mark (James, 1892, p. 293).

This quotation hardly does full justice to James's conception of

memory, but it does serve to illustrate that permanent memory
was a part of his theoretical beliefs.

Psychoanalysis

Sigmund Freud's interest was motivated forgetting (Freud,
1943), in which an error in recall or failure to recall occurs for
reasons that have meaning to the mental life of the person. The
forgetting of a name may be because the individual is unpleasant,
and the fact is censored from conscious recall. In more dramatic
cases of severe trauma, memories could be totally repressed in
the unconscious because their recall would be anxiety-producing.
Sometimes a person's psychic needs result in the distortion of
memories when they are recalled. Of more interest here is the
fate of memory traces over time, even though they lie deep in
the unconscious, and in a footnote it is evident that Freud believed in the permanence of memory. Recall may be inhibited
or distorted, but beneath it all are the original, unsullied traces.

> As these processes of condensation and distortion continue
> for long periods, during which all fresh experiences act upon
> the transformation of the memory content, it is our belief that
> it is time that makes memory uncertain and indistinct. It is quite
> probable that in forgetting, there can really be no question of a
> direct function of time. From the repressed memory traces, it can
> be verified that they suffer no changes even in the longest periods.
> The unconscious, at all events, knows no time limit. The most
> important, as well as the most peculiar character of psychic
> fixation consists in the fact that all impressions are, on the one
> hand, retained in the same form as they were received, and also
> in the forms that they have assumed in their further develop-
> ment. This state of affairs cannot be elucidated by any compari-
> son from any other sphere. By virtue of this theory, every former
> state of the memory content may thus be restored, even though
> all original relations have long been replaced by newer ones
> (Freud, 1938, pp. 174–175, Footnote).

The virgin memory traces lie in the unconscious unchanged by time, whatever form conscious memory might take. Through psychoanalytic methods the store of original memories can be entered and illuminated.

Modern Learning Theory

Learning theorists of substance have sometimes implied the permanence of habit, although they rarely phrased the matter in such terms. Hull (1943, 1951, 1952) defined no conditions for the weakening of habit strength. Performance, as momentary behavior which all relevant variables can influence, could be lowered by changing the values of such nonhabit variables as motivation or work inhibition. Habit strength itself, however, was only subject to increases through reinforcement. No operations were ever specified for lessening of habit strength; thus habit, or memory, is permanent. Mechanisms were specified for lowering performance, but not habit. It is unclear why Hull did not consider forgetting, particularly since he sought a behavior theory with generality.

Kimble (1961), in his book on the experimental psychology of learning, writes that, "There has always been general agreement among authorities on the subject that *learning refers to a more or less permanent change in behavior which occurs as a result of practice*" (p. 2; italics are Kimble's). This statement hedges a bit on the permanence of memory, but Kimble nevertheless reflects a prevalent sentiment among learning theorists. One of Hull's legacies to modern learning theory is a disinterest in forgetting which is reflected in these feelings about the permanence of habit. Perhaps there is the implicit assumption that forgetting will be easily understood once the laws of acquisition and experimental extinction are known and that forgetting per se need not be studied.

Penfield's Work on Brain Stimulation

Wilder Penfield is a clinical surgeon, and so far his research has not had much impact on experimental psychology. When an investigator deals with clinical case histories, reports his findings in books and journals on the fringes of the intellectual life of most experimental psychologists, and presents his findings in an offbeat combination of physiological and clinical interview terms, it is understandable that he has little influence on behavioral research in the psychological laboratory. In fairness to experimental psychologists, it must be said that Penfield's work is important only for its far-reaching implications and not for its immediate value in suggesting explicit hypotheses for the behavior laboratory. Penfield does not perform experiments in the sense that we usually mean this activity in psychology, but in observing over 1,000 clinical cases he is in a position to discern empirical regularities. His provocative work speaks for far more detail in the brain's memory record than we are able to recall, and it can be interpreted as relevant for a permanent and detailed memory that retains events long after they have been unavailable to recall. Penfield's paper entitled "The Interpretive Cortex" (Penfield, 1959) is perhaps the most readable overview of his research, but other papers also deserve to be read as more detailed reports of his work (Penfield, 1951, 1954, 1955, 1958a, 1958b, 1958c, 1960; Penfield & Jasper, 1954; Penfield & Roberts, 1959).

Penfield was intellectually stimulated by the work of John Hughlings Jackson, a British medical scientist of the nineteenth century. Jackson's first professional interest was epilepsy, and his papers (Taylor, 1938) are filled with case histories, descriptions of symptoms, and hypotheses about relationships between the brain and epileptic manifestations. Jackson believed epilepsy to be "the name for occasional, sudden, excessive, rapid and local discharges of grey matter" (Taylor, 1938, p. 100). He saw epilepsy as a disease entity caused by brain lesions, and he surmised the size of the lesion to be quite small. Epileptic seizures can differ widely in their effects on motor movements, speech, and hallucinatory conscious experiences, and so Jackson reasoned that the lesion had no standard locus in the brain. The position of the lesion should vary in accord with the particular behavioral pattern of the patient during seizure.

Forming a bond with Penfield's later work is Jackson's discussion of "intellectual auras," or "dreamy states" as he preferred to call them because patients often mentioned them in this way (e.g., Taylor, 1938, pp. 385–405). Crude sensations like smells and intellectual auras can be immediate precursors of epileptic attacks. These auras are conscious images or experiences, sometimes imaginary and sometimes memories of past events, sometimes fragmentary and sometimes meaningful sequences, and sometimes with emotional content and sometimes without. Jackson's descriptive research methods resulted in an extensive reporting of these mental states that accompany the cortical storms of an epileptic attack. An important lead for Penfield was that Jackson reported autopsies of several patients with histories of intellectual auras, and they all had tumors that were partly or wholly in the temporal lobes of the cortex (Taylor, 1938, pp. 406–411, 458–473). Stimulation of the temporal lobes seemed to have something to do with epilepsy and intellectual auras.

Penfield uses the technique of unilateral removal of a portion of the temporal lobes and adjacent areas for relief of focal epilepsy when medication fails, and it has had moderate success (Penfield, 1958c, p. 150). The operation, called a craniotomy, is performed with local anesthetic on the conscious, aware patient. A portion of the skull is removed and the side of the brain is laid bare. Being a scientist as well as a clinician seeking a cure, Penfield conducts systematic electrical stimulation of the open brain, and the patient, being conscious, reports his subjective experiences. In an early case, Penfield stimulated the temporal lobe and re-created the memory of a childhood experience that formed the intellectual aura accompanying the epileptic attack each time (Penfield, 1959, p. 1723). In the more than 1,000 craniotomies that followed, Penfield liberally explored the surface of the brain available to him, and these extensive observations have given him a theory of memory.

Stimulation of sensory areas of the cortex produces verbal reports of experiences that lack meaningful content. The auditory cortex produces ringing, buzzing, blowing, and thumping sounds, but never meaningful music or voices, for example. The visual area on stimulation gives unstructured lights, colors, etc. Stimulation of the motor area results in bodily movements or feelings of numbness. *Only* stimulation of the temporal lobes leads to reports of meaningful, integrated experiences; and these are often of haunting reality because they can be complete with color, accurate sounds, and emotional content. Some of the experiences accurately involve extensive sequences of the present or past; others are bizarre hallucinations and illusions that are fragmentary or distorted elements of the past or present, as in a dream. Only one stimulated experience occurs at a time (Penfield, 1954, pp. 140–141).

Penfield calls these manifestations of the temporal lobes "psychical responses," and he has labeled the temporal lobes the "interpretive cortex." The interpretive cortex is not considered the seat of memory because surgical removal of the temporal lobe from which a recollection has just been evoked by stimulation does not abolish an individual's memory of the event just recalled (Penfield, 1951, pp. 23–24; 1959, p. 1724). Obviously, however, the interpretive cortex must be intimately connected to a physiological seat of memory (if there is any such single place).

Of great interest for the study of memory is the fact that

some of the stimulated experiences of great detail had long been unavailable in normal recall, and Penfield reports numerous case histories that show the detailed complexity of these events. The vividness and detail of an electrically stimulated experience can be very compelling and deserves contrasting to the normal recall of the intact subject. Penfield says:

> What a man remembers when he makes a voluntary effort is apt to be a generalization. If this were not so, he might be hopelessly lost in detail. On the other hand, the experiential responses described above are detailed reenactments of a single experience. Such experiences soon slip beyond the range of voluntary recall. A man may summon to mind a song at will. He hears it then in his mind, not all at once but advancing phrase by phrase. He may sing it or play it too, and one would call this memory.
>
> But if a patient hears music in response to the electrode, he hears it in one particular strip at a time. That time runs forward again at the original tempo, and he hears the orchestration, or he sees the player at a piano "over there." These are details he would have thought forgotten (Penfield, 1959, p. 1724).

Penfield's theorizing about memory is less extensive than his empirical work, and his theoretical views are best represented in a single paper (Penfield, 1951). Penfield is understandably captivated with the almost unbelievable completeness of the experiences which his electrode can evoke. He says:

> When the electrode is applied to the memory cortex [The interpretive cortex as he later came to call it—J. A.] it may produce a picture but the picture is not usually static. It changes, as it did when it was originally seen and then the individual perhaps altered the direction of his gaze. It follows individual observed events of succeeding seconds or minutes. The song produced by cortical stimulation progresses slowly, from one phase to another and from verse to chorus (Penfield, 1951, pp. 24–25).

He goes on to say:

> The thread of continuity, in evoked recollections, seems to
> be time. The original pattern was laid down in temporal succes-
> sion. And it is the thread of temporal succession that later seems
> to hold the elements of evoked recollection together (Penfield,
> 1951, p. 25).

Penfield believes that

> whenever a normal individual is paying conscious attention to
> something he is simultaneously recording it in the temporal cortex
> of each hemisphere (Penfield, 1951, pp. 23–24).

In other words, *all* stimulation which is given attention is recorded
in the brain. There is no doubt that Penfield has a far richer
conception of the memory record than anyone else, and with
justification. Moreover, he believes in an intrinsic permanent
memory record even when forgetting processes forbid recall.

> Thus it would appear that the memory record continues
> intact even after the subject's ability to recall it disappears (Pen-
> field, 1951, p. 22).

And he believes this splendidly detailed record to be potentially
recoverable:

> A provocative research question is whether we could de-
> velop techniques which could elicit far more detail than hereto-
> fore (Penfield, 1951, p. 23).

How does one judge Penfield's research and interpretations?
His work is clinical in the sense that subjects are not freely
chosen and organized into an experiment, and so it may not be
fully palatable to some laboratory investigators. Yet Penfield's
studies are systematic, and he has made a number of fascinating
observations about the brain and memory. A greater scientific
security would prevail if he had independent verification of the

events which are remembered by electrical stimulation, but all in all, it is hard not to be impressed by Penfield's exploitation of a rare research opportunity. Penfield's ideas on the permanence of all events given attention may be a bit extreme, but even if seen relatively as a big discrepancy between recall and stored events, his point of view contains ideas of large promise. If true, the discrepancy between storage and recall may be due to an inhibition barrier whose penetration by techniques yet unknown could give us an increment in remembering that would be of inestimable theoretical value and practical service.

Conclusion on the Permanent Memory Hypothesis

The chapters with their empirical data that follow have no evidence on the permanent memory hypothesis. Penfield's studies contain the main research strength of the hypothesis—the conjectures by James and Freud being more speculative and based on informal observations. James was taken with the excellent recall that some individuals have of events in the distant past, and similarly Freud was impressed with the recollection of past occurrences that could be elicited in psychoanalysis. Hull seemed to have even less cause when he assumed the stability of habit strength. The hypothesis of permanent memory is of large potential significance, however, and should be a stimulus for behavioral research even though ways of testing it are foggy at the moment.

COMPARTMENTS OF MEMORY

The discussion in Chapter 2 would be oversimplified for some because it said that the operations of acquisition put the trace directly in memory where the forces of forgetting begin to work on it. In its essentials no one would disagree with this, but most would say that the process is more complex. For them the time has come to enlarge the initial conception. The embellished interpretation, centered almost wholly in the findings of verbal recall, is a distinction between *short-term memory* (STM) and *long-term memory* (LTM). A to-be-remembered event, like a series of letters, numbers, or words, is presented to a subject for later recall after a few seconds or minutes. With one or a few reinforcements, the event is assumed to be in STM and operating according to its laws. After a number of reinforcements, however, the event is considered transferred to LTM and subject to a different set of laws. Depending upon the nature of the material, the event in STM may or may not be independent of LTM. If the event in STM has well-learned associations from past experience, it can draw on these mediated connections and relate them to the memory task at hand.

Operationally, what must prevail for the STM–LTM distinction to be scientifically secure? The basic requirement is the demonstration that STM and LTM obey different laws—that is, different variables affect retention in STM and LTM, or the same variables operate in quite different ways for the two compartments. Not everyone believes the distinction to be defensible (Melton, 1963a, 1963b), primarily because interference affects retention in both STM and LTM (Chapters 5 and 7), but the following section takes the opposite tack with arguments to show why an STM–LTM distinction is sound. The arguments are mostly based on verbal recall data (Chapter 5), which is the domain of most STM studies.

Evidence for the Dual Conception of Memory

There are three main lines of evidence which imply that STM and LTM are different:

1. *Capacity.* The STM component of memory is customarily assumed to have a small capacity relative to LTM. No one knows how to express the capacity of LTM, but certainly it is vast considering the tremendous number of things we can remember. The huge discrepancy between STM and LTM capacities is one reason for believing in two memory compartments. With practice, a subject's capacity can increase, and this can be interpreted as transfer from the STM to the LTM store.

A usual experimental arrangement for assessing the capacity of STM is to give the subject a brief presentation of a perceptual array of stimuli like letters or numbers, or for the experimenter to give him the letters or numbers orally, and then have the subject recall as many of them as he can. Immediate recall is ordinarily the requirement because the experimenter's interest is the subject's maximum STM capacity under the particular experimental conditions, not the residual after a retention interval. In a typical experiment, a subject will recall about seven units (e.g., Miller 1956; Woodworth, 1938, Ch. 27; Averbach, 1963) although, like any other behavior, recall is a function of a number of experimental variables. Experiments of this sort were being conducted long before psychologists distinguished STM and LTM. Over one hundred years ago early psychologists were concerned about the limited capacity of the mind to apprehend stimuli, and they undertook simple experiments on "span of apprehension," or "span of attention" (Woodworth, 1938, Ch. 27). Later the term "memory span" came into vogue, and it became (and still is) a topic of interest for differential psychologists because of individual differences in capacity.

2. *Interference.* As we shall see in Chapters 5 and 7, the interference theory of forgetting has explanatory status for both STM and LTM. That common mechanisms apply to both compartments of memory has led some psychologists (e.g., Melton, 1963a, 1963b) to conclude that the STM–LTM distinction is in-

valid, and there is a kind of justification for this position. However, the view can be challenged on the grounds that STM and LTM respond to different kinds of interference. It is as if a very general nonspecific principle of interference applies to both compartments of memory, but in the specific sense the same variables do not cause interference in the same way for STM and LTM.

Most of our principles of interference (Chapter 4) are derived from the study of well-learned responses stored in LTM. The exact conditions of interference are far from clear, but in one way or another, they are based on competition between opposing responses. Consider an example from a retroactive inhibition experiment with paired associates, in which a pair from a first list of word pairs learned is HOUSE-TENSE. A second list, with the pair HOUSE-RELAXED, whose learning interpolated between the first list and its recall, will most likely cause a decrement in recall of the response TENSE when the stimulus term HOUSE is presented. Here the relevant dimension is a semantic one, with interference produced by responses opposed in meaning (Osgood, 1953, Ch. 12).

This brief commentary on interference and LTM is background for the position that STM is also subject to interference but not in the same way as LTM. Interference in STM is now known to occur along a dimension of *acoustic similarity,* and this is so different from LTM that it seems reasonable to see STM as a distinct memory compartment with special properties and features. Items which interfere in STM are those that sound alike (e.g., Conrad, 1964; Conrad & Hull, 1964; Conrad, Freeman, & Hull, 1965; Wickelgren, 1965a, 1965b). With practice, the laws of interference shift from acoustic to semantic, and this is an empirical meaning of transfer from the STM to the LTM compartment. Baddeley (1964, 1966) and Baddeley and Dale (1966) present evidence that acoustic, not semantic, relationships between words are the main source of interference in STM, and that semantic interference operates primarily in LTM. At our present state of knowledge there seems good cause to assume different laws of interference for STM and LTM, and the different laws encourage the conviction that STM and LTM are separate memory compartments.

It is with practice that the material being remembered moves from STM to LTM. With the potential for interference high when amount of practice is low (Chapter 4), the chances of forgetting are greater for material in STM, and according to the interference theory of forgetting, more and rapid forgetting is likely. The rapid forgetting of material in STM is true empirically, and so the tag "short-term memory." At the outset of STM research in the late 1950s, it seemed as if trace decay theory might be operating for STM and not LTM, but this does not seem to be so (Chapter 5).

3. *Physiological evidence.* Penfield and his associates were mainly interested in the excision of portions of the temporal lobes to relieve severe epilepsy, and the first point to clarify is that a deeper surgical penetration into the hippocampus is necessary to produce a memory deficit (Penfield, 1959, p. 1724). Milner, a colleague of Penfield's who has conducted extensive study of memory and the hippocampus, believes that bilateral hippocampal lesions are necessary for the memory deficit (Milner, 1959). But Walker (1957) reports contrary evidence, and Victor et al. (1961), who have a good discussion of the medical literature and a very extensive case history in their paper, believe that unilateral lesions can impair memory. Whatever the merits of unilateral versus bilateral excision and memory, the kind of defect customarily produced is one that helps the distinction between STM and LTM.

Well-known and useful papers on memory and the hippocampus are Milner and Penfield (1955), Penfield and Milner (1958), and Milner (1958); but the most readable general reference is Milner (1959). The gist of the hippocampal effect on memory is that the patient has trouble with new learning. The IQ as a measure of established responses remains about the same as before the operation, as do other well-learned skills and knowledge. However, the consequences of the operation for acquiring new responses are devastating and are best illustrated by one of Milner's case histories of an epileptic patient. She writes:

> This was a 29-year-old motor-winder who had been rendered incapable of work by his frequent severe seizures. Because of his desperate condition, Dr. Scoville carried out radical bilateral medial temporal-lobe resection on Sept. 1, 1953. I first saw him 20 months later, at which time he gave the date as March, 1953, and his age as 27. He knew that he had had a brain operation, but I think only because the possibility had been entertained for so many years before the operation was actually performed. He kept saying "It is as though I am just waking up from a dream; it seems as though it has just happened."
>
> As far as we can tell this man has retained little if anything of events subsequent to operation, although his I.Q. rating is actually slightly higher than before. Ten months before I examined him his family had moved from their old house to one a few blocks away on the same street. He still has not learned the new address, though remembering the old one perfectly, nor can he be trusted to find his way home alone. He does not know where objects constantly in use are kept; for example, his mother still has to tell him where to find the lawn-mower, even though he may have been using it only the day before. She also states that he will do the same jigsaw puzzles day after day without showing any practice effect and that he will read the same magazines over and over again without finding their contents familiar (Milner, 1959, p. 49).

In general, this case history contains the essentials of most that are reported in the literature on the hippocampus—a stability of IQ and preoperative behavioral patterns and tremendous instability of postoperative responding. The postoperative deficit in memory does not seem to be a deficit in STM per se, because the patient can hold items in temporary store by concentrating intensely and continuously repeating the material (a commonly reported device used by these patients to forestall forgetting). What is most significant is that practice repetitions fail to produce learning or, in the parlance of this chapter, to transfer material from STM to LTM. There is an STM loop available for the circulation of new material, but the material never seems to stamp in. The change to relatively long-term stability, which we ordinarily call learning, is missing. In the case history of the motor winder, commerce with everyday details like the address of his new house or the location of a commonplace object like the lawn mower, failed to produce learning. As we shall see in Chapter 5, practice is the variable that gives material stability with respect to time and moves it from STM to LTM, and removal of the hippocampus prevents this transfer. Milner writes of the relationship between the hippocampus and new and old learning:

> But it seems logical to suppose (in view of the many memories and habits which survive hippocampal destruction) that eventually (perhaps due to frequent rehearsal) the cortical linkage becomes autonomous, and recall is no longer dependent upon the simultaneous activity of cortical and hippocampal cells. On this view, then, removal of the hippocampal region will leave these well-established associations to be built up, and those not yet independent of hippocampal activity will be lost (Milner, 1959, p. 52).

Weiskrantz (1964, p. 25) reemphasized these ideas of Milner's.

The focus of this section was on a defense of the STM–LTM distinction, and the work on the hippocampus has been a source of valuable evidence for this defense. By showing that short-term and long-term retention both occur, but that transfer from STM to LTM is absent with hippocampal excision and new learning is thereby denied, there is the clear implication that two memory compartments exist and that stable learning involves transfer from one to the other.

SUMMARY

This chapter has laid the foundation for two topics that in various ways will occupy most of the data-laden chapters that follow. First, there was broad sketching of three theories that attempt to explain why there is a change in responsiveness after a retention interval that we call forgetting. Second, there was added the complexity of STM and LTM as compartments of memory. Enough data were cited to give substance to some of the viewpoints, but the details of empirical argument will be developed subsequently.

We should keep in mind the empirical possibility, largely unproved, that compartments of memory may be more elaborate than suggested in this chapter. Chapters 9 and 10 will suggest that recognition and recall are based on different habit states (perceptual versus memory traces) and that each may have an STM and LTM compartment. Furthermore, research on memory has been largely with verbal materials. Is it possible that other response classes like motor, touch, and smell follow different laws and have memory compartments of their own? Speculative to be sure, but nature does not always abide parsimony, and memory ultimately may prove far more complex than we now believe.

REFERENCES

Averbach, E. The span of apprehension as a function of exposure duration. *J. verbal Learn. verbal Behav.*, 1963, **2**, 60–64.

Baddeley, A. D. Semantic and acoustic similarity in short-term memory. *Nature, London,* 1964, **204**, 1116–1117.

Baddeley, A. D. Short-term memory for word sequences as a function of acoustic, semantic and formal similarity. *Quart. J. exp. Psychol.,* 1966, **18**, 362–365.

Baddeley, A. D., & Dale, H. C. A. The effect of semantic similarity on retroactive interference in long- and short-term memory. *J. verbal Learn. verbal Behav.,* 1966, **5**, 417–420.

Bartlett, F. C. *Remembering: A study in experimental and social psychology.* London: Cambridge Univer. Press, 1932.

Broadbent, D. E. *Perception and communication.* New York: Pergamon Press, 1958.

Brown, J. Some tests of the decay theory of immediate memory. *Quart. J. exp. Psychol.,* 1958, **10**, 12–21.

Conrad, R. Acoustic confusions in immediate memory. *Brit. J. Psychol.,* 1964, **55**, 75–84.

Conrad, R., Freeman, P. R., & Hull, A. J. Acoustic factors versus language factors in short-term memory. *Psychon. Sci.,* 1965, **3**, 57–58.

Conrad, R., & Hille, B. A. Decay theory of immediate memory and paced recall. *Canad. J. Psychol.,* 1958, **12**, 1–6.

Conrad, R., & Hull, A. J. Information, acoustic confusion and memory span. *Brit. J. Psychol.,* 1964, **55**, 429–432.

Freud, S. *The basic writings of Sigmund Freud.* (Trans. by Brill.) New York: Random House, 1938.

Freud, S. *A general introduction to psychoanalysis.* New York: Garden City, 1943.

Gomulicki, B. R. The development and present status of the trace theory of memory. *Brit. J. Psychol. Monogr. Suppl.,* 1953, No. 29.

Hebb, D. O., & Foord, E. N. Errors of visual recognition and the nature of the trace. *J. exp. Psychol.,* 1945, **35**, 335–348.

Hull, C. L. *Principles of behavior.* New York: Appleton-Century, 1943.

Hull, C. L. *Essentials of behavior.* New Haven: Yale Univer. Press, 1951.

Hull, C. L. *A behavior system.* New Haven: Yale Univer. Press, 1952.

James, W. *Psychology.* New York: Holt, 1892.

Kimble, G. A. *Conditioning and learning.* New York: Appleton-Century-Crofts, 1961.

Koffka, K. *Principles of Gestalt psychology.* New York: Harcourt, Brace, 1935.

Köhler, W. *Gestalt psychology.* New York: Liveright, 1947.

McGeoch, J. A. Forgetting and the law of disuse. *Psychol. Rev.,* 1932, **39,** 352–370.

Melton, A. W. Comment on Professor Peterson's paper. In C. N. Cofer & Barbara S. Musgrave (Eds.), *Verbal behavior and learning.* New York: McGraw-Hill, 1963. Pp. 353–370. (a)

Melton, A. W. Implications of short-term memory for a general theory of memory. *J. verbal Learn. verbal Behav.,* 1963, **2,** 1–21. (b)

Miller, G. A. The magical number seven, plus or minus two: Some limits of our capacity for processing information. *Psychol. Rev.,* 1956, **63,** 81–97.

Milner, B. Psychological defects produced by temporal lobe excision. *Res. Publ., Ass. Res. Nerv. Ment. Dis.,* 1958, **36,** 244–257.

Milner, B. The memory defect in bilateral hippocampal lesions. *Psychiat. res. Rep.,* 1959, **11,** 43–52.

Milner, B., & Penfield, W. The effects of hippocampal lesions on recent memory. *Trans. Amer. Neurol. Ass.,* 1955, **80,** 42–48.

Nagel, E. *The structure of science.* New York: Harcourt, Brace & World, 1961.

Osgood, C. E. *Method and theory in experimental psychology.* New York: Oxford, 1953.

Penfield, W. Memory mechanisms. *Trans. Amer. Neurol. Ass.,* 1951, **76,** 15–31.

Penfield, W. Studies of the cerebral cortex of man: A review and an interpretation. In J. F. Delafresnaye (Ed.), *Brain mechanisms and consciousness.* Springfield, Ill.: Charles C Thomas, 1954. Pp. 284–304.

Penfield, W. The permanent record of the stream of consciousness. *Acta Psychol.,* 1955, **11,** 47–69.

Penfield, W. *The excitable cortex in conscious man.* Springfield, Ill.: Charles C Thomas, 1958. (a)

Penfield, W. Functional localization in temporal and deep Sylvian areas. *Res. Publ., Ass. Res. Nerv. Ment. Dis.*, 1958, **36**, 210–226. (b)

Penfield, W. The role of the temporal cortex in recall of past experience and interpretation of the present. In G. E. W. Wolstenholme & C. M. O'Connor (Eds.), *Neurological basis of behaviour.* Boston: Little, Brown, 1958. Pp. 149–182. (c)

Penfield, W. The interpretive cortex. *Science,* 1959, **129**, 1719–1725.

Penfield, W. Neurophysiological basis of the higher functions of the nervous system: Introduction. In J. Field (Ed.), *Handbook of physiology.* Section 1: Neurophysiology. Vol. 3. Washington: American Physiological Society, 1960. Pp. 1441–1445.

Penfield, W., & Jasper, H. *Epilepsy and the functional anatomy of the human brain.* Boston: Little, Brown, 1954.

Penfield, W., & Milner, B. Memory deficit produced by bilateral lesions in the hippocampal zone. *AMA Arch. Neurol. Psychiat.,* 1958, **79**, 475–497.

Penfield, W., & Roberts, L. *Speech and brain mechanisms.* Princeton: Princeton Univer. Press, 1959.

Peterson, L. R., & Peterson, Margaret J. Short-term retention of individual verbal items. *J. exp. Psychol.,* 1959, **58**, 193–198.

Taylor, J. (Ed.) *Selected writing of John Hughlings Jackson.* Vol. 1. *On epilepsy and epileptiform convulsions.* New York: Basic Books, 1938.

Thorndike, E. L. *Educational psychology.* New York: Teachers College Press, Columbia Univer., 1913.

Tolman, E. C. There is more than one kind of learning. *Psychol. Rev.,* 1949, **56**, 144–155.

Underwood, B. J. Interference and forgetting. *Psychol. Rev.,* 1957, **64**, 49–60.

Victor, M., Angevine, J. B., Mancall, E. L., & Fisher, C. M. Memory loss with lesions of hippocampal formation. *Arch. Neurol.,* 1961, **5**, 244–263.

Walker, A. E. Recent memory impairment in unilateral temporal lesions. *AMA Arch. Neurol. Psychiat.,* 1957, **78**, 543–552.

Weiskrantz, L. Impairment of learning and retention following experimental temporal lobe lesions. In M. A. B. Brazier (Ed.), *Brain function.* Vol. 2. Berkeley: Univer. of California Press, 1964. Pp. 203–231.

Wickelgren, W. A. Acoustic similarity and intrusion errors in short-term memory. *J. exp. Psychol.*, 1965, **70**, 102–108. (a)

Wickelgren, W. A. Acoustic similarity and retroactive interference in short-term memory. *J. verbal Learn. verbal Behav.*, 1965, **4**, 53–61. (b)

Woodworth, R. S. *Experimental psychology*. New York: Holt, 1938.

The Laws of Verbal Interference 4

Interference is such a prominent theory of forgetting that a chapter must be devoted to the laws that govern it. Since most of the experimental work appearing in subsequent chapters is concerned with verbal responses, this chapter concentrates on verbal interference to make the recurring theme of interference and forgetting easier to understand. Research on interference and motor behavior will be covered in Chapter 8 on the retention of motor responses. Moreover, the present chapter will be developed in terms of the recall measure in which the subject attempts to repeat his originally learned response. Recognition as a special case is to be covered in Chapter 9.

The interference theory of forgetting says that certain classes of responses occurring before the acquisition of criterion responses to be later tested for retention, or between acquisition and test, cause a decrement in criterion behavior. The decrement is the loss that we call forgetting. The interference theory of forgetting is an active theory because it is based on the experiencing of certain kinds of events, and should be contrasted to the passive theory of trace decay. An implication of interference theory is that forgetting may be small or large depending on the type and amount of interfering experience. Trace decay, on the other hand, produces forgetting solely as a function of time and independently of experience.

The prominence of the interference theory of forgetting does not mean that it stands without a flaw to pale its scientific virtue. Later chapters will discuss studies that give one pause in whole-heartedly accepting interference theory, but nevertheless the evidence in favor of the theory would make one foolhardy to discount it. One, a few, or even a good many instances of negative findings are often not enough to displace a theory from the superstructure of a science. Enough negative evidence can, of course, cause rejection of a theory, but this final act is usually preceded by two prudent courses of scientific action. First, scientists ask if the experimental situations which generated the negative evidence fulfill the defining conditions required by the theory and constitute a strict test of the theory's implications. Second, if the negative evidence is judged methodologically adequate, the question is asked whether one can refine the theory and adjust it to embrace the new findings. The direction that psychology will take to accommodate negative findings for the interference theory of forgetting remains to be worked out. Regardless of eventual direction, the interference theory of forgetting is very important today, and this chapter will examine the principles that are its foundation.

INTERFERENCE PARADIGMS

The only kind of interference that will be examined in this chapter will be that which is revealed in measures of retention. Transfer, or associative inhibition (Underwood, 1945, p. 1), in which the concern is the effect of one activity on the *learning* of another, will be sidestepped (e.g., Wimer, 1964). Only proactive inhibition (PI) and retroactive inhibition (RI), in which the focus is the effect of one activity on the *retention* of another, will be considered.

Proactive Inhibition

PI takes place when interfering responses occur before acquisition of criterion responses, and these interfering events are said to act forward, or proactively, on the remembering of criterion responses. Actually, "proaction" is an inappropriate term if taken literally to mean forward action because nothing of the sort happens. Prior responses leave their traces which interact with the criterion responses that are learned later, and the interaction produces an effect on retention. This is not a forward action of events but the interplay of habits that are laid down successively in time.

The basic paradigm for PI is:

	Learn	Learn	Retention interval	Retention test
Experimental group:	*AC*	*AB*	. . .	*AB*
Control group:	*DE*	*AB*	. . .	*AB*

Paired associates are represented in this schema (usually a list of paired associates is used), with double letters like *AB* signifying the two words, syllables, or numbers that make up the pair. The subject's task is to learn to give the second term of the pair as a response when the first term is presented as a stimulus. In the schema above, the same stimulus term *A* is used throughout, and *B* and *C* are different response terms that interfere with each other. Although different stimulus terms could be used, it is generally acknowledged that the most interference is found when different responses *B* and *C* are required for the same stimulus term *A*. Two completely separate sets of responses might be used if two lists of paired associates were used, or the responses of list 2 might be the list 1 responses assigned to different stimulus terms in list 2. The convention of emphasizing paired associates in schematizing paradigms of this sort has some justification because so much research is done with paired-associate verbal materials, but the general outlines of the PI paradigm can be considered applicable to other tasks in which the double-letter designation does not apply.

The paradigm shows that an experimental group learns *AC* prior to the learning of *AB*. The amount by which the experimental group scores below the control group on the retention test is a measure of PI. Some investigators omit *DE* learning as a requirement for the control group on the premise that a control group's purpose is to be a baseline for general processes that occur over the retention interval. This premise is dubious because *AC* learning also provides opportunities for nonspecific learning-how-to-learn and warm-up effects, and these must be controlled if the specific interfering effects of *AC* are to be determined. The learning of *DE* material, of the same class as *AC* but neutral, provides equal opportunity for these nonspecific factors to affect control subjects. Comparison of the two groups in the retention test is then on sound footing because all experience is the same for both groups except *AC* interference, which is the object of study.

Another variable to control is interference from contextual sources. Superficially, the effective stimuli are the *A* and *D* terms which the experimenter has explicitly defined. This is not strictly true because the general context stimuli of the whole experimental situation impinge on the subject, as well as proprioceptive stimuli arising from within, and provide a stimulus set that combines with those defined by the experimenter to form a compound to which responses are learned (e.g., Bilodeau & Schlosberg, 1951; Greenspoon & Ranyard, 1957). In other words, the *nominal stimuli* defined by the experimenter are not always the same as the *functional stimuli* which operate as the actual cues for learning (Underwood, 1963). Thus, the *A* terms are not the only common stimuli to which the experimental group learns *B* and *C* responses—there are the context stimuli also. The control group also has context stimuli common to *B* and *E* responses, which are different responses learned to the same stimuli and would be sources of interference and decrement running counter to the positive effects of warm-up and learning-how-to-learn. The presence of composite positive and negative factors makes the control group necessary if the specific interfering effects of *AC* learning for the experimental group are to be assessed. If there were an interest in assessing the effect of *DE* learning on the recall of *AB*, a second control group could be added which would simply learn and recall *AB*.

The activity that fills the retention interval depends upon the length of the interval. In the usual laboratory session, in which all learning takes place in an hour or so, the interval's length is a few minutes, and it is a good control to fill the interval with a noninterfering task to prevent the rehearsal of *AB*. When the intervals are longer, and run to hours or days, the subject is released from the laboratory to his normal activities. The opportunity is available for rehearsal, but the consequences might not bias retention appreciably if it is assumed that both groups have equal opportunity to rehearse. Actually very little voluntary rehearsal may occur. Most subjects have more to do outside the laboratory than rehearse word pairs.

Retroactive Inhibition

Using the RI paradigm, the experimenter attempts to determine the effect of *AC* materials interpolated between *AB* learning and recall:

	Learn	*Retention interval: learn*	*Retention test*
Experimental group:	**AB**	**AC**	**AB**
Control group:	**AB**	**DE**	**AB**

Here the retention interval is deliberately filled with interfering activities, which is the substance of an RI design. The arguments for the learning of *DE* materials as a necessary control apply to RI as they did to the PI design. The amount by which the experimental group scores below the control group on the retention test is a measure of RI. As with the PI paradigm, a second control group with *AB* learning and recall could assess the effects of *DE* learning for the first control group.

As in the discussion of the term "proaction," the term "retroaction" is misleading in suggesting that *AC* somehow works backwards in time to affect *AB*. The *AB* and *AC* materials have their habits laid down successively in time, and their interaction is the interference that produces the decrement found in the retention test.

Concluding Remarks

Neither a pure PI nor a pure RI design can be achieved. In the PI case there is some chance that interfering events will occur in the retention interval, producing a joint PI–RI situation, particularly if the interval is long and no neutral filler task is used. Similarly, in the RI case, events prior to *AB* learning can interfere and produce a joint PI–RI design. Prior events are liable to have a substantial influence in the RI case because *AB* learning is preceded by a lifetime of verbal behavior, some of which is interfering (Underwood, 1957). Despite these contaminating effects we are not prevented from discovering salient properties of PI and RI, any more than a physicist is denied an understanding of vacuum because he can never achieve a pure instance of it. The learning of *AC* in both the PI and RI cases will have an effect that is large relative to other sources of interference, and it is this effect which we study. These other influences that might affect interference for the experimental group are revealed by control groups, which are the baseline for measuring experimentally induced interference.

Not all experiments discussed in this chapter exactly fit the PI and RI paradigms presented in this section. Commonly, the control group simply has been Learn *AB*—Recall *AB*, with no *DE* control activity. In most instances the dereliction should be regarded with charity; the investigators were in harmony with the extant research practices of their time. A less than optimum design does not always negate research findings. Often the conclusion about the effect of a variable can be essentially correct, or the form of a function correct, but the *amount* of an effect may be influenced by a slightly improper design. In some ways this is a minor sin for a young science that is less concerned with the absolute amount of change in behavior than it is with the general form of functions. Often a focus is whether an experimental manipulation produces an effect on behavior and deserves status as a variable.

THE EXTINCTION HYPOTHESIS OF INTERFERENCE

Basic Assumptions

By what process does interference occur? How does the learning of one material interact with the learning of another and cause a decrement in retention? One explanation is the *extinction hypothesis* of interference decrement. It says that the same phenomena which are observed in the experimental extinction of relatively simple animal and human responses are also observed in verbal PI and RI paradigms. Kimble (1961) reviews findings on experimental extinction for simple organisms and responses in some detail.

Consider a simple learning situation in which a rat is reinforced with a pellet of food each time it presses the bar of a Skinner box. With repeated reinforcement there is an orderly increase in the rate of bar presses. During extinction, when the reinforcement is withdrawn and the animal no longer receives a pellet when the bar is pressed, the rate of bar-pressing behavior steadily declines. If extinction is carried on long enough, the animal will stop pressing the bar. Suppose a rest period is given after extinction and the animal is taken from the box for a period of time. Upon return to the box, it will demonstrate a marked (but not full) recovery of the extinguished response. The reappearance of extinguished responses after rest, as all students of elementary psychology know, is called "reminiscence," or "spontaneous recovery." And when reinforcement is given on postextinction trials, the animal will regain the original performance level at a more rapid rate than it was acquired originally.

Interference is produced by the learning of different responses to the same or similar stimuli, and it is seemingly quite unlike experimental extinction. Yet it involves the withdrawal of reinforcement and is a special case of experimental extinction, according to the extinction hypothesis. Consider the PI design in which AC learning precedes the learning of AB and its retention test. An AC verbal pair (assume only one pair for ease of discussion, rather than a list) is systematically reinforced and learned. When learning of the AB pair begins, the presentation of the A stimulus term evokes the C response term because it is the response most strongly associated with A, but the B response term is now correct and receives the reinforcement. The C term is an error and is no longer reinforced. With repeated presentation of AB, the C term will continue to occur for several trials, but systematic nonreinforcement eventually extinguishes it, and B replaces C as the response most strongly associated with A. Now assume that a rest (retention) period is given after the AB learning. The extinguished response C will have an opportunity for spontaneous recovery, and in a retention test for AB after rest, the presentation of A will result in some probability of occurrence for C.

Figure 4-1 shows these expected relationships for PI. The learning of AB, which follows AC learning, brings extinction of AC, and the AC pair shows spontaneous recovery over rest. The first postrest trial is a retention test, and both *B* and *C* now have response potential and are in a competitional situation in which their respective probabilities of occurrence are proportional to their relative strengths. The extent of this competition is revealed in the *AB* decrement at recall. In the relearning trials that follow, the *B* term is again reinforced, and *AC* once again undergoes extinction. Relearning of *AB* is rapid in comparison to original learning, which is the case for animal behavior also.

Figure 4-2 poses the question of whether retention in a PI situation is a function of length of the interpolated rest period. The extinguished *AC* pair is assumed to have a negatively accelerated spontaneous recovery over the rest period. Its strength increases relative to *AB* and in the competition for occurrence at recall lowers the probability of occurrence of *B*. Since *B* is the criterion response being measured, the extinction hypothesis predicts PI to be an increasing function of time between *AB* learning and its retention test.

Fig. 4-1. Hypothetical performance curves for a PI paradigm showing the extinction of *AC* during the learning of *AB*. A decrement in *AB* is shown, as is some spontaneous recovery of *AC* over the retention interval.

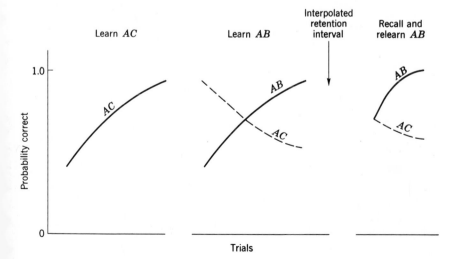

The same empirical principles of extinction shown in Figure 4-1 for PI also apply to RI, and Figure 4-3 shows the expectations.

Fig. 4-2. Hypothetical recall function showing *AB* as a decreasing function of the retention interval in a PI paradigm. The spontaneous recovery function for *AC* is also shown.

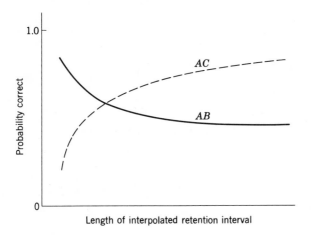

Fig. 4-3. Hypothetical performance curves for an RI paradigm showing the extinction of *AB* during the learning of *AC*. A decrement in *AB* is shown, as is some spontaneous recovery of *AC* over the retention interval.

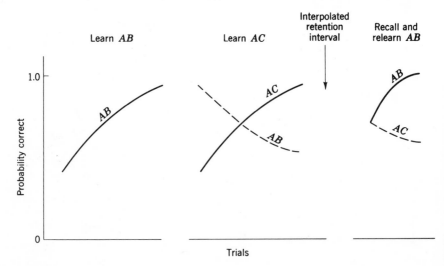

Figure 4-4 shows the predicted influence of the time interval between end of *AC* learning and beginning of the retention test for the RI paradigm. The criterion pair is *AB,* and its increased strength at the retention test because of spontaneous recovery results in a prediction that RI is a decreasing function of the interval.

Empirical Evidence

The extinction hypothesis of interference had its beginnings with Melton and Irwin (1940), whose ideas about the interference process are a cautious challenge to the competition-of-response theory held by McGeoch and his associates (see a summary in McGeoch & Irion, 1952, Ch. 10). McGeoch held, for example, that decrement of *AB* retention in the RI paradigm is a matter of the direct competition between *B* and *C* responses. The learning of *C* does not alter the strength of *B* as in the extinction hypothesis. Rather, when *A* is presented, the *B* and *C* responses compete for occurrence, and to the extent that *C* responses are stronger,

Fig. 4-4.   Hypothetical recall function showing *AB* as an increasing function of the retention interval in an RI paradigm. The spontaneous recovery of *AB* results in a corresponding decrease of *AC*'s availability.

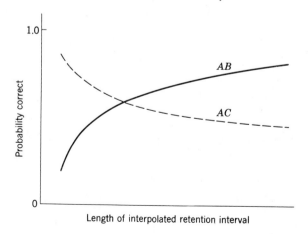

they intrude and momentarily dominate some or all of the *B* responses. The extent to which *B* responses are dominated in the retention test is a measure of the amount of RI, and the decrement in *B* responses should mainly be due to *C* responses which have the upper hand in the competition and are now error intrusions. Important for McGeoch's position is the fact that *AC* does not fundamentally change *AB;* the two response systems are assumed to remain independent. In fact, Barnes and Underwood (1959, p. 98) called it the "independence hypothesis," and this is now the commonplace label for McGeoch's point of view.

Melton and Irwin (1940) used serial learning of consonant-vowel-consonant syllables such as DAK (known as CVCs) in an RI design. The experimental variable was the number of practice trials given list 2, the list interpolated between the original learning and recall of list 1. They found that amount of RI was rather directly related to amount of interpolated learning but, contrary to McGeoch's hypothesis, that overt intrusion errors from list 2 only accounted for a minor portion of the decrement. Most of the decrement was omitted responses, and omissions increased as a function of amount of interpolated activity. Of course, one might keep McGeoch's hypothesis intact with the ad hoc assumption that omissions were covert intrusions, but Melton and Irwin entertained the "unlearning hypothesis" instead. "Unlearning" meant a direct weakening of the original responses when interpolated responses are learned, and according to this view, the extinction hypothesis would be a special form of the unlearning hypothesis. Melton and Irwin, however, did not say that unlearning *is* experimental extinction, but they did suggest that interference may be a process of weakening the original responses and not merely the competition of independent response systems.

The unlearning hypothesis stimulated little interest until Underwood sharpened its outlines with two significant papers

(Underwood, 1948a, 1948b). He found evidences for spontaneous recovery of paired adjectives and for PI to increase and RI to decrease over the retention interval. Underwood suggested that unlearning may well be a matter of experimental extinction. His 1948 data and ideas were the first to give substance to the extinction hypothesis, which was explained in the preceding section. It would be laborious to document all the evidence for the extinction hypothesis, which is formidable by now. However, two of the best studies (Briggs, 1954; Barnes & Underwood, 1959) will be reviewed to give the flavor of the findings and research approaches in the area. Other studies and reviews that support the extinction hypothesis are Goggin, 1963; Houston et al., 1965; McGovern, 1964; Postman, 1961, 1962a, 1962b, 1965; Postman & Stark, 1964, 1965; and Saltz, 1965.

The Briggs Study. Briggs (1954) used an RI paradigm with two lists of 12 paired adjectives having common stimulus terms. The gist of the study was that each subject learned the first list to a criterion of one perfect trial. The second, interfering list was learned to the same criterion 24 hours later. Subgroups of subjects then relearned the original list after retention intervals of 4 minutes, 6, 24, 48, or 72 hours. An important innovation was that Briggs used test trials throughout original and interpolated learning for modified free recall (MFR). In MFR the stimulus terms are presented alone. The subject is asked to give the first response that comes to mind, but only one response. The advantage of MFR is that the subject is free to give any response from either list, or from outside the list if he wishes, and the frequency of each type of response reflects its relative strength. Information about relative response strengths becomes important when the simultaneous acquisition of one response class and the weakening of another, as well as spontaneous recovery, are at the heart of the extinction hypothesis. An MFR test was given after 3 responses ($\frac{1}{4}$ criterial level), 6 responses ($\frac{1}{2}$ criterial level), 9 responses ($\frac{3}{4}$ criterial level), or 12 responses ($\frac{4}{4}$ criterial level) had been given correctly. Also, a free association test for the 12 stimuli was given prior to the experiment so that changes in these preexperimental responses could be charted throughout the experimental learning.

The results are given in Figure 4-5. Notice that in original learning, when there is the expected increase in the reinforced responses of list 1, there is an accompanying decrease in preexperimental responses, which were the ones most strongly attached to the stimuli at the start of the experiment. And in the 24-hour interval between original and interpolated learning, the preexperimental responses show spontaneous recovery. During acquisition of list 2 responses the strength of list 1 responses steadily declines.

Of most interest in Figure 4-5 is the retention function. Because the MFR method allows all response classes to occur freely,

Fig. 4-5. The left and center sets of curves are the acquisition and extinction functions when lists 1 and 2 are learned successively in an RI paradigm. Recall as a function of time from the end of list 2 learning is shown in the right-hand set of curves. Adapted from Briggs (1954).

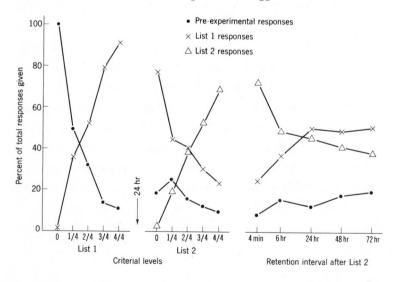

we see the changing strengths of each as a function of time between the end of interpolated learning and the retention test.
The extinguished list 1 responses exhibit a negatively accelerated
spontaneous-recovery function, and correspondingly, list 2 responses decrease in number. The curve for list 1 closely parallels
the ideal curve for the recall of *AB* in the RI design shown in
Figure 4-4, and the curve for list 2 parallels the *AB* curve for the
PI design in Figure 4-2. The preexperimental responses, which
underwent a second extinction during the learning of list 2, show
a small amount of spontaneous recovery.

The Barnes-Underwood Study. The Briggs experiment has all
the functions necessary for support of the extinction hypothesis,
but Briggs himself and Barnes and Underwood (1959, pp. 97–
98) urge restraint in acclaiming the Briggs study fully in behalf
of the extinction hypothesis. The decrease in frequency of list 1
responses during the learning of list 2 responses does not necessarily mean that list 1 responses were extinguished and unavailable for recall. List 2 responses may have only become stronger
relative to those of list 1 without making list 1 responses genu-
inely unavailable. This is another way of saying that McGeoch's
independence hypothesis could be valid. Briggs's method of MFR
allowed the giving of only one response to a stimulus, but the
other response could have been available.

Barnes and Underwood had groups of subjects stop at different points in the learning of list 2 and attempt to recall *both*
list 1 and list 2 responses for each stimulus. If list 1 responses
become increasingly unavailable as list 2 learning increases, even
when given full opportunity to occur, the extinction interpretation becomes more palatable. The opportunity to give both responses is a modification of MFR, and is known as MMFR. The
lists were eight paired associates, with CVCs as stimuli and adjectives as responses. Both lists had the same stimuli. All subjects

learned list 1 to a criterion of one perfect trial, and four groups practiced list 2 for 1, 5, 10, or 20 trials before the MMFR test. The procedure for MMFR was written recall. The answer sheet had the eight stimuli printed on it and spaces to write the two responses associated with each stimulus. The subjects were told to write the responses as they came to mind, making no attempt to recall one list first and then the other. Following this, the subjects were asked to go through the responses they had written and attempt to indicate whether they were from list 1 or list 2.

The mean number of correct responses from list 1 as a function of trials on list 2 is shown in Figure 4-6. The response had to be recalled correctly and identified with its proper list. Even when given a full chance to occur on the MMFR test, list 1 responses are seen to be less and less available as list 2 learning proceeds. Barnes and Underwood conclude that list 1 responses become truly unavailable and extinguished. Because of the work done by Barnes and Underwood, the Briggs study is now on

Fig. 4-6.   Mean number of responses correctly recalled and identified with list by the MMFR Method. From Barnes and Underwood (1959).

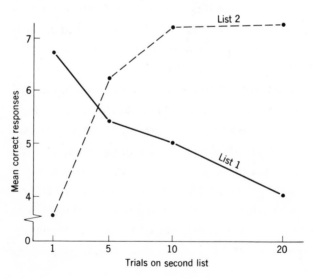

firmer ground as evidence for the extinction hypothesis, and the independence hypothesis is rejected.

General Remarks on the Extinction Hypothesis.   The extinction hypothesis for PI and RI situations is a good example of increasing the generality of empirical laws which govern experimental extinction in simple organisms and responses. Laws with limited domain are not to be discounted, but laws gain in usefulness if their predictive power is widened to new situations. It is as if gravitational force was thought to have value only for balls rolling down inclined planes and was suddenly found to apply to free-falling bodies, from sticks to meteorites. Gravity as a concept in physics most certainly would gain in significance.

Chapter 3 discussed interference as one theory of memory, and it was pointed out that the interference theory of forgetting says nothing of how competing responses affect the state of the underlying habit. In particular, the extinction hypothesis mentions nothing about the fate of the trace. Nor does it suggest whether competing responses permanently erode or merely inhibit the criterion habit. The extinction hypothesis is a good general principle of interference theory, but it leaves untouched the nucleus of the whole forgetting problem—fate of habit.

EFFECTS OF AMOUNT OF TRAINING ON PI AND RI

The extinction hypothesis implies that amount of learning for *AB* and *AC* would be an important variable for PI and RI. Less retention loss should occur as amount of practice (reinforcement) on the criterion *AB* list is increased and *AB* becomes more resistant to the interfering effects of *AC*. And increases in the amount of *AC* practice should heighten the likelihood of interference with *AB*, with increases in retention loss resulting.

Proactive Inhibition

Most verbal interference research has been on RI, but this is largely a matter of the kind of emphasis that has been given the interference theory of forgetting over the years. Until Underwood's article (1957), thinking on the interference theory of forgetting emphasized interference in the interval between learning and recall of *AB* in accordance with the RI design. It was a natural line of thinking. When material is fully learned and can be only partly recalled after the retention interval, it is good common sense to infer that events in the retention interval have causal status. An emphasis on the RI aspects of the interference theory of forgetting is not the least bit wrong, but it is neglectful of PI, and it did lead to a slighting of PI in laboratory studies. As late as 1945 Underwood said, "In fact, the amount of data available on PI is exceedingly scant when compared with the enormous mass of data available on RI" (1945, pp. 4–5); and he went on to say that the dearth of PI data led McGeoch, as an eminent protagonist of the interference theory of forgetting, to relegate it to a minor role in forgetting. Underwood (1957) subsequently made a major case for PI, and since then it has loomed larger in research on forgetting.

Serial Learning.   The topic of serial learning and PI is virtually untouched except for a major experiment by Postman and Riley (1959). They gave either 5, 10, 20, or 40 trials of practice on a criterion list and either 0, 5, 10, 20, or 40 trials on a prior list. Findings for recall of the criterion list after 30 minutes were mixed and uncertain. Amount of prior list learning was a statistically significant variable for recall, but the effects were small and there was no clear pattern to the results.

Paired Associates.   Underwood (1945) conducted the first important investigation on amount of practice and PI as part of a series of studies on verbal interference. Over several sessions, he had the same group of subjects learn either zero (control condition), two, four, or six *AC* lists each time prior to the learning and retention of an *AB* criterion list. All lists were 10 paired adjectives, and all lists had common stimulus terms but dissimilar response terms. The retention interval was 25 minutes. With recall on the first trial of the retention test as the measure, amount of PI increased as a function of number of prior lists learned. Underwood (1949) found a similar function when amount of *AC* learning was defined in terms of number of correct responses on a single list.

Greenberg and Underwood (1950) used a different approach to the problem of amount of prior learning and PI. Previous studies defined amount of prior practice in terms of number of *AC* lists (Underwood, 1945), or number of correct responses on a single *AC* list (Underwood, 1949) before learning and recall of an *AB* list, but Greenberg and Underwood used four stages of practice for each of three groups. A stage of practice was defined as the learning, and recall and relearning, of a given list. Each group had a different list at each stage, but the same retention interval of either 10 minutes, 5 hours, or 48 hours was used for a group throughout. For example, a subject in the 10-minute group would learn a list and then recall and relearn it after 10 minutes as stage 1, return the next day for stage 2 and repeat the sequence with a different list and the same interval, etc. Each list was 10 paired adjectives, with different stimuli and response terms for the pairs of each list.

The results of the Greenberg-Underwood study are shown in Figure 4-7. Retention is unaffected by prior stages of practice when the retention interval is brief, but the loss is apparent at the longer intervals, particularly 48 hours. A curious feature of the Greenberg-Underwood findings, and implicit in Underwood's

1957 analysis also, is that PI occurs even though lists have markedly dissimilar stimuli. Most interference studies have identical stimuli for the lists. In the Greenberg-Underwood experiment, the lists were quite different, however; thus they should have had virtual independence and no PI. Yet, PI occurred. What, then, were the common stimuli to which the different responses became attached and which created the conditions of interference? Greenberg and Underwood were sensitive to this problem, and they suggested that context stimuli of the general experimental situation were part of the functional stimuli. According to this hypothesis, which was mentioned before, the context stimuli of the general experimental surroundings which impinge on the subject supplement the functional stimuli of pairs learned in stage 1. In stage 2 the responses of the new list are also learned to the context stimuli. In so doing, they compete

Fig. 4-7.   Performance as a function of time between the learning of a list of paired associates and its recall in a PI paradigm. The abscissa is stage of practice, in which each stage was learning and recall of a different list. From Greenberg and Underwood (1950).

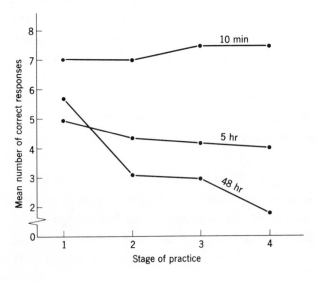

with the responses of stage 1 to these same stimuli and bring about their extinction. As these extinguished responses recover in the retention interval, they produce PI. The greater the number of prior stages, the more extinguished responses there are to recover and interfere with the recall of criterion responses, and the greater the PI. That responses become attached to context stimuli is established experimentally (Bilodeau & Schlosberg, 1951; Greenspoon & Ranyard, 1957).

Prose Passages.   So much verbal learning research is concerned with serial and paired-associates learning that one sometimes has the uneasy feeling that laws are being uncovered with too much narrowness for general interest and applicability. There is nothing basically wrong with laws for paired associates per se, but such laws are trivial goals in and of themselves. Science is more interested in laws of wide scope—and the wider the better. It is refreshing, therefore, to have an experiment like Slamecka's (1961) in which the general expectations for PI are met with prose passages as the learning material. Slamecka had subjects learn paragraphs like, "Any generalized statement of relationship between variables requires specification of some reference class or universe from which the material comes." His subjects learned zero, one, two, or three prior passages before the learning and recall of a criterion passage. Practice was with a memory drum by the serial anticipation method, in which the words of the passage were presented sequentially at a 3-second rate. The subject had to anticipate the next word of the passage while the present word was being displayed. Once through the passage was a trial, and the criterion of learning was one errorless trial. Retention intervals were 15, 30, and 60 minutes, and 24 hours. The results are shown in Figure 4-8, and they nicely fit the expectations for PI and the extinction hypothesis. The PI increases with number of prior passages and length of the retention interval.

Summary. Despite Underwood's analysis (1957), which brought a new focus on PI and forgetting, research lags on basic PI functions. RI has always dominated the research effort, and still does, and the result of our lesser attention to PI is reduced understanding. For example, the interest has been on number of prior lists learned, which is understandable, but there has been little emphasis on amount of practice for the criterion materials being remembered. The notable exception was the serial-learning work of Postman and Riley (1959) who studied amount of practice on both lists, but their findings were inconclusive. What there is of PI research in the paired-associates realm, however, supports the extinction hypothesis.

Retroactive Inhibition

Serial Learning. McGeoch and his associates did much to stim-

Fig. 4-8. In a PI paradigm, the recall of prose passages as a function of retention interval and number of prior passages learned. The score is number correctly anticipated on the first relearning trial. Adapted fom Slamecka (1961).

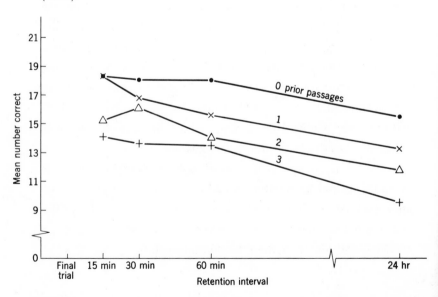

ulate interest in verbal interference and its mechanisms, and their work on amount of practice and RI used serial verbal learning. McGeoch (1929) found that RI decreased as a function of number of repetitions of the first list, and McGeoch (1936) found that increasing the repetitions of an interpolated list increased the RI. Melton and Irwin (1940), in a study on amount of interpolated learning that is better known because it contained the germ of the extinction hypothesis, also found that amount of RI increased with amount of interpolated learning, but only up to an intermediate degree of interpolation. With a comparatively large amount of interpolation the RI decreased just slightly, but not enough to alter the conclusion that RI is a negatively accelerated increasing function of amount of interpolated learning.

Postman and Riley (1959) have performed the most comprehensive experiment on RI and amount of serial learning. The experimental variables were amounts of first-list learning and interpolated learning. The first list was practiced for either 5, 10, 20, or 40 trials and the interpolated list for either 0, 5, 10, 20, or 40 trials. Recall of the first list increased with amount of original learning and decreased with amount of interpolated learning.

Paired-associate Learning. Number of practice trials is the primary approach to manipulating the amount of training on the first or *AB* list in an RI paradigm. But amount of training for the interpolated *AC* list can be defined by either the number of trials given a single *AC* list or the number of different interpolated lists (*AC, AD, AE,* etc.). Both of these approaches should produce some extinction of responses of the *AB* list, and findings for these two methods show this to be the case.

Thune and Underwood (1943) were the first to study the relationship between amount of practice and RI with paired associates. They varied the number of trials on an *AC* list and found that RI was a negatively accelerated increasing function of degree of interpolation. Barnes and Underwood (1959), in a study reviewed earlier in this chapter, manipulated amount of practice on a single interpolated list and, using the MMFR method, convincingly demonstrated that increasing amounts of *AC* learning resulted in increasing extinction of responses from the *AB* list (see Figure 4-6). Postman (1965) also used MMFR, but he manipulated the number of interpolated lists in which stimulus terms were the same as the original *AB* list but response terms were different. Consistent with Barnes and Underwood, Postman concluded that extinction of first-list responses was an increasing function of amount of interpolated learning.

The most comprehensive study on this topic was done by Briggs (1957), and it is worthwhile to present his experiment in detail. Briggs manipulated amount of both *AB*- and *AC*-list learning in the same experiment, which allowed the plotting of RI as a joint function of the two variables. Amount of interpolated learning was defined in terms of number of trials on a single *AC* list. Lists of 10 paired adjectives were used. The originally learned *AB* list was given either 2, 5, 10, or 20 trials. The *AC* list was given either 0 (control), 2, 5, 10, or 20 trials and was followed by recall of the *AB* list by the MFR method. Figure 4-9 is a three-dimensional plot of his findings in terms of relative RI. The amount of relative RI is a percentage defined as (Rest − Work/Rest) × 100. Briggs used number correct on the first recall trial as the score in the formula. The formula expresses how much the interpolated learning reduces recall of *AB* below the control condition that had only rest during the interim between *AB* learning and recall (Briggs did not use a *DE* control condition). For example, in Briggs's data, a control group with 20 trials on the *AB* list (and zero *AC*-list trials) had 9.44 syllables correct on the first recall trial. An experimental group with 20 trials on the *AB* list (and 20 trials on the *AC* list) recalled 4.38 responses. Thus, $(9.44 - 4.38/9.44) \times 100 = 54$ percent relative RI.

Figure 4-9 shows data that are consistent with the extinction hypothesis and with other experimental findings for these variables. We would expect the *AB* list to have its responses increasingly resistant to extinction and to show increasing recall (and thus less RI) as amount of practice increases, and this is clearly evident in Figure 4-9 for all levels of *AC*-list learning. Similarly, increasing the amount of *AC* learning should increase the amount of *AB* extinction and lower recall (more RI). Figure 4-9 shows this also.

Prose Passages. Slamecka, as part of his research program on interference for prose passages, investigated the effect of amount of original and interpolated learning in an RI design. Prose passages, of the kind that Slamecka used in his study of PI described earlier in this chapter (Slamecka, 1961), were used. One of the

Fig. 4-9. Relative retroactive inhibition (see text for definition) as a function of amount of original and interpolated learning. From Briggs (1957).

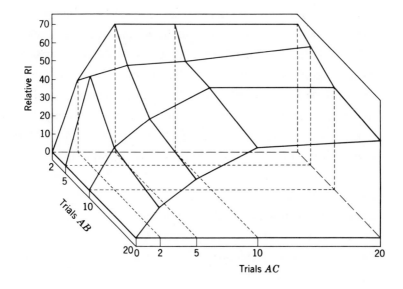

studies (Slamecka, 1960) had three amounts of original and interpolated learning. The amount of interpolated learning was defined as number of practice trials on an interpolated passage. RI was a decreasing function of the strength of the original passage and an increasing function of amount of practice on the interpolated passage—a result fully consistent with the work on serial lists and paired associates.

In a second experiment on the same theme (Slamecka, 1962), level of training on the original passage was held constant and amount of practice on the interpolated passage was varied both by the number of trials on a single passage and by the number of different passages. Amount of RI increased regardless of how amount of interpolated learning was defined, and Slamecka concluded that the way of defining amount of interpolated learning makes scant difference in the outcome of the experiment. Although Underwood (1945) found minor differences in amount of RI as a function of these two methods for defining interpolated learning, it seems fair to conclude that interference for prose passages and paired associates follows the same laws.

Summary. The data on amount of original and interpolated learning for RI are orderly and consistent, and there are enough to be secure in the generalization that (1) RI decreases with increasing practice on the original material, which strengthens against the extinguishing action of interpolated learning; and (2) RI increases as a positive function of the amount of interpolated learning, the extinguishing agent for the original material. These laws are fully in accord with the extinction hypothesis.

SIMILARITY AND VERBAL INTERFERENCE

Paradigms involving *AB* and *AC* have been used in discussions of interference in this chapter so far. The terms *AB* and *AC* mean that stimulus members of corresponding verbal pairs in successive lists are the same and response terms are different, but the nature of the difference that produces interference has not been defined. Furthermore, *AB* and *AC* represent the special case for reliable interference and hardly do justice to the range of stimulus-response variation that is possible. Both the stimulus and response terms of successive pairs can vary through a full range of similarity, and comprehensive laws should include all similarity values, not just the special ones that are known to produce interference. Any combination of stimulus and response similarity is possible. The interference theory of forgetting requires a delineation of materials that interfere with one another, those that are neutral, and those that benefit one another positively. Ideally, psychology would like to have laws which show how RI and PI vary as a function of the systematic manipulation of both stimulus and response similarity. Osgood (1949) and Bugelski and Cadwallader (1956) have attempted this extensive mapping for RI, but the task of working out the corresponding relationships for PI has yet to be undertaken. Even more ideally, one could hope for a family of laws that show RI and PI as a function of stimulus and response similarity, amount of practice on each list, retention interval, etc.

The definition of similarity has had a checkered history. Early studies often used subjective definitions of the similarity relationship between two words. In the case of CVC syllables (consonant-vowel-consonant combination like DAK) or numerals, the number of letters or numerals in common for two verbal units was sometimes used. Synonyms or antonyms were employed. Some of the definitions satisfactorily suited the requirements for objectivity, such as number of common elements, but their application was limited to certain classes of materials. In more recent years there has been a reliance on quantitative scaling of similarity. Haagen (1949) had judges scale word pairs for similarity on a seven-point scale, and his values are often used for expressing the degree of similarity.

There is a provocative move toward defining the relatedness between two words in terms of the number of associations they have in common (Cofer, 1957; Marshall & Cofer, 1963; Garskof & Houston, 1963). Judged similarity and an index of mutual associations correlate highly—Garskof and Houston (1963) report a correlation of .94. A high correlation suggests that a measure of mutual associations has processes in common with judged similarity, and it may be interchanged with measures of judged similarity for experimental purposes. However, the implications for an index of relatedness based on joint associations goes beyond interchangeability with scaled similarity. Number of associations for single words is an important definition of meaningfulness (e.g., Noble, 1963), and it is an established variable for verbal learning. To now use number of common associations as an index of similarity for two words creates a lawful relation with meaningfulness and establishes number of associations as a more fundamental determinant of verbal behavior. The new definition of similarity has yet to receive systematic use in research on learning and retention. All the research discussed in this chapter employs judged similarity.

Similarity and Proactive Inhibition

The data on PI and the similarity of verbal materials are scant, and those which are available are not completely consistent. The studies that are worthy of review involve only the experimental manipulation of response similarity, not stimulus similarity; thus only a start has been made in this field.

Morgan and Underwood (1950) used paired adjectives in a PI design, with stimulus terms the same from list 1 to list 2 and response terms varying in similarity. A control group learned and recalled a single list. Five experimental groups each had the response members of their two lists in a different similarity relationship (Haagen, 1949), ranging from dissimilarity (e.g., NOISELESS-SINCERE for list 1, NOISELESS-LATENT for list 2) to high similarity (WILLING-DIRTY for list 1, WILLING-UNCLEAN for list 2). The retention interval was 20 minutes. The results are easily stated—only the experimental group with dissimilar responses had significant PI.

The earlier discussion of the extinction hypothesis, and evidence presented for it, made the point that PI increases with length of the retention interval. Dallett (1962) argued that a PI effect with similar responses would be stronger if a longer retention interval were used, and so he tested recall after 48 hours. Paired associates were used that had the same stimulus terms (CVCs) in both list 1 and list 2, and three levels of response similarity for adjectives (Haagen, 1949) that ranged from dissimilarity to high similarity. The outcome of his study was the same as that of Morgan and Underwood (1950). Only dissimilar responses gave a significant PI effect. However, a later study of Dallett's (1964) gave contradictory results. A portion of the study (his experiment II) reported findings for PI as a function of two levels of response similarity and a retention interval of 48 hours. The level of similarity between list 1 and list 2 was reasonably high in both conditions and represented the conditions which did not induce significant PI in his 1962 study. A significant loss in list 2 performances was found for both levels of similarity, and there was no significant difference between them.

If one is inclined to take a probabilistic point of view and tabulate the percentage of studies that weigh in a particular direction, Morgan and Underwood (1950) and Dallett (1962) lead one to the conclusion that PI occurs only when the stimuli of paired associates are the same and responses are dissimilar. Yet

Dallett (1964) urges us to be cautious. Rather than speculate on reasons for this discrepancy, it is perhaps best to accept the probabilistic viewpoint, use the weight of evidence in our thinking, but keep the exception in mind as a guide for future experimentation.

Similarity and Retroactive Inhibition

Osgood's Transfer and Retroaction Surface. The interest in verbal similarity and RI has been far greater than for PI. Off and on, there has been research on this topic since the 1920s, and in 1949 Osgood gave it an elegant summarization in his transfer and retroaction surface (Osgood, 1949). Rather than dwell on the individual experiments of the pre-1949 era, a more useful expository tactic is to discuss Osgood's surface as it integrates all the findings on similarity, transfer, and retroaction until 1949. Osgood organized the findings of a number of diverse empirical studies into three general laws. The surface is a composite of these empirical generalizations. The transfer and retroaction surface applies to both transfer, or the effect of list 1 on the learning of list 2, and RI, or the effect of interpolating list 2 between the learning of list 1 and its recall. The similarity to which the surface refers is between the stimuli or responses of corresponding word pairs of two lists, or interpair similarity.

Osgood's three laws of transfer and retroaction are:

1. Where stimuli are varied and responses are functionally identical, positive transfer and retroactive facilitation are obtained, the magnitude of both increasing as the similarity among the stimulus members increases.

2. Where stimuli are functionally identical and responses are varied, negative transfer and retroactive interference are obtained, the magnitude of both decreasing as similarity between the responses increases.

3. When both stimulus and response members are simultaneously varied, negative transfer and retroactive interference are obtained, the magnitude of both increasing as the stimulus similarity increases.

Figure 4-10 is the surface Osgood based on the three laws, showing relative amounts of negative or positive transfer and retroaction as a function of stimulus and response similarity [the dashed line is a revision suggested by Bugelski and Cadwallader (1956), to be discussed shortly]. The vertical dimension represents degree of transfer and retroaction, ranging from maximum positive to maximum negative. Response similarity is on a second dimension and stimulus similarity on a third. The medial plane is the region of zero effect. The peak point of maximum positive

Fig. 4-10. Except for the lower dashed line, the transfer and retroaction surface of Osgood (1949). The primary symbols S and R stand for stimulus and response. The subscripts *I, S, N, O,* and *A* signify identical, similar, neutral, opposed, and antagonistic as degrees of similarity in meaning. The lower dashed line is contradictory evidence by Bugelski and Cadwallader (1956).

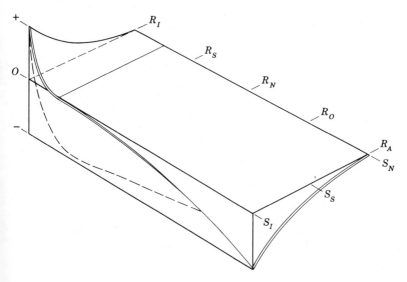

effect occurs when stimuli and responses are identical, which is another way of saying that list 1 and list 2 are the same and that continued practice on the same list is optimum for transfer. Negative transfer is greatest when the stimuli of the two lists are identical and responses are antagonistic in meaning (BLACK-WHITE), according to Osgood's surface. Osgood had no data for antagonistic responses, however; therefore this area of the surface is conjectural.

The Bugelski-Cadwallader Revision of Osgood's Surface. Bugelski and Cadwallader (1956) properly pointed out that Osgood's transfer and retroaction surface is a composite derived from heterogeneous experiments that used different materials, measures, indices of similarity, subjects, and experimental conditions. They believed that an important test of the surface would be a single major experiment with a common method and homogeneous materials, and their experiment was just such a test. Visual forms scaled for similarity were used as stimulus terms of the pairs, and adjectives scaled for similarity were the response terms. Four similarity values ranging from identical to opposite in meaning were used. All possible combinations of four levels of stimulus and response similarity were employed, with an independent group (N-9) for each combination. Each list had 13 pairs. All groups learned the same first list, and each had a prescribed stimulus- and/or response-similarity variation for the interpolated list. The retention interval between the end of interpolated learning and recall of the first list was 2 minutes. The method of adjusted learning was used, in which a pair was dropped from the list when it was successfully anticipated twice in a row (Madden, Adams, & Spence, 1950; Battig, 1965). This is a methodological advance over the anticipation method (e.g., memory drum) because each pair is raised to a common criterion of performance rather than having the criterion, like one errorless trial, relate to the list as a whole. When the criterion is defined for the list, the easy pairs are learned quickly and become overlearned as the subject practices the more difficult pairs, but difficult pairs may only have correct anticipations on the final trial and be of comparatively low strength. The method of adjusted learning is considered superior for a PI or RI design because the items of both lists are closely equated for level of performance (implying a similar level of associative strength), which is a desirable control when other variables like similarity are being studied.

It will suffice to say that the findings of Bugelski and Cadwallader agreed with Osgood's surface except for the dashed curve drawn in Figure 4-10 (based on the recall measure). They say, on the basis of this disagreement, that Osgood's second empirical law should be modified to read:

> Where stimuli are functionally identical and responses are varied, negative transfer and retroactive interference are obtained, the magnitude of both first increasing and then decreasing as similarity between the responses increases.

And Bugelski and Cadwallader agree that transfer and retroaction can be described by the same surface. They found a high correlation (−.85) between number of trials to learn the second list and recall of the first list.

Whose Surface Shall We Choose?   The surface of Bugelski and Cadwallader has the advantage of being derived from a study in which stimulus and response similarity are manipulated under common experimental conditions, in contrast to the data from mixed sources that Osgood had to rely on. Yet, the rejection of Osgood's surface, and the acceptance of Bugelski and Cadwallader's, may be hasty. The proposed revision of Osgood's second law may not be sound. The recommended reason for casting out the second law is that with identical stimuli and response variation Osgood specifies substantial interference for opposing responses, whereas Bugelski and Cadwallader say that interference is the greatest with similar responses. In a relevant experiment, Gladis and Braun (1958) used identical stimuli and variation of response similarity and found the *least* amount of interference for highly similar responses. Gladis and Braun saw their data in agreement with Osgood's surface insofar as they tested it. Barnes and Underwood (1959), in a part of their experiment that was omitted in the earlier discussion of their study, used identical stimuli and similar responses for the two lists as one of their experimental treatments. For this experimental condition, Bugelski and Cadwallader found the most interference, but Barnes and Underwood found high positive transfer in the learning of list 2 and high retroactive facilitation in the recall of list 1. Barnes and Underwood report evidence for mediation when responses are similar. A response to a list 1 stimulus is used as an implicit aid for learning the highly similar response to the same stimulus in list 2. Of 96 subjects in the Barnes-Underwood study, 94 reported using mediation when responses were similar.

There are other reasons why we should not reject Osgood's surface hastily. The experiment of Bugelski and Cadwallader is methodologically sound, but one cannot conceal wonder about so major an experiment using only nine subjects in a group. Merely because our statistical techniques countenance small samples and allow us to detect population differences does not mean that they should be used when the verification of functional form is at stake. The variance of the mean is inversely proportional to the number of observations N, and when a function is plotted in terms of group means, we should strive to stabilize the means in all ways possible. Large N is a primary way of doing this. If the supply of subjects is limited, it is wise to reduce the scope of an experiment and do a better job of estimating fewer functions. Also, Bugelski and Cadwallader used visual forms as stimuli. Osgood's surface could conceivably apply to the combination of perceptual and verbal learning that Bugelski and Cadwallader used, but it is unmistakable that Osgood intended his surface to describe functions for verbal behavior only.

Considering all things, Osgood's transfer and retroaction surface is not wholly unusable. Osgood's surface does have the weakness of being partly speculative and of being derived from heterogeneous experiments. Bugelski and Cadwallader were sound to check a portion of it in a single homogeneous experiment. There is cause, however, to doubt the Bugelski-Cadwallader undertaking, meritorious though it was. Certainly further investigations are in order. New experiments can profitably go beyond the empirical variables of stimulus and response similarity that define the surface. Being descriptive and empirical, the transfer and retroaction surface does not ask, for example, about underlying mediational behavior that can influence the amounts of negative or positive transfer that can be obtained (mediation will be discussed later in this chapter). The trend for the future appears to be analysis of the processes which lie beneath the amounts of positive and negative transfer that define the surface, rather than working out an accurate empirical description of the surface, useful though this description might be. Martin (1965) attempts an explanation of the surface in terms of three processes which he identifies as underlying verbal learning. Battig (1966) discusses issues for the transfer and retroaction surface, and his work can be profitably read.

Acoustic Similarity and Short-term Memory

Chapters 3 and 5 discuss acoustic similarity as one of the grounds for distinguishing short-term memory from long-term memory. It deserves mention because it is a kind of similarity that relates

to interference. The studies on similarity that have been discussed in this chapter so far have dealt with semantic similarity
along a dimension of meaning and, implicitly, with LTM because
well-practiced verbal responses are involved. The studies of
acoustic similarity and STM (e.g., Conrad, 1964; Conrad & Hull,
1964; Conrad, Freeman, & Hull, 1965; Wickelgren, 1965a, 1965b)
were qualitative in demonstrating that interference occurs when
sounds are similar, but as yet there has been no scaling of acous-
tical similarity that could lead to a transfer and retroaction surface for STM.

VERBAL MEDIATION AND INTERFERENCE

There are limitations to the laws of interference, apart from the
usual needs for more research and the occasional experiments
whose findings do not agree. The principal fault of interference
theory is that it is based on an oversimplified conception of how
verbal paired associates are learned, and it fails to consider the
actual complexity of the verbal behavior that takes place when
a subject learns a word pair. Depending upon the theory, habit
is all-or-none and formed in one trial (e.g., Estes, 1960) or is
incremental and requires multiple trials (e.g., Hull et al., 1940;
Underwood & Keppel, 1962). The position is, in effect, one of
rote (nonmediated) learning, whatever the theory. This is not
to say that modern workers ignore mediation, but it seems fair to
say that most experimenters see the learning of a word pair as
the strengthening of a direct habit bond between the stimulus
and response term. This is another way of saying that learning
is achieved by rote.

In actuality, many pairs are not learned by rote at all, as
evidence presented later in this chapter will show. Instead, a
subject will very often *mediate*, or impose implicit verbal re-

sponse chains between the stimulus and the response. Using his very complex language habits from a lifetime of learning, the subject may link the members of a pair with a one-word association or a more elaborate language sequence like a sentence, or he may rely on similarities between the sounds of the two words. When the stimulus term is presented, the mediator is elicited which in turn arouses the response. In a more complex case, which is poorly understood, the response is imbedded in the mediator and somehow must be retrieved.

To illustrate mediators of this kind, suppose the subject was given the pair CAT-RAT to learn. Through his mediational mechanisms he may impose the association that CAT sounds like RAT, that CAT and RAT have two letters in common, or that CAT is an animal that likes to eat a RAT. When CAT is presented alone as a stimulus in a retention test, the mediator and RAT are run off as an integrated response sequence, with the mediator covert and RAT overt. Mediators are idiosyncratic and often take imaginative forms from subject to subject. Although some subjects might have mediators in common because of common language habits, the varieties of past experience among subjects impart strong uniqueness to the mediator for a word pair. Underwood and Schulz (1960, pp. 296–300), Clark, Lansford, and Dallenbach (1960, p. 33), and Bugelski (1962, p. 411) all report on the frequent occurrence of mediators. A mediator of this sort for a word pair has been called an "associative aid" (Reed, 1918), but this is a loaded label as it implies benefits for verbal behavior. In the absence of more evidence than we now have on the beneficial effects of self-imposed mediators, it would seem best to use *natural language mediator* (NLM) as a more neutral tag. To identify them as self-imposed mediators from the natural language keeps them separate from mediators which are trained in the laboratory (Jenkins, 1963).

Some experimenters would label mediational learning as

"cognitive" or "learning with understanding" or "relational learning," and certainly it is their scientific privilege to assign tags freely. Whatever the name, it is a reasonable hypothesis that NLMs represent a case of transfer of training in which the skills of past language learning are applied to the new learning, a point of view in agreement with Underwood (1964, pp. 68–70) and Björgen (1964, p. 105). A transfer-of-training view hardly denies rote learning, for certainly there are word pairs which must be learned from the beginning, as a zero transfer case.

The Adams-Montague Experiment. An experiment by Adams and Montague (1967) illustrates the presence of NLMs in paired-associate learning and demonstrates their role in an *AB–AC–AB* paradigm for RI. Lists of eight paired adjectives were used, with identical stimuli and different response terms. Questionnaires given after original and interpolated learning were the source of the mediational device, if any, that the subjects used in learning the pairs. Table 4-1 is a tabulation for 60 subjects (480 pairs) of the joint relative frequency for *AB* and *AC* of the four kinds of NLMs that occurred, the evidences of rote learning, and the occasional instances of subjects forgetting how they learned a pair. Table 4-2 shows the four NLM categories that were used and examples of each. An impressive fact about Table 4-1 is the large amount of mediation that took place. The proportion of pairs learned by rote in original learning was only 0.332, and this value dropped to 0.128 in interpolated learning. The reduction in rote learning from original to interpolated learning (also found by Martin & Dean, 1966) was mostly absorbed by an increase in number of sentence NLMs. Perhaps the interpolated list was more amenable to NLM formation, although subjects could have learned how to learn and become more facile after the experience of the first list.

Table 4-3 shows the effect of NLM versus rote in original

Table 4-1. Joint Probability of Occurrence of Method of Association Used in Original (AB) and Interpolated (AC) Learning. Based on 480 Pairs in Original Learning and 480 Pairs in Interpolated Learning. From Adams and Montague (1967)

Method of association	Interpolated learning (AC)						
	Sentence association	Word association	Sound association	Letter association	Rote	Forgot how pair was learned	Total
Sentence association	0.233	0.035	0.004	0.015	0.067	0.004	0.358
Word association	0.075	0.023	0.010	0.004	0.050	0.0	0.162
Sound association	0.046	0.021	0.002	0.0	0.006	0.0	0.075
Letter association	0.023	0.012	0.006	0.006	0.010	0.002	0.059
Rote	0.112	0.037	0.017	0.006	0.158	0.002	0.332
Forgot how pair was learned	0.006	0.0	0.0	0.002	0.002	0.0	0.010
Total	0.495	0.128	0.039	0.033	0.293	0.008	

Original learning (AB)

Table 4-2.   The Four Categories to Which Mediators Were
Assigned in the Adams and Montague (1967) Study

Mediator category	Word pair	Sample of mediator reported on questionnaire
Sentence association	INSHORE-VICTOR	I thought of troops landing on a shore
Word association	RETAIL-WEALTHY	Money
Sound association	RETAIL-FATAL	The two words sound alike
Letter association	PORTLY-UNEARNED	P–U

Table 4-3.   Proportion of Items Correct at Recall as a Function of
Method of Association Used in Original (*AB*) and Interpolated
(*AC*) Learning. The Proportion Is Obtained from the Ratio Given, in
Which the Ratio Is Number Correct at Recall Relative to the Total
Number of Pairs in the Category. From Adams and Montague (1967)

		Interpolated learning (*AC*)		
		Mediated	Rote	
Original learning (*AB*)	Mediated	66:82 0.804	23:26 0.884	89:108 0.824
	Rote	17:28 0.607	14:24 0.583	31:52 0.596
		83:110 0.755	37:50 0.740	Total: 120:160 0.750

and interpolated learning on the recall of *AB*. In the recall data
in Table 4-3, 20 subjects (160 pairs) are represented, which is
a group that had standard MFR recall in contrast to other groups
that had specialized recall treatments and need not concern us
here. Table 4-3 shows the four mediation subcategories collapsed
into one main mediation category; thus the comparison is simply

between rote learning and mediation. Overall, the number of pairs correctly recalled was 120 out of 160. The row proportions, showing the effects on recall of mediation and rote in the original learning of *AB*, have an impressively higher proportion correct for mediated pairs. The column totals do not show a corresponding difference in recall for mediation versus rote in interpolated learning, however. Apparently the critical matter for correct recall of *AB* is whether *AB* was mediated or not when originally learned. When mediated, the *AB* pairs have good resistance to interference from *AC*. Notice that mediation for *AB* does not give immunity to interference. The proportion of mediated *AB* items not recalled is 0.176.

Issues and Implications for NLMs and Interference Theory. Some difficult methodological questions are raised in an experiment like that of Adams-Montague in which NLMs were collected with questionnaires after original and interpolated learning. Was the NLM a genuine part of the associative process and an intrinsic part of the learning for a pair, or was it only an epiphenomenon whose effects occurred because of their correlation with another, more basic variable? Stated another way, was the NLM actually used to form the association between the elements of the pair, or was it added after the basic association was formed? There are three possibilities for a relationship between NLMs and the associative process when NLMs are collected after the learning of a list has been completed.

The first possibility would assume that an NLM occurs at the time the questionnaire is administered and is not an intrinsic part of the associative process in the practice trials. Some variation in associative strength would be expected among items, and it is possible that the stronger items tended to produce NLMs. Since higher levels of learning result in less RI, such items would tend to have less interference decrement—not because of NLMs but because of the associative strength with which an NLM is correlated.

The second possibility would assume that NLMs are a close correlate of the associative process during the practice trials but not a direct determinant of it. When the associative strength for a pair builds up to a certain level in the practice trials, the subject can begin to perceive relationships with his well-learned language sequences and perhaps find an NLM at that time. Here again would exist the possibility that NLMs relate to RI because they are a correlate of associative strength as a more fundamental variable.

The third possibility is to consider NLMs a direct determinant of associative strength, not a correlate of it. The adult subject capitalizes on the relationship between elements of a pair and integrated sequences in his language repertoire and brings these sequences to bear on the learning of the pair. This is the transfer-of-training view which was discussed before and which says that verbal units are learned in relation to a vast matrix of existing language habits. Admittedly the postlearning method of questioning about NLMs has methodological shortcomings in securing the transfer hypothesis and allows the counter hypothesis of NLMs as correlates of the associative process. However, the shortcomings may only be a deficiency in experimental method, and hopefully the procedures can be improved. One potential improvement might be to have the subject verbalize his NLM as it occurs to him when a pair is presented on a trial, rather than after the criterion of learning for the list has been reached. This would reduce the criticism that an NLM was formed after the fact, although it would not eliminate it because a rote association could conceivably occur first, followed by an NLM, even in the few seconds available to study a pair on a trial. Until these problems are worked out, the transfer hypothesis, which assumes a relevance of NLMs for the associative process, will be preferred. Chapter 7 will add evidence for the transfer hypothesis in showing a positive relationship between recall of the NLM and recall of the criterion response.

Assuming the empirical truth of the transfer hypothesis, what are its explanatory implications for the Adams-Montague findings and for interference theory in general? One implication is that NLMs, representing well-learned language habits, give items that have for them a greater associative strength, and less RI occurs for the items as a result. A second possibility is that an NLM makes a response in its totality far more complex and unique than is customarily considered for the extinction hypothesis and the transfer and retroaction surface. When two successive lists with identical stimuli are learned in a PI or RI paradigm, the conventional conception involves a single response for each stimulus:

List 1	*List 2*
$S_1 - R_1$	$S_1 - R_2$

The two responses interfere as list 2 is learned and the responses to list 1 undergo experimental extinction, as we have seen. But, with NLMs, the schema becomes:

List 1	*List 2*
$S_1 - NLM_1 - R_1$	$S_1 - NLM_2 - R_2$

The response for each list involves the NLM plus the response term of the pair. This response composite is relatively unique for corresponding pairs in each list, and the likelihood of competition between the composites is reduced. Less interference should occur. That less interference sometimes occurs than might be expected bothers some interference theorists (Postman, 1963). This is exemplified in Figure 4-6 in which the data of

Barnes and Underwood (1959) show that even after extended list 2 learning the recall of list 1 responses is about 50 percent and is showing a distinct tendency to level off. Why is extinction only partial? One reason could be that some pairs have NLMs and little or no interference occurs for them.

The occurrence of NLMs in verbal interference paradigms hardly negates interference theory because the theory says nothing about the complexity of responses. Because contemporary research assumes that the single response elements of word pairs are the interacting responses does not mean that the theory (and the thinking of theorists) cannot be enlarged to accommodate greater response complexity. Foremost, we must work toward a better understanding of what interferes with what—toward a new conception of a transfer and retroaction surface that considers the similarity of responses that actually occur, explicit or implicit, not merely the responses that the experimenter presents to a subject. The similarity of overt response members is hardly irrelevant, because the transfer and retroaction surface shows a definite lawfulness with respect to it. Yet, it appears that we must consider the similarity of *all* verbal responses that are taking place, and how they interact, not just the response members which the experimenter defines.

It is difficult at this early stage of understanding to see how interference theory will be affected by NLMs, but it is becoming increasingly evident that our conception of response has been naïve. Earlier, a distinction was made between nominal stimuli which the experimenter assumes the subject is using as cues for responding, and the functional stimuli which he actually uses. A corresponding distinction for response seems justified. The *nominal response* of the word pair is not always the same as the *functional response* which the subject makes and which can include a covert NLM along with the overt response of the word pair.

A Methodological Comment on Retrospective Reports. An NLM is obtained through interviews or questionnaires that ask a subject how he learned each pair. This procedure may not appeal to many experimental psychologists in the stimulus-response tradition who are rather strictly inclined to present a stimulus and record the overt response that occurs. Verbal reports may smack of clinical practices that are scientifically dubious from a tough laboratory viewpoint, or they may hark back to the old phenomenological days of introspection, and stimulus-response psychologists are reluctant to embrace clinical practices or regress. Yet, the strong reliance of stimulus-response psychology on observable events does not mean disinterest in the unobservable mediational states that determine behavior. The label "stimulus-response" mostly means that the psychologist is in the behaviorist tradition of dealing with objective, operationally defined variables rather than vague, elusive entities like consciousness that were pursued in prebehaviorist times. As far as verbal mediators are concerned, the stimulus-response psychologist prefers to infer them from their effects on criterion responses rather than from verbal reports that hopefully are correlated with mediational states. Effects on criterion responses are observed as a function of the experimental circumstances that define the presence or absence of a particular mediational event, or different amounts of it. The present-day approach to mediation in verbal learning is to have subjects learn a sequence of lists. Through learning, some responses become mediators that facilitate the learning of other responses (Earhard & Mandler, 1965; Jenkins, 1963). For example, the three-list paradigm AB–BC–AC trains B as a mediator between A and C in the first two lists which in turn is an influence on the learning of AC in the third list. The subject is almost never questioned about his use of B as a mediator in the learning of AC. The presence of B is inferred when the AC learning is compared with proper control groups who have not had prior

AB–BC learning. There is nothing wrong with this procedure; it is methodologically above reproach. However, Montague and Kiess (in press) have shown that paradigms of the *AB–BC–AC* sort vastly oversimplify the mediational behavior that is actually operating. Over half of their subjects imposed NLMs on the pairs and used them as a supplement or a substitute for the mediators being trained. With all the self-imposed mediation occurring, the effect of experimental mediators was greatly obscured. For other experiments that use mediation paradigms and question the subjects, see Martin and Dean (1964, 1966).

If it is necessary to attach a label to the verbal report method for gathering NLMs, it might be called "stimulus-response$_1$-response$_2$," in which response$_1$ is the verbal report which gives the internal verbal chain that is the mediator, and response$_2$ is the response word presented by the experimenter. The NLM should be seen as an independent variable, response-defined, that joins other independent variables to predict the criterion response$_2$. As a response-defined independent variable that specifies under-the-skin mediational events, it is directly comparable to certain uses of printed tests in experimental psychology. The Taylor Manifest Anxiety Scale is a printed test that yields responses which supposedly reflect a mediational anxiety state. These test scores, along with practice and task variables, are used for the prediction of conditioned eyeblinks (e.g., Spence, 1964). NLMs come from interviews or questionnaires, but they are response-defined variables that specify under-the-skin states also; thus they have the same methodological status as test scores. Like any other independent variable, their value lies in the contribution they make to the prediction of criterion behavior. The degree to which NLMs from verbal reports define relevant mediational events for behavioral prediction, and the degree to which relevant mediators are "unconscious" and incapable of verbalization, is a matter for empirical research, just as the degree to which the Taylor Manifest Anxiety Scale measures anxiety is a matter for research. Whatever the weight of NLMs in behavior prediction, there is no need to be apprehensive about regression to phenomenology as long as objective measures from verbal reports are used in the prediction of objective criterion behavior.

CONCLUSION

This chapter has reviewed the laws of interference as background for subsequent discussions of the interference theory of forgetting. Our level of scientific understanding is moderate for verbal interference, but it nevertheless is rather good as areas go in experimental psychology. A delicate problem in understanding the worth of the interference theory of forgetting is that we do not know whether a failure to confirm a prediction from the theory (see Chapter 7, for example) occurs because the theory is fundamentally wrong (i.e., trace decay may really be the explanation) or because the theory is fundamentally correct but we do not know enough about interference to define a hypothesis explicitly enough to be tested. Only improved laws of interference can solve such a problem.

REFERENCES

Adams, J. A., & Montague, W. E. Retroactive inhibition and natural language mediation. *J. verbal Learn. verbal Behav.*, 1967, in press.

Barnes, Jean M., & Underwood, B. J. "Fate" of first-list associations in transfer theory. *J. exp. Psychol.*, 1959, **58**, 97–105.

Battig, W. F. Procedural problems in paired-associate learning research. *Psychon. Monogr. Suppl.*, 1965, **1**, No. 1.

Battig, W. F. Facilitation and interference. In E. A. Bilodeau (Ed.), *Acquisition of skill.* New York: Academic, 1966. Pp. 215–244.

Bilodeau, Ina McD., & Schlosberg, H. Similarity in stimulating conditions as a variable in retroactive inhibition. *J. exp. Psychol.*, 1951, **41**, 199–204.

Björgen, I. A. *A re-evaluation of rote learning.* The Norwegian Research Council for Science and the Humanities, 1964.

Briggs, G. E. Acquisition, extinction, and recovery functions in retroactive inhibition. *J. exp. Psychol.*, 1954, **47**, 285–293.

Briggs, G. E. Retroactive inhibition as a function of the degree of original and interpolated learning. *J. exp. Psychol.*, 1957, **53**, 60–67.

Bugelski, B. R. Presentation time, total time, and mediation in paired-associate learning. *J. exp. Psychol.*, 1962, **63**, 409–412.

Bugelski, B. R., & Cadwallader, T. C. A reappraisal of the transfer and retroaction surface. *J. exp. Psychol.*, 1956, **52**, 360–366.

Clark, L. L., Lansford, T. G., & Dallenbach, K. M. Repetition and associative learning. *Amer. J. Psychol.*, 1960, **73**, 22–40.

Cofer, C. N. Associative commonality and rated similarity of certain words from Haagen's list. *Psychol. Rep.*, 1957, **3**, 603–606.

Conrad, R. Acoustic confusions in immediate memory. *Brit. J. Psychol.*, 1964, **55**, 75–84.

Conrad, R., Freeman, P. R., & Hull, A. J. Acoustic factors versus language factors in short-term memory. *Psychon. Sci.*, 1965, **3**, 57–58.

Conrad, R., & Hull, A. J. Information, acoustic confusion and memory span. *Brit. J. Psychol.*, 1964, **55**, 429–432.

Dallett, K. M. The role of response similarity in proactive inhibition. *J. exp. Psychol.*, 1962, **64**, 364–372.

Dallett, K. M. Proactive and retroactive inhibition in the *A–B, A–B'* paradigm. *J. exp. Psychol.*, 1964, **68**, 190–200.

Earhard, B., & Mandler, G. Mediated associations: Paradigms, controls, and mechanisms. *Canad. J. Psychol.*, 1965, **19**, 346–378.

Estes, W. K. Learning theory and the new "mental chemistry." *Psychol. Rev.*, 1960, **67**, 207–223.

Garskof, B. E., & Houston, J. P. Measurement of verbal relatedness: An idiographic approach. *Psychol. Rev.*, 1963, **70**, 277–280.

Gladis, M., & Braun, H. W. Age differences and retroaction as a function of intertask similarity. *J. exp. Psychol.*, 1958, **55**, 25–30.

Goggin, J. Influence of the written recall measure on first-list associations. *J. exp. Psychol.*, 1963, **65**, 619–620.

Greenberg, Ruth, & Underwood, B. J. Retention as a function of stage of practice. *J. exp. Psychol.*, 1950, **40**, 452–457.

Greenspoon, J., & Ranyard, R. Stimulus conditions and retroactive inhibition. *J. exp. Psychol.*, 1957, **53**, 55–59.

Haagen, C. H. Synonymity, vividness, familiarity and association value ratings of 400 pairs of common adjectives. *J. Psychol.*, 1949, **27**, 453–463.

Houston, J. P., Garskof, B. E., Noyd, D. E., & Erskine, J. M. First-list retention as a function of the method of recall. *J. exp. Psychol.*, 1965, **69**, 326–327.

Hull, C. L., Hovland, C. I., Ross, R. T., Hall, M., Perkins, D. T., & Fitch, F. B. *Mathematico-deductive theory of rote learning.* New Haven: Yale Univer. Press, 1940.

Jenkins, J. J. Mediated associations: Paradigms and situations. In C. N. Cofer & Barbara S. Musgrave (Eds.), *Verbal behavior and learning.* New York: McGraw-Hill, 1963. Pp. 210–245.

Kimble, G. A. *Conditioning and learning.* New York: Appleton-Century-Crofts, 1961.

McGeoch, J. A. The influence of degree of learning upon retroactive inhibition. *Amer. J. Psychol.*, 1929, **41**, 252–262.

McGeoch, J. A. Studies in retroactive inhibition: VII. Retroactive inhibition as a function of the length and frequency of presentation of the interpolated lists. *J. exp. Psychol.*, 1936, **19**, 674–693.

McGeoch, J. A., & Irion, A. L. *The psychology of human learning.* (2d ed.) New York: Longmans, 1952.

McGovern, Jean B. Extinction of associations in four transfer paradigms. *Psychol. Monogr.*, 1964, **78** (Whole No. 593).

Madden, Marian S., Adams, J. A., & Spence, Shirley A. Memory-drum vs. adjusted-learning techniques in the study of associative interference in learning by paired-associates. *Amer. J. Psychol.*, 1950, **63**, 186–195.

Marshall, G. R., & Cofer, C. N. Associative indices as measures of word relatedness: A summary and comparison of ten methods. *J. verbal Learn. verbal Behav.*, 1963, **1**, 408–421.

Martin, E. Transfer of verbal paired associates. *Psychol. Rev.*, 1965, **72**, 327–343.

Martin, R. B., & Dean, S. J. Implicit and explicit mediation. *J. exp. Psychol.*, 1964, **68**, 21–28.

Martin, R. B., & Dean, S. J. Reported mediation in paired-associate learning. *J. verbal Learn. varbal Behav.*, 1966, **5**, 23–27.

Melton, A. W., & Irwin, J. M. The influence of degree of interpolated learning on retroactive inhibition and the overt transfer of specific responses. *Amer. J. Psychol.*, 1940, **53**, 173–203.

Montague, W. E., & Kiess, H. O. Effect of mediation training on the acquisition and retention of paired associates, in press.

Morgan, R. L., & Underwood, B. J. Proactive inhibition as a function of response similarity. *J. exp. Psychol.*, 1950, **40**, 592–603.

Noble, C. E. Meaningfulness and familiarity. In C. N. Cofer & Barbara S. Musgrave (Eds.), *Verbal behavior and learning*. New York: McGraw-Hill, 1963. Pp. 76–119.

Osgood, C. E. The similarity paradox in human learning. *Psychol. Rev.*, 1949, **56**, 132–143.

Postman, L. The present status of interference theory. In C. N. Cofer (Ed.), *Verbal learning and verbal behavior*. New York: McGraw-Hill, 1961. Pp. 152–179.

Postman, L. The temporal course of proactive inhibition for serial lists. *J. exp. Psychol.*, 1962, **63**, 361–369. (a)

Postman, L. Retention of first-list associations as a function of the conditions of transfer. *J. exp. Psychol.*, 1962, **64**, 380–387. (b)

Postman, L. Does interference theory predict too much forgetting? *J. verbal Learn. verbal Behav.*, 1963, **2**, 40–48.

Postman, L. Unlearning under conditions of successive interpolation. *J. exp. Psychol.*, 1965, **70**, 237–246.

Postman, L., & Riley, D. A. Degree of learning and interserial interference in retention. *Univer. of California Publ. Psychol.*, Berkeley, 1959, **8**, 271–396.

Postman, L., & Stark, Karen. Proactive inhibition as a function of the conditions of transfer. *J. verbal Learn. verbal Behav.*, 1964, **3**, 249–259.

Postman, L., & Stark, Karen. The role of response set in tests of unlearning. *J. verbal Learn. verbal Behav.*, 1965, **4**, 315–322.

Reed, H. B. Associative aids: I. Their relation to learning, retention, and other associations. *Psychol. Rev.*, 1918, **25**, 128–155.

Saltz, E. Spontaneous recovery of letter-sequence habits. *J. exp. Psychol.*, 1965, **69**, 304–307.

Slamecka, N. J. Retroactive inhibition of connected discourse as a function of practice level. *J. exp. Psychol.*, 1960, **59**, 104–108.

Slamecka, N. J. Proactive inhibition of connected discourse. *J. exp. Psychol.*, 1961, **62**, 295–301.

Slamecka, N. J. Retention of connected discourse as a function of duration of interpolated learning. *J. exp. Psychol.*, 1962, **63**, 480–486.

Spence, K. W. Anxiety (drive) level and performance in eyelid conditioning. *Psychol. Bull.*, 1964, **61**, 129–139.

Thune, L. E., & Underwood, B. J. Retroactive inhibition as a function of degree of interpolated learning. *J. exp. Psychol.*, 1943, **32**, 185–201.

Underwood, B. J. The effect of successive interpolations on retroactive and proactive inhibition. *Psychol. Monogr.*, 1945, **59** (Whole No. 273).

Underwood, B. J. Retroactive and proactive inhibition after five and forty-eight hours. *J. exp. Psychol.*, 1948, **38**, 29–38. (a)

Underwood, B. J. "Spontaneous recovery" of verbal associations. *J. exp. Psychol.*, 1948, **38**, 429–439. (b)

Underwood, B. J. Proactive inhibition as a function of time and degree of prior learning. *J. exp. Psychol.*, 1949, **39**, 24–34.

Underwood, B. J. Interference and forgetting. *Psychol. Rev.*, 1957, **64**, 49–60.

Underwood, B. J. Stimulus selection in verbal learning. In C. N. Cofer & Barbara S. Musgrave (Eds.), *Verbal behavior and learning.* New York: McGraw-Hill, 1963. Pp. 33–48.

Underwood, B. J. The representativeness of rote verbal learning. In A. W. Melton (Ed.), *Categories of human learning.* New York: Academic, 1964. Pp. 47–78.

Underwood, B. J., & Keppel, G. One-trial learning? *J. verbal Learn. verbal Behav.*, 1962, **1**, 1–13.

Underwood, B. J., & Schulz, R. W. *Meaningfulness and verbal learning.* New York: Lippincott, 1960.

Wickelgren, W. A. Acoustic similarity and intrusion errors in short-term memory. *J. exp. Psychol.*, 1965, **70**, 102–108. (a)

Wickelgren, W. A. Acoustic similarity and retroactive interference in short-term memory. *J. verbal Learn. verbal Behav.*, 1965, **4**, 53–61. (b)

Wimer, R. Osgood's transfer surface: Extension and test. *J. verbal Learn. verbal Behav.*, 1964, **3**, 274–279.

Serial Recall of Verbal Responses in Short-term Memory 5

Studies of long-term memory completely dominated forgetting research until the 1950s. At the start of this century, Strong (1913) had the essentials of short-term memory phenomena in hand, but the spirit of the scientific times was unreceptive to his observations. Strong was studying the recognition of meaningful words over retention intervals of 15 seconds to 42 days, and he commented (p. 342) that subjects could rarely recall words a few minutes after their presentation. Recognition was high, but quick forgetting in recall is the stuff from which modern research on STM is made. Strong failed to see the implications of his casual observations and exploit them in research. He was bound by the interests and ideas of his time, just as surely as are most of us. An idea must have a receptive intellectual environment, and there is a splendid chance for it to die if its historical timing is wrong. Later, Pillsbury and Sylvester (1940) came forward with implications similar to Strong's. They showed forgetting over a 10-second retention interval, but again the time was wrong. The scientific climate did not become favorable until 1959 when Peterson and Peterson reported an STM experiment that started a steady flow of studies that shows no sign of slowing.

Chapter 3 presented a panoramic view of the ways that distinguish STM and LTM. With the exception of Milner's physiological work (e.g., 1959), the reasons for the distinction are behavioral, and it is the behavioral side of STM that will be examined in detail in this chapter. The data of Milner's were covered in some detail in Chapter 3, and they will be given no further discussion.

Most STM experiments have been with verbal materials, and responses at recall can be required either in the original order in which they were administered (serial recall) or any order (free recall). This chapter is about the *serial recall of verbal responses*. Free recall will be examined in Chapter 6. And short-term recall of motor responses will be examined in Chapter 8 in which motor behavior is a featured topic in its own right.

THE DISTINCTION BETWEEN SERIAL AND FREE RECALL

An experimenter can require either serial recall or free recall at the retention test, and the implications for each are different.

Serial Recall

A subject is given a series of criterion items to learn, such as eight digits. He is given an opportunity to read, see, or hear them, and after a brief retention interval, usually less than a minute, a signal is given for recall. An error is counted if a digit is omitted, if a digit in a particular serial position is given wrongly because a new digit was introduced that was not in the criterion set, or if one or more of the eight digits was transposed and recalled in an order different from the prescribed one. The eight digits must be recalled in their original positions to be scored fully correct.

Free Recall

Order of items is ignored in free recall. A subject receives the items in an order defined by the experimenter, but there are no restrictions on their order at recall. This means that the subject can impose organization and structure on items that may seemingly be random and meaningless. By "organization and structure" is meant the reordering of newly learned items at recall in accord with past learning. Thus, four animal words from a list of randomly presented words may be grouped together in free recall as if the subject's previously acquired concept behavior is the organizing agent. A basic measure of retention is the number of items correctly recalled, but measures of organization and structure are commonly used also.

BASIC DATA ON SHORT–TERM SERIAL RECALL

The effects of length of the retention interval and amount of practice on recall are fundamental for any area of forgetting, and STM is no exception. The empirical findings for these two variables are examined in this section without much comment. Later sections of this chapter will provide explanatory substance for these empirical findings because it took a research effort on interference and STM before a theoretical niche was found for them.

Effects of the Retention Interval

The Peterson-Peterson Study. This is one of the landmark studies, of which there are few in psychology, or any other science for that matter. The experiment by Peterson and Peterson (1959) unleashed a flood of interest and experiments on STM, and reawakened theorizing about immediate memory and its relation to LTM. Studies by Brown (1958) in England were a bit prior in time to the Peterson-Peterson work and closely similar in method and outcome, but it was the Peterson-Peterson paper that gave impetus to modern STM research.

Peterson and Peterson began by doing a simple and elegant thing—they dispensed with the ubiquitous list of verbal items that since Ebbinghaus had stood astride psychology like a colossus. This seemingly minor change in procedure may not seem elegant to some, particularly neophytes, but it is a drastic change for experienced hands who remember the legions of subjects who have sat in front of memory drums and learned lists. By eschewing the list, Peterson and Peterson were able to pose the simple question of how well a subject can remember the elements of a single item that are presented to him. The list, with all its inter-item interactions, was no longer the unit for remembering.

Their procedure had the experimenter spell a three-unit consonant syllable (e.g., QFZ) to be remembered and then immediately say a three-digit number as a cue for the subject to begin counting backwards by 3s or 4s. The counting began the retention interval. The backward counting was a necessary control to prevent covert rehearsal of the syllable. A metronome ticking at two beats per second paced the backward counting at a brisk rate to minimize pauses and hesitations in which rehearsal might occur. The subject attempted recall when a signal light came on. The retention intervals were 3, 6, 9, 12, 15, and 18 seconds. Each of 24 subjects was given eight syllables at each of the intervals. A particular syllable was never presented more than once to a subject. The results are shown in Figure 5-1. The

Fig. 5-1. Short-term retention function for trigrams. Adapted from Fig. 2 in Peterson and Peterson (1959).

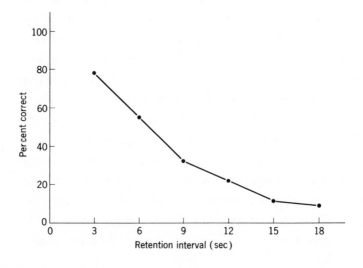

striking feature of the curve is the extremely rapid forgetting over 18 seconds. Psychologists had been accustomed to thinking of the temporal function for forgetting in units no smaller than hours, and it was exciting to see conditions where forgetting was almost complete in 18 seconds. Murdock (1961) replicated the Peterson-Peterson study in its essentials and obtained about the same curve as shown in Figure 5-1. Other investigators have also confirmed the rapid forgetting with the Peterson-Peterson paradigm or one similar to it, and there is no doubt about its reality.

Theoretically, Peterson and Peterson were thinking in terms of Estes' stimulus fluctuation model (Estes, 1955) from which Estes deduced the behavioral phenomenon he called "spontaneous regression," or response loss over short time intervals. Estes (1955, p. 148, footnote 4) distinguished spontaneous regression from forgetting over longer time intervals. Thus he seemed to be making a distinction between short-term and long-term memory phenomena. It was in this theoretical context that Peterson and Peterson viewed their results. They did not particularly see their findings in terms of trace decay theory as defined in Chapter 2. However, many were sorely tempted to see Figure 5-1 as the embodiment of the speedy forgetting we might expect according to ideas about decay of memory traces. If so, this experiment would be the first real evidence for trace decay theory, which has always been a hypothesis stronger on the speculative than on the empirical side. The matter is not this simple, though, as we shall shortly see in the section on interference and STM.

Effects of Practice

It is an established fact that retention increases as amount of practice increases (Ebbinghaus, 1913; Krueger, 1929, 1930; Postman, 1962; Underwood & Keppel, 1963). With the exception of Krueger's 1930 study which used a finger maze, these studies have used verbal lists, and the degree of learning varied from intermediate to overlearning. Does the same relationship hold for the single-item STM paradigm?

There are two basic ways in which practice can be manipulated in STM studies. After being shown or told an item, the subject can be required to repeat it aloud more than once. Each response occurrence defines a practical trial. Let such a method be called "overt practice." The other method will be called "covert practice," and its occurrence relies on an unfilled time interval after item presentation in which a subject may practice the material privately. By instructions the experimenter can encourage the subject to use his time for covert rehearsal, or the experimenter can count on the reliable fact that many subjects voluntarily indulge in covert rehearsal whenever they get a chance. Covert rehearsal is the reason that activities like backward counting are imposed in the retention interval so that forgetting processes, not counterforgetting processes like practice, can operate.

Not everyone has agreed that amount of practice is a variable that influences the associative strength of the item and thereby increases its resistance to forgetting processes. Brown (1958), a trace decay theorist, believes that rehearsal merely serves to delay the onset of trace decay. If so, different amounts of practice given before the retention interval should not influence retention curves because the same decay process goes on once the last response is made and regardless of how many times it was practiced. But if practice repetitions increase resistance to forgetting, the number of practice repetitions before a retention interval should have a decided effect on the curves. To find an effect of practice on the curves would disprove Brown's particular hypothesis about practice and decay, but it would not bear on the validity of trace decay theory in general. One could be a trace theorist

and argue that the role of practice is to increase resistance to
forgetting by slowing down the rate of decay, not to delay onset
of decay as Brown argues.

Overt Practice.   The most thorough study of number of overt response repetitions before the retention interval was done by
Hellyer (1962). Three-unit consonant syllables were used and
digit naming was the filler activity to prevent rehearsal in the
retention interval. Hellyer had the subjects say the criterion
item one, two, four, or eight times aloud (number of reinforcements) before a retention interval of either 3, 9, 18, or 27 seconds. Over five days, all subjects contributed data to all 16
experimental conditions. Figure 5-2 is a graph of the results. It
is evident that practice has a strong effect on short-term retention.
As number of repetitions (or reinforcements) increase, the resistance to forgetting increases. The curve for one reinforcement, incidentally, is essentially the same situation that Peterson and
Peterson (1959) used for their data in Figure 5-1, and the results
are about the same. Actually, Hellyer's experiment is a partial
replication and extension of a portion of Peterson and Peterson's
earlier study (1959) that also found a positive effect of overt
practice repetitions on retention.

  Figure 5-2 refutes Brown's hypothesis (1958) that rehearsal
only stalls decay of the memory trace and that all curves will be
independent of number of responses prior to the retention interval. Practice definitely slows down the rate of forgetting.

Covert Practice.   Brown (1958, Experiment III) increased the
silent study period before the retention interval from 0.78 to 4.68
seconds, and over a retention interval of 7 seconds, the correct
recall rose from 41 to 59 percent. However, Sanders (1961) had
the most comprehensive study on covert practice and short-term

retention. He varied the covert study period for sets of digits from 8 to 40 seconds, and the retention interval ranged from 15 to 120 seconds. Forgetting was large with only 8 seconds of silent rehearsal and was about the same for all retention intervals. Rehearsal of 120 seconds, however, virtually eliminated retention loss for all intervals. Pollack's findings (1963) confirm Sanders'. Hebb (1961), Melton (1963), and Murdock (1963) used the somewhat different procedure of varying study time by repeating an item within a long series of items. In all cases retention increased as amount of study time increased.

In general, covert practice works like overt practice to increase short-term retention, and there is nothing to say about it that has not already been said about overt practice. Overt practice has the advantage of assuring the experimenter that the response was made a definite number of times, which is often a necessary control procedure.

Fig. 5-2. Short-term retention functions for trigrams, with reinforcements, or number of repetitions before the retention interval, as the curve parameter. Adapted from Table 1 in Hellyer (1962).

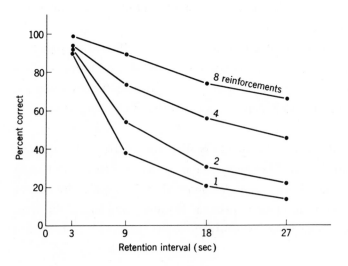

INTERFERENCE AS AN EXPLANATION OF FORGETTING IN SHORT–TERM SERIAL RECALL

Interference theorists did not delay long in attacking the trace implications of the Peterson-Peterson findings. The consequences of a trace explanation for STM were considerable. Despite the difficulties that interference has as an explanation of forgetting in LTM (see Chapter 7), it is the only theory that has ever had any empirical justification and status. With trace decay as a possibility for STM, there was a much stronger chance that human memory would require at least two fundamental compartments. Heretofore, the issue had not arisen in any systematic way, and there was always the implicit theoretical assumption that all memory could be described by a unitary set of laws. That a unitary explanation is desirable is beyond doubt, but that laws often fail to fulfill our hopes for elegant simplicity is also undeniable. Our hopes remain, however, and in the face of threats they provide the motive for counterattack. Those interference theorists who believed in one general set of laws for memory, therefore, sought to prove that rapid forgetting is a function of interference.

Proactive inhibition and retroactive inhibition are the basic paradigms for interference, and the Peterson-Peterson experiment had possibilities for both. The RI likelihood in the form of backward counting was less possible because of the great dissimilarity between the consonant syllable and the numbers that were interpolated between its learning and recall. Keppel and Underwood (1962) showed no RI effects of counting. Neimark et al. (1965) have explored the consequences of similarity of materials interpolated in the retention interval, and they showed that backward counting has small or no effects on the retention of CVC syllables when compared to other kinds of interpolated activities. The possibility for PI in the Peterson-Peterson experiment was much greater, however. Their design required each subject to learn and recall eight syllables at each of the six retention intervals; thus a learn-recall sequence could have anywhere from 0 to 47 prior learn-recall sequences, which is a pregnant possibility for PI. For well-learned lists, Greenberg and Underwood (1950) demonstrated that retention was a decreasing function of the number of prior learn-recall sequences. It is likely that the same effect could have been operating for Peterson and Peterson. Of course, they had number of prior sequences counterbalanced with respect to retention interval, but nevertheless most items had a number of preceding sequences and the overall effect would be to lower average forgetting. Under the laws of interference discussed in Chapter 4, the learning of any particular syllable would bring some extinction of prior-learned syllables, and their spontaneous recovery in the retention interval would produce competition with the criterion syllable which would lower its recall. The greater the number of prior learn-recall sequences, the greater the decrement (Greenberg & Underwood, 1950); and the longer the retention interval, the greater the spontaneous recovery of the extinguished responses. If STM is explained by the laws of interference at all, the experimental design chosen by Peterson and Peterson should have PI operating.

Proactive Inhibition

There was evidence for PI in the experiments by Brown (1958), but as a trace decay theorist, Brown was not inclined to make much theoretical use of it. Keppel and Underwood (1962), however, being workers in the interference tradition, were fully aware of interference and its implications and produced a solid experiment to show its influences in STM. In one of the experiments which they reported (Keppel & Underwood, 1962, Experiment II), only three consonant trigrams were used, and each was tested at three retention intervals of 3, 9, and 18 seconds. Through counterbalancing, each trigram was tested at each interval in the first, second, and third learn-recall sequence; and this design enabled them to assess PI by plotting retention curves as a function of ordinal number of the learn-recall sequence. Figure 5-3 shows the results; they are splendid in their explanatory simplicity. The items tested in the first position, with no prior learn-recall sequences and no PI, have *no* decrement at all. Both one and two prior sequences, however, induce the rapid forgetting which characterizes the Peterson and Peterson data. In other experiments in this same paper, Keppel and Underwood further verified and extended the findings in Figure 5-3. Loess (1964) performed a very similar STM experiment that manipulated number of prior learn-recall sequences and length of retention interval, and his results were fully consistent with those of Keppel and Underwood. Wickens, Born, and Allen (1963) demonstrated that PI is a function of the similarity of the prior-learned mate-

Fig. 5-3. Short-term retention functions for trigrams, with the order of the item in the test series as the curve parameter. Adapted from Fig. 3 in Keppel and Underwood (1962).

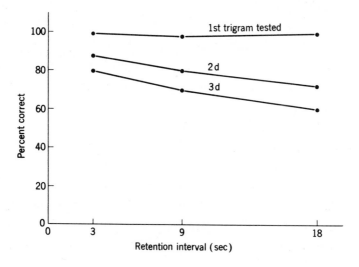

rials. When prior-learned material was of a different form class than the criterion material that was learned and recalled (e.g., digit sets as the prior events, consonant trigrams as the criterion events), forgetting was less than when both event classes were the same.

There is little doubt that STM is subject to laws of interference just like LTM, and that a temptation to interpret the Peterson-Peterson findings in terms of trace decay should be resisted. The very rapid forgetting that is so striking in the Peterson-Peterson study is virtually absent when number of prior learn-recall sequences, and thus PI, is controlled. The rapid forgetting occurs only when PI is present. Studies like Hellyer's (1962) on amount of practice are consistent with interference theory also. Hellyer's study had the same methodological flaw as that of Peterson and Peterson. A long series of learn-recall sequences was given to the same subjects, and precipitous forgetting decrements were obtained. Forgetting decreased as number of practice trials for an item increased. This is interpretable in terms of an increase in the resistance to interference due to practice (Chapter 4).

That interference is vindicated as an explanation of forgetting in STM should not necessarily lead to the conclusion that verbal STM and LTM are covered by the same laws. Interference could work for both memory systems, but the nature of interfering activities could differ in each case and justify two memory systems. The next section on acoustic interference supports this point of view.

Acoustic Interference

Sperling (1963) said that some subjects reported they could "hear" material being held in short-term storage, and he suggested that short-term memory for verbal materials may be in the form of an auditory loop not present in LTM. The first major laboratory studies of this topic were by Conrad (1962, 1964). Conrad (1964) reported two experiments that secured the point nicely. In the first experiment, Conrad determined the confusability of letters of the alphabet. He had the letters recorded on tape with a background of white noise, and when they were presented at a rate of one per 5 seconds, the subjects wrote down the letter they thought had been spoken. Not surprising was the finding that subjects confused letters that sounded alike. When *B* was spoken, the subjects would often respond with *P, T,* or *V.* Using the first experiment as a point of departure, Conrad then conducted a second experiment using the standard format of an STM study. Six-letter sequences were presented visually at the rate of one letter per 0.75 seconds. When presentation of the six letters had been completed, the subject wrote them down immediately. Conrad found that the errors in recall were of the same type as in the first experiment. The subjects confused letters that sounded alike. The correlation between errors in the two experiments was .64, indicating that errors in an *auditory* discrimination test can predict errors in short-term recall for *visually* presented material. In a confirming investigation, Conrad and Hull (1965) had sets of three and nine letters that were either aurally similar or dissimilar. Rapid visual presentation was again used, and recall was immediate. Error rate for aurally similar letter sets ran twice as high.

Wickelgren's results (1965a) fully supported Conrad's work. Eight items, four letters and four digits, were presented visually and the subject had to recall them immediately in writing. All 26 letters of the alphabet and the digits 1 through 9 were used. Wickelgren felt that if Conrad's thesis was valid there should be a significant tendency for confusions to occur among letters, and digits and letters, whose vowels or consonants sound alike. The results supported the hypothesis. There was a significant tendency for units with sound-alike elements to be confused. Wickelgren found that the probability of making an intrusion error was related to the number of similar sounding letters in the alphabet. A letter that shares a common sound with many letters is more error-prone than a letter which shares auditory similarity with only a few letters.

It might have been subjectively obvious all along that we often use auditory-verbal encoding in the short-term remembering of visually presented verbal material, but the pioneering work of Conrad, and the supporting research of Wickelgren, put the laws of interference for STM on a sound empirical footing. Some experiments have demonstrated the confusion of similar auditory items when the material is presented in the auditory mode (Wickelgren, 1965b, 1966), but this is a bit less fascinating than sound-alike errors for visual material. At this stage of knowledge it seems reasonable to say that STM is an auditory system distinct from LTM. Both are subject to interference but not the same kind. Acoustic similarity governs interference in STM, and semantic similarity determines it in LTM (Chapter 4).

Acoustic and Semantic Similarity

Baddeley (1964, 1966) and Baddeley and Dale (1966) contrasted acoustic and semantic similarity as variables for interference and emphasized explicitly what it means for the STM–LTM distinction. Baddeley and Dale (1966) had subjects learn lists of paired associates in an RI paradigm that was intended to show interference for semantic similarity of well-practiced material in LTM. The two groups of subjects in the experiment learned two lists of eight paired adjectives each, followed by recall of the first list. An experimental group learned two lists of paired adjectives, in which corresponding pairs in the two lists had highly similar stimuli and different responses. A control group had neutral stimuli and different responses for its two lists. Eight trials of practice were given each list, which brought attainment to about two-thirds of the items correct. Considering the laws of verbal interference in Chapter 4, it is not surprising that the RI group showed significantly more decrement than the control group. Although not startling, this experiment provided a necessary reference for the next one. Baddeley and Dale, in another experiment in the same paper, used the same materials as before but this time in an STM experiment. Lists of 2, 4, or 6 pairs were presented once, followed by a test trial presentation of the stimulus term for one of the pairs. Both PI and RI paradigms were used. Consider the two-pair case. If the stimulus for the first pair is presented, there is one pair intervening between learn and test, and the paradigm is RI. If the second pair is tested, one pair precedes its learning, and the paradigm is PI. The results showed that semantic similarity of interfering pairs, regardless of their number, was not a variable when comparisons were made with neutral pairs. Semantic similarity is an interference variable for LTM, not STM.

Baddeley (1966) went on to dovetail with the work of Conrad and Wickelgren on acoustic interference in STM. Just as Baddeley and Dale (1966) demonstrated that semantic similarity applied only to LTM, Baddeley (1966) showed that acoustic similarity applied only to STM. In his experiment I, Baddeley employed auditory presentation of material, which was followed by written recall. One group was presented sets of five acoustically similar words (MAN, MAD, MAT, etc.) for immediate recall, as well as acoustically different control words (COW, DAY, BAR, etc.) of equal frequency of occurrence in the language (Thorndike & Lorge, 1944). A second group was presented sets of eight adjectives for learning and immediate recall, with some sets being similar in meaning (BIG, LONG, BROAD, etc.) and others being semantically different words (OLD, DEEP, FOUL, etc.) of equal frequency of occurrence in the language. The results showed a big effect for acoustic similarity. Only 9.6 percent of the acoustically similar sequences were correctly reproduced, compared with 82.1 percent of the control sequences. On the other hand, semantically similar sequences were 64.7 percent correct and little different from their control sequences with 71.0 percent correct. In another experiment in the same paper, Baddeley showed that the strong interference effects of acoustic similarity in STM were not merely because words like MAN, MAD, and MAT had letters in common and were somewhat perceptually similar—it was, indeed, their acoustic similarity.

Interference versus Trace Decay

Scientifically, it is not enough to show that interference operates for STM; it is also desirable to demonstrate that other theoretical explanations do not apply. The possibility is always open that retention losses with interference paradigms may have little to do with normal forgetting. Interference is one way of producing a retention loss, but it may not be the usual way for a forgetting decrement in the everyday world. We must guard against uncritical acceptance of the syllogism:

> A decrement in retention is caused by interference.
> Forgetting is a decrement in retention.
> Therefore, all forgetting is caused by interference.

This *may* be empirically true, but may not be.

One way of testing the empirical truth of the syllogism is to test interference theory outside the laboratory and within the context of normal forgetting processes. This is an impossibility for STM because of the very short retention intervals involved, but it is an approach that has been used in testing interference theory for LTM. These experiments will be discussed in Chapter 7. Another way is to design experiments that discriminate the various theoretical possibilities in the laboratory. Systematic support for one explanation and disproof of others would increase the strength of our belief in the principle that is supported. Platt (1964) makes the telling argument that a science advances most decisively by testing rival hypotheses and choosing between them. One of Platt's main points is that science advances vigorously by disproof, and that rival hypotheses should be expressed so that a clear choice can be made between them. Empiricism that collects facts without a plan would not be considered worthless, according to Platt's position, but it would be a quasi-random approach that would lead us to laws and theories clumsily.

Waugh and Norman (1965) report an experiment with an RI paradigm which discriminates the trace decay and interference theories of forgetting. The STM task was auditory, and lists of 16 digits were used. The last digit of the list was called a "probe digit," and it had occurred only once before in the list. The probe digit was accompanied by a tone to ensure its identification, and at its occurrence the subject was to recall the digit that had immediately preceded it when it first occurred in the list. Using different lists, all positions of the list were tested in this fashion. One experimental condition was a slow rate of presentation of one item per second, and the other was a fast rate of four per second. The main interest was in recall as a function of time (trace decay), and number of items between the first occurrence of the probe digit and its second occurrence as a signal for recall (interference). If the trace decay hypothesis is correct, forgetting should be a function of time between the two occurrences of the digit irrespective of number of interpolated digits. For any given amount of interference, the rate of one per second should produce more forgetting than the rate of four per second because more intervening time was involved. But, if the interference hypothesis is correct, forgetting should be a function of number of interpolated digits regardless of time.

Figure 5-4 shows the results. Number of interfering items is the sole determiner of recall, and the data bear strongly in behalf of the interference explanation. If trace decay has validity, the list presented at the rate of four items per second should have had better recall than the list presented at the rate of one item per second because the former events occurred in one-fourth the time. As Figure 5-4 shows, presentation rate made no difference whatsoever. A criticism of this experiment is that the rate of four per second might have been so fast that some digits were not adequately learned, thus lowering the level of recall. Conversely, recall level under the condition of one per second might have been raised because the rate was slow enough to allow occasional covert practice repetitions. The result of these opposing effects would have been to bring together two curves that otherwise would have been separated. However, this criticism of the Waugh-Norman study is a speculative one, and it uses the dis-

Fig. 5-4.   Short-term retention functions for digits as a function of presentation rate and number of interpolated digits. Adapted from Fig. 1 in Waugh and Norman (1965).

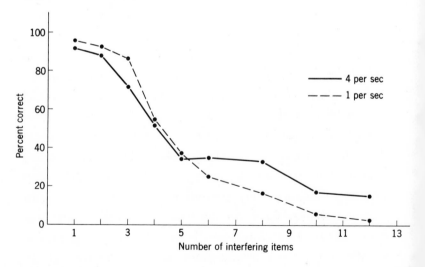

honorable device of assuming two equal and opposing processes to explain no difference, and all without evidence. Until evidence emerges to the contrary, these findings stand as evidence for interference theory and against trace decay in STM. This experiment, along with the various other STM experiments on interference, emphasizes that interference has no challenger as an explanation of forgetting in verbal STM.

VERBAL MEDIATION AND SHORT-TERM SERIAL RECALL

What Is Learned

The understanding of STM cannot be separated from the central problem of what is learned and remembered, and how it relates to LTM. For the adult human subject, there is no such thing as verbal material being held solely in STM without an interacting bond with LTM. In order to make the responses at all, the subject must have them high in his behavioral repertoire. Letters, digits, and words are common materials for STM experiments, and all are overlearned in the adult human who is the usual subject. Being overlearned, they have ties with LTM.

The typical serial-learning task for short-term recall has a series of things to remember, like several letters or digits. This produces two features that are new and which must be held in STM independently of LTM. One is which elements, independently of their serial order, out of all the available elements of the class, are in the item. The subject must remember that out of the 26 letters of the alphabet QXZ was presented. Second, the serial order of elements must be remembered. The subject must remember that X follows Q and Z follows X. Peterson and Peterson (1959, pp. 197–198) present data on these two kinds of learning. A portion of their paper was concerned with one, two, or four response occurrences as amounts of practice used before the retention interval and recall of consonant trigrams. They expressed serial learning of the three elements in terms of the conditional probability of a letter being correct, given correctness of the preceding letter. The general trend of the conditional probabilities was the same for all retention intervals. The 9-second retention interval, for example, had a probability of 0.64 for one, 0.72 for two, and 0.85 for four response occurrences. And looking at the first element of the syllable, which is a case of learning only what element to give out of the 26 in the alphabet, the probabilities correct for the three levels of practice were 0.60, 0.65, and 0.72. Thus, practice increases both aspects of serial learning in STM. Overall, there has been only mild concern with the characteristics of intraitem learning for STM (Crossman, 1961; Conrad, 1959, 1960, 1965; Jahnke, 1963).

Learning the elements of an item and their serial order can be done by rote practice, but mediation is another way in which the human subject preserves the elements and their order for later recall. Through past experience a subject can develop associations for the item, and our evidence so far shows that these associations are a powerful variable for short-term retention. Natural language mediation was discussed in Chapter 4 as a variable for interference, and it appears potent for STM also. For example, if a subject named David was given the syllable DIT to remember, he might encode it as "David is tired" and then remember this sentence at recall and decode it to recover DIT. Or if the subject was given the binary number set 000111000, he might encode it as "3 zeros, 3 ones, 3 zeros." Some experiments have deliberately trained mediational mechanisms, but others have relied on idiosyncratic NLMs from the subject's particular past experience. The use of encoding in STM represents interplay between new material in STM and well-learned associations in LTM. A theoretical implication is that STM and LTM are separate memory systems in dynamic interplay which cannot be kept tidily apart.

Natural Language Mediation

Groninger (1966) has conducted the only explicit study so far on the role of NLMs in short-term recall. His experimental design was essentially the same as that of other STM experiments except that he asked subjects to report the associations, if any, that they used in remembering the item. One group of subjects had consonant trigrams of low association value, and a second group had trigrams of high association value. The syllable was presented for 2 seconds and the subject was required to spell it aloud. The experimenter then spoke a three-digit number from which the subject began counting backwards by 3s as the filler activity for the retention interval, which was 30 seconds for both groups. At the end of the retention interval the signal for recall was given and the subject attempted recall. Recall was followed by an interview request for any association that came to the subject when he first saw the syllable. Each subject was given four items in a counterbalanced order.

Both groups reported a substantial number of NLMs. The group with low association-value syllables had NLMs for 10 percent of its items on trial 1 and 43 percent on trial 4. The group with high association-value syllables had NLMs for 49 percent on trial 1 and 69 percent on trial 4. As might be expected, high association-value material had more NLMs than low association value, which is consistent with LTM research on NLMs (Montague, Adams, & Kiess, 1966; Chapter 7).

The effect of NLMs on short-term recall is shown in Figure 5-5, and it is impressive. For both high and low association-value items, NLMs facilitate recall relative to the same class of items without NLMs. High association-value syllables with NLMs

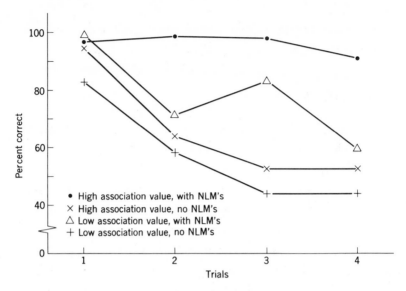

Fig. 5-5. Short-term retention as a function of the association value of the trigram and the presence or absence of natural language mediation (NLM). The four trials represent the learn and recall of four different trigrams, with a constant retention interval of 30 seconds on each trial. Adapted from Fig. 2 in Groninger (1966).

have almost perfect recall over all four trials. Another important way of looking at these data is noting that NLMs decrease PI effects in STM. Figure 5-3 from Keppel and Underwood (1962) shows that recall is a decreasing function of number of prior items. They used low association-value syllables, with no breakdown in terms of NLMs versus no NLMs; thus their data would correspond to a union of Groninger's second and the fourth curves (counting from the top) in Figure 5-5. However, Figure 5-5 shows that when the data are sorted in terms of NLMs versus no NLMs, the PI effect on recall occurs mainly when NLMs are absent and is sharply reduced when NLMs are present. The explanation for these data is essentially the same as for the Adams and Montague (1967) experiment on NLMs and interference. Through transfer of training, the past language skills represented in an NLM integrate with the stimulus syllable, and it is this verbal complex which is remembered. The reduced PI for items with NLMs could occur, therefore, for two reasons in the Groninger experiment. First, the NLM is based on well-learned language habits, and this imparts a high degree of learning to the NLM-syllable complex and gives resistance to interference from prior items. Second, each NLM-syllable complex is a relatively unique verbal entity, and lower interference would be a product of this uniqueness.

Exercising a bit of license, we can use Groninger's findings to account for other STM findings that have been unexplained or given other explanations. Peterson, Peterson, and Miller (1961) found that meaningful words had almost perfect short-term recall, whereas low association-value syllables had rapid forgetting. From Groninger's study it is reasonable to surmise that NLMs were formed for a good many of the words, and high retention was the result. Few NLMs would be expected for the syllables. A similar explanation would apply to McNulty's experiment (1965) in which words of high meaningfulness had better short-term retention than words of low meaningfulness. Neimark et al. (1965) used an RI design in which low- and high-meaningfulness syllables were interpolated between the learning and short-term recall of either low- or high-meaningfulness criterion syllables. Interference, and thus lowered recall, occurred when the criterion syllables were of low meaningfulness, but not when the syllables had high meaningfulness. The recall of high-meaningfulness syllables was virtually perfect for retention intervals of 3, 9, and 18 seconds. Groninger found that NLMs increased resistance to interference in a PI paradigm and this resistance was particularly strong for high association-value material with frequent NLMs. The results of Neimark et al. could be similarly explained.

The conservative investigator may think these explanatory extensions of Groninger's findings unwarranted, and might prefer to test them explicitly in the laboratory. In the absence of such explicit research, however, Groninger's experiment provides a unifying theme for previously unrelated facts. As a minimum, his experiment points to NLMs as a strong variable for STM that should command more attention in the future. Chapter 7 will show that NLMs are equally important for LTM.

Recoding and Decoding

Lindley and his associates, in a series of interesting papers (Lindley, 1963, 1965; Schaub & Lindley, 1964; Lindley & Nedler, 1965), were concerned with the problem of recoding a quasi-meaningful trigram syllable into a meaningful word and then subsequently decoding it at recall to retrieve the syllable. Rather than working with freely associated NLMs, these investigators controlled recoding by giving the subject a word association at the outset. This line of research attacks the problem of the kind of NLM that can be effectively remembered and easily decoded to produce the to-be-remembered syllable.

Schaub and Lindley (1964) first administered 72 trigrams of both low and high meaningfulness in a free association test in which the subjects were asked to give associations that would help them learn or remember the trigram. The associations were then divided into common and uncommon recoding words to be used as associative aids for new subjects in the STM experiment that followed. For example, a high-meaningfulness trigram like BOM had a common association of "Bomb" and an uncommon association of "Bowman." A low-meaningfulness trigram like VUJ had a common cue of "View" and an uncommon one of "Virgin." In the STM experiment, the experimenter spoke the recoding cue, spelled the trigram syllable, and then spoke a three-digit number for counting backwards by 3s during the retention interval. At the end of the retention interval the experimenter spoke "Recall," and the subject attempted to spell the syllable. Retention intervals of 8, 14, and 20 seconds were used. There were two levels of meaningfulness and common and uncommon recoding cues.

Any recoding cue was found to be better than no recoding cue at all, and the retention of high-meaningfulness syllables was the highest and about the same whether the recoding cue was common or uncommon. Low-meaningfulness syllables had lower retention, with common cues producing higher retention than uncommon ones. The authors' explanation for these results was that both the common and uncommon associations for high-meaningfulness items frequently had the letters of the trigram in the same, or nearly the same, sequence as the trigram itself, and so the subjects had little difficulty in decoding the association and retrieving the syllable. Low-meaningfulness trigrams, on the other hand, had more associations which lacked one or more of the letters of the trigram or had letters which were not in the same sequence as the trigram. This tendency was greater for uncommon associations. The consequences were poorer retention for low-meaningfulness material and poorer retention for uncommon than common associations.

This experiment by Schaub and Lindley is important because it inquires about the characteristics of associative aids and how they relate to recall. Groninger's study (1966) shows that mediators help remembering. An important question is to ask the characteristics of mediators that help or hinder retention. Important for the future also is the extent to which the decoding procedure is forgotten or the mediator itself is forgotten or transformed over the retention interval. Being responses, they too can be forgotten. Montague, Adams, and Kiess (1966), in an LTM study using paired associates, found that NLMs had a strong positive effect on recall only when they were remembered in substantially their original form.

CAPACITY OF SHORT-TERM MEMORY

The Memory Span

"Memory span" is a term that refers to limitations in the amount of data which a subject can absorb in STM in a single, brief learning opportunity and then recall immediately. Briefly show a subject a display of letters or numbers, or read him a series of letters or numbers. Depending upon the subject's ability and the type of material, about five to nine items will be correctly reported in an immediate recall test. A typical experiment of the kind discussed so far in this chapter deliberately avoids overloading the limited capacity of STM by using items that are well within capacity, such as three-element trigrams.

Figure 5-6 shows representative data on capacity (Sperling, 1963). Two subjects were tachistoscopically presented arrays of letters for different exposure periods, and Figure 5-6 shows the accuracy of their immediate recall. With the very short exposures there is insufficient time to read out the stimulus trace and fill STM to capacity, but with 100 milliseconds or more the capacity of five or so items is attained and the curve levels off. Other sources of typical data are Blankenship (1938), Woodworth and Schlosberg (1954), Sperling (1960), and Averbach (1963). The notion of the memory span is important for memory theory because it defines a property of STM that does not seem to apply to LTM. Short-term storage has a distinct limit in its capacity to hold material for recall, but LTM has a very large and unknown capacity.

Capacity and Mediation

Capacity in the last section intended a one-to-one correspondence between the items presented and the items remembered and recalled. The stimulus unit is encoded directly and held in STM.

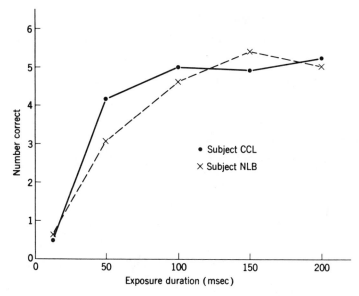

Fig. 5-6. Retention of tachistoscopically presented arrays of letters as a function of exposure duration for two subjects. Adapted from Fig. 5 in Sperling (1963).

However, sometimes the subject mediates and imposes structure on the material, and the mediator then becomes the stored unit. Through mediation the subject can transcend the restraints that STM capacity imposes on nonmediated material by embodying the material in a smaller number of mediators. Miller (1956) calls the unit of STM the "chunk," whether it is a mediated entity or not. According to his thinking, the capacity of STM is limited, but we must think in terms of number of chunks occupying STM. The chunk may be a stimulus item or a mediator. Natural language mediation and trained mediation are the two ways that a stimulus array can be encoded, and these two sources of chunks will each be discussed in turn.

Natural Language Mediation. NLMs are idiosyncratic, as we have already discussed. The investigator might present a string of seemingly meaningless letters like HMLTFTHR, and the subject might break down the series as HMLT/FTHR and use the mnemonic aid "Hamlet's father." In some cases longer sentences may be required, or maybe one word could be used.

Glanzer and Clark (1963b) report an excellent series of studies on verbal encoding of strings of binary numbers. In one of their experiments (1963b, Experiment II) they used a slide projector to present eight-place binary numbers. A number was presented for 0.5 seconds. One group of subjects had to recall the number immediately in writing, and a second group wrote their verbalization, or their NLM, of the number. For example, if the number was 00001111, a subject might write "4 zeros, 4 ones." Or 11000000 might become "Eleven million." Some numbers were verbally complex, and six or eight words would be used to describe them. The accuracy score for the group writing the number was correlated with the number of words used by the other group to describe the same number, and the results are shown in Figure 5-7. On the assumption that the subjects reporting the numbers directly were using about the same kinds of verbalizations as the subjects who verbalized the number, Figure 5-7 shows the accuracy of immediate recall and length of the verbalization to be highly correlated (.83). The ellipse represents the pattern of the individual data points around a straight line fitted to the data. An intriguing aspect of these data is that memory span is expressible in terms of the number of words that subjects use to describe the number. Accuracy was almost perfect when the number of descriptive words was four or so, and was negligible when the number of words was seven to nine and pushed the limits of capacity. These findings deserve interpretation in terms of the chunk as the unit of STM—the number of words or recoded units that is occupying STM. Glanzer and Clark (1963a) have made a closely related study with a similar outcome that uses geometric shapes as stimuli.

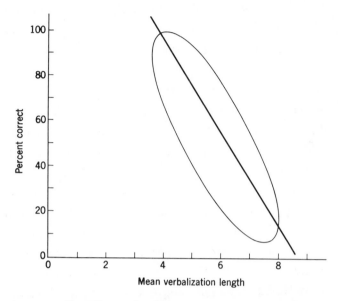

Fig. 5-7. Accuracy of recalling eight-place binary numbers as a function of the number of words used to describe them. The line of best fit is drawn through the data points for individual eight-number stimuli whose scatter around the line is approximated by the ellipse. Adapted from Fig. 2 in Glanzer and Clark (1963).

Melton (1963), in a follow-up of Murdock (1961), argued strongly in behalf of the chunk and hypothesized that the rate of forgetting in STM is a function of interference between chunks. His data appear in support of this hypothesis, with two or more consonants forgotten more readily than one. However, he related short-term recall to the number of consonants and did not get at the verbal mediator which a subject might have used and which would have been the "real" chunk. Actually, Melton's results can be viewed in terms of Groninger's findings (Figure 5-5). Single-consonant stimuli, like the letter *B*, are amenable to NLMs and should have high retention as a result. Multiple consonants like BXCDF would certainly have fewer associations in the natural language and more forgetting.

Trained Mediation.   Natural language mediation is fallible. Not all subjects have freely available mediators for all items, and some have inefficient or weak ones. A much better scheme is the teaching of an efficient mediator. We have yet to appraise thoroughly the variables for teaching effective mediators, but the practical implications of this method are large. There is no reason why schoolteachers of future generations should not show students ways of learning materials that will result in their high recall. At present, students are given materials for learning and are left to their own memory devices. How much better it would be if an instructor told the students about proved mnemonic devices and saw that they used them in systematic ways.

It is discouraging to report that this provocative idea is supported by data from only one subject. Ordinarily one would hurry by data from one subject with only a quick glance because the power of generalization is so limited. But in this case the importance of the underlying idea is strong, and the findings cannot be dismissed lightly. Miller (1956) reports findings by Smith who taught himself efficient ways of encoding binary digits and improving his memory span for them. An attempt to use a group of naïve subjects who had familiarization training with the coding methods had only minor success because extensive training is necessary; therefore Smith gave the intensive training to himself. Table 5-1 shows the recoding scheme, which Miller explains as follows:

> Along the top row is a sequence of 18 binary digits, far more than any subject was able to recall after a single presentation. In the next line these same binary digits are grouped by pairs. Four possible pairs can occur: 00 is renamed 0, 01 is renamed 1, 10 is renamed 2, and 11 is renamed 3. That is to say, we recode from a base-two arithmetic to a base-four arithmetic. In the recoded sequence there are now just 9 digits to remember, and this is almost within the span of immediate memory. In the next

line the same sequence of binary digits is regrouped into chunks of three. There are eight possible sequences of three, so we give each sequence a new name between 0 and 7. Now we have re-coded from a sequence of 18 binary digits into a sequence of 6 octal digits, and this is well within the span of immediate memory. In the last two lines the binary digits are grouped by fours and fives and are given decimal-digit names from 0 to 15 and from 0 to 31 (Miller, 1956, pp. 93–94).

Figure 5-8 shows the results. With the 4:1 and 5:1 recoding Smith was able to recall 40 binary digits! Miller (p. 94), under-stating, says, "It is a little dramatic to watch a person get 40 binary digits in a row and then repeat them back without error."

The potential significance of trained mediators is great. But it is unnecessary to urge verification and extension of Smith's data with groups of subjects who receive extensive training in recoding. Ways of training and recoding for different types of materials are badly in need of research. One study attempted to replicate Smith's work, but it failed (Klemmer, 1964). Klemmer flashed his binary displays for only 0.10 seconds and then asked for immediate recall. Because learned mediators undoubtedly take more time than this to operate, Klemmer's study cannot be taken as a satisfactory test.

Table 5-1. Ways of Recoding Sequences of Binary Digits. From Miller (1956)

Binary digits (bits)	*1 0 1 0 0 0 1 0 0 1 1 1 0 0 1 1 1 0*							
2:1 Chunks	10	10	00	10	01 11		00 11	10
Recoding	2	2	0	2	1 3		0 3	2
3:1 Chunks	101		000	100	111		001	110
Recoding	5		0	4	7		1	6
4:1 Chunks	1010			0010	0111		0011	10
Recoding	10			2	7		3	
5:1 Chunks	10100			01001		11001		110
Recoding	20			9		25		

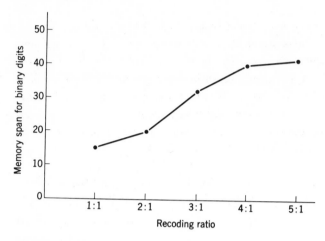

Fig. 5-8. Number of binary digits recalled as a function of the coding mechanism, or recoding ratio, which is explained in Table 5-1. Adapted from Fig. 9 in Miller (1956).

SUMMING UP

General Status of Short-term Memory

Early thinking on STM has undergone revision. Rapid forgetting per se is not a property of STM. The study by Peterson and Peterson (1959), and others like it, led to the understandable temptation to give STM the special property of rapid forgetting and led some experimenters to think of it in terms of a decaying memory trace. The possibility of this interpretation collapsed with the research of Keppel and Underwood (1962) and Loess (1964) on PI which showed rapid forgetting to be a function of the number of prior learn-recall sequences—a variable that was generously present in experiments like that of Peterson and Peterson. In the absence of prior learn-recall sequences, forgetting is negligible in STM. And Waugh and Norman (1965) demonstrated that STM is subject to RI effects because the number of responses that intervenes between learning and recall clearly affects short-term retention. Findings such as these are what might be expected by an interference theorist who sees all memory phenomena, short-term and long-term, as falling under one set of interference laws. Interference theorists also are comforted by the fact that short-term recall is a positive function of amount of practice (e.g., Hellyer, 1962) which is true for long-term recall also. But are these similarities between STM and LTM sufficient to proclaim a unity of all memory phenomena under the banner of interference? The vigor of the interference explanation cannot be denied, but there are reasons, nevertheless, to doubt that STM and LTM are one and the same memory system. It is hoped that these reasons will eventually disappear because one unifying set of laws for all memory is parsimonious and scientifically desirable. Still, the reasons are with us, and they stand as foundation of theory for the moment.

Chapter 3, and this chapter, gave three main reasons for thinking of verbal STM and LTM as different memory systems:

1. Hippocampal removal is associated with deficiencies in transition of stored material from STM to LTM, according to physiological evidence (e.g., Milner, 1959, discussed in Chapter 3).

2. Interference in STM is based on acoustic similarity of materials, but interference in LTM is based on semantic similarity. That both memory systems are susceptible to interference is a kind of unity of explanation, but the different defining conditions for interference in each case are adequate grounds for contending that two systems exist.

3. Capacity is very limited in STM; LTM has a very large and unspecifiable capacity.

The effects of practice do not discriminate the unified and the two-compartment views of memory. According to the unified view, practice performs a "stamping in" function in which the response becomes increasingly resistant to forgetting processes. The STM experiments on practice, such as Hellyer (1962), can be interpreted in this way. Within interference theory and the unified conception of memory, practice can be seen as the variable which increases the resistance of the verbal materials to interference (e.g., Briggs, 1957). On the other hand, if we admit to an STM–LTM distinction, an added function of practice is to produce transfer from STM to LTM.

And finally, regardless of which view of memory we hold, practice can be the variable that defines the time available to form an NLM. Bugelski (1962) and Bugelski and Rickwood (1963) see time as fundamentally a practice variable which the subject uses both covertly and overtly to practice the responses and/or find NLMs for them. The time available to the subject is the variable for practice, and when the experimenter gives a series of discrete practice trials and plots his findings in terms of them, he is really expressing the total time in another way (actually a crude way because he is omitting the time between items and between trials, which the subject also uses for practice). Both Bugelski (1962) and Montague, Adams, and Kiess (1966) have shown that number of NLMs increases as total time increases, and Groninger (1966) and Montague, Adams, and Kiess have shown NLMs to benefit retention.

When practice benefits retention by increasing the number of NLMs formed, we can interpret it in terms of either the unified or the two-compartment view. If the unified view is held, NLMs are part of a network of associations in the single memory system, and the verbal events arouse one of these which the subject uses as his mnemonic aid. Essentially the same thinking applies to the two-compartment view, except that NLMs are considered in LTM and the enhancement of retention resides in the interplay of events in STM with NLMs in LTM. Thus, no matter whether practice is a device for stamping in the memory trace, a means of accomplishing the transition from STM to LTM, or a method for allowing time for NLM formation, it fails to discriminate the two views. In all cases, practice increases retention.

Accepting that the two-compartment position is dictated by present evidence, what does the schema for *verbal memory* look like? It seems reasonable to assume that at low levels of practice a verbal event is coded as a memory trace which resides in an auditory loop of limited capacity and which is the STM subsystem. There is no rapid decay in STM. The memory trace is stable as long as there are no interfering events, and in this sense the label "short-term memory" is inapplicable. However, the material in STM, being at a low level of practice, is highly susceptible to interference. The interference comes from other verbal events which have similar sounds. Certainly there are generous sources of acoustic interference in the human being's verbally rich environment, and so his retention can often be expected to be short-lived. In this sense, the label of short-term memory *is* appropriate. With practice, in cases of rote learning in which associations with past learning (NLMs or trained mediators) are absent, the memory trace grows stronger and enters LTM where it is now susceptible to interference based on semantic, not acoustic, similarity. When an item in STM arouses an NLM or a trained mediator, STM and LTM interact and retention of the item in STM can benefit from its associative bond with LTM.

Methodological Problems

Sensitivity to methodological issues is a new emphasis for STM research, and most of the studies that have been reviewed in this chapter have ignored one or more of them. This dereliction must be seen with sympathy because the issues only recently have been emphasized in the literature (Keppel, 1965; Underwood, 1964).

Control of Associative Strength. "Associative strength" is a term equivalent to "habit strength," and it is a function of number of reinforcements. Everything else equal, a verbal item with greater associative strength will have a higher probability of recall or a shorter latency. The measurement of associative strength has two purposes: (1) to determine the strength of the item in original learning so that recall can be interpreted in terms of the associative strength at the start of the retention interval and (2) to determine the strength of the item at recall so that the weakening effects of the forgetting process can be known.

Assuming that no NLM or learned mediator is present and the item is rote learned, the assessment of associative strength must separate the act of learning from the assessment of strength (Battig, 1965). When an item is given one or more trials, an increment of habit develops on each trial which adds to the habit strength from preexperimental reinforcements. Assessment of total associative strength, therefore, must take place after the learning trials and just before start of the retention interval. One way to do this might be to give an immediate test trial in which a stimulus is presented and recall is elicited. But the test trial would require several seconds, and it would offer an opportunity for covert rehearsal. Also, one cannot be totally confident that an unreinforced test trial would not induce an increment of habit strength that would positively benefit performance in the later test after the retention interval (see the section on subjective reinforcement in Chapter 10). A better method would be to have one of the experimental treatments be a zero retention-interval condition in which performance would provide the measure of associative strength and the baseline from which other interval treatments could be gauged. The assumption is that forgetting is negligible in immediate recall and the response reflects item strength at the end of the learning period. The occurrence of the response at the zero-interval test also assures the experimenter that the response has entered memory and is available for remembering over the retention interval—a precaution not observed in most STM experiments. The subsequent absence of the response on the recall trial can then be attributed to forgetting processes and not to the failure of the response to enter the behavioral repertoire in the first place. And by objectively testing for response occurrence at the zero interval, an empirical baseline from which to measure forgetting is established. In experiments of the past, when this baseline was usually omitted, it is unlikely that any serious bias occurred because immediate recall is customarily very high and nearly 100 percent correct when the material is within memory span. Nevertheless, the use of the zero-interval baseline is a sound scientific practice, and its use is recommended.

But the mere occurrence of a response at immediate recall is a crude measure of associative strength because it says only that the response is strong enough to occur, but it does not say how much stronger. If one's theory uses the concept of a threshold, the occurrence of the response at immediate recall says that the response is above threshold, but it does not say how far above threshold. This problem comes into sharp focus in an experiment in which two or more types of material are being studied for their effects on retention. In order to know their consequences for retention, it is necessary that the items used for each variable be equated for associative strength so that the effects can be interpreted in terms of type of material, not differences in associative strength. Suppose that short-term retention of two levels of verbal meaningfulness is being studied, with meaningful words being compared with low association-value syllables. Higher retention of words does not necessarily mean that highly meaningful material is remembered better than that with low association value, even when both occur at immediate recall. Meaningful words may be remembered better simply because they have greater associative strength. If equated for strength, both kinds of material might well have the same recall level. Both Keppel (1965) and Underwood (1964) have suggested response latency as an additional and more sensitive measure of associative strength at immediate recall. Latency is an established measure of strength, with stronger responses being given faster than others. In this hypothetical experiment on meaningfulness it would not be possible to preequate the two conditions for associative strength, but latency measures at zero-interval recall are thought to provide indices of differential associative strength, and later recall after the retention interval could be interpreted in terms of them. The problem for associative strength at recall is somewhat similar. We are interested in change in item strength from learning to recall as a function of forgetting variables, but because two items are recalled with equal probability does not necessarily mean that they have equal associative strength and are equally affected by forgetting processes. Here again response latency might be used to discriminate differences in associative strength.

All the foregoing remarks about assessment of associative strength apply to rote-learned items only. This constraint was deliberate because the problem is different and more difficult with NLMs and learned mediators. With mediated items, as with rote ones, a zero-interval recall test is necessary to guarantee that the response has entered memory, but this is about all the meaning that can be given these responses or all the measurement that can be meaningfully made of them. A measure of response latency is virtually impossible to interpret directly in terms of associative strength, as in the rote case, because when the subject invokes a mediator, a response complex of the mediator plus the item is created whose overall strength is embodied in the latency. The latency reflects the strength of a response chain, not the single criterion response. Suppose a subject is shown the criterion syllable VCL which arouses the NLM "Vanilla and Chocolate are Luscious." Latency at the zero-interval test, in which VCL must be given in recall, is undoubtedly a compound effect of the strength of the NLM and the speed with which it can be decoded to VCL. Similar reasoning would apply to latency measures for mediated recall after the retention interval.

What is a solution to the problem of measuring associative strength for an item? If one could be confident that an item would be learned by rote, a zero-interval test with latency of response recorded, as well as latency recorded at recall after the retention interval, could use probability correct and latency as meaningful indices of associative strength. However, there is no assurance that an item will not be mediated by at least a few of the subjects, and these measures then become of dubious value. Bluntly, there is no good solution at this time to the control of associative strength. Many experimental problems with variables under study, like the length of the retention interval, can use the same items from treatment to treatment, and in this way the issue illustrated by the example of two levels of meaningfulness is sidestepped. But when different types of items enter each treatment condition, the experimenter must face the problem that differences at recall may be as much an effect of differences in associative strength as of other variables being manipulated.

Controlling for Proactive Inhibition. Keppel and Underwood (1962) and Loess (1964) demonstrated unmistakable PI in STM, and an implication of their work for experimental design is that experiments which administer learn-recall sequences for more than one item must assess the PI potential in the number of preceding items. It would be ideal if only one item could be administered to each subject. In some cases this might be done, but ordinarily the cost is prohibitive. Practically, a number of items will be given to each subject and the experiment should be designed to account for number of prior items and their effect on the recall of any particular item. Prior to the findings on PI it was assumed that items were independent, and the result of this assumption was misinterpretation of the amount of forgetting in STM. Peterson and Peterson (1959) ignored number of prior items, and they demonstrated precipitous forgetting. But Keppel and Underwood (1962) and Loess (1964) showed that this only occurs when there has been a number of prior items and PI effects are strong. Number of prior items is a variable in STM that cannot be ignored.

Controlling for Rehearsal.   The resourceful human subject will grasp his opportunities to practice the to-be-remembered material in the retention interval (Keppel, 1965), and when he does, experimental control weakens. The experimenter wants the amount of practice under his explicit direction, and unknown amounts of practice upset his research intentions. There have been experiments in which amount of practice time for covert rehearsal is an experimental variable (e.g., Sanders, 1961), but most of the time the experimenter wants to restrict covert practice. The typical way of doing this in STM experiments is to have subjects count backwards by 3s. The rationale for using this particular task is not completely clear, but it is usually presumed that counting backwards is thought to be difficult enough to fully occupy the subject and leave him no time to rehearse. A task, like rote counting "1, 2, 3, 4, . . . etc.," might be so easy that the subject could slip in a repetition of the criterion item from time to time without appreciable pauses in his counting.

The efficacy of counting backwards by 3s as a control technique has largely been assumed, but Groninger (1966) attempted an evaluation of it. The main purpose of his STM experiment was to assess the role of NLMs for short-term recall (Figure 5-5), but he also asked subjects in postexperimental interviews whether they rehearsed while counting backwards by 3s. When the syllables were of low meaningfulness, 59 percent of the subjects admitted to rehearsal on trial 1 and 37 percent on trial 4. The percentages were about the same for high-meaningfulness material, being 63 percent on trial 1 and 37 percent on trial 4. Assuming the validity of the interviewing technique for tapping this phenomenon, it is apparent that counting backwards is an inadequate control for covert rehearsal. Just what might be an effective control is unclear. Subjects are observed to stumble and hesitate occasionally while counting backwards; thus maybe the task is too difficult. A task intermediate in difficulty between rote counting and counting backwards by 3s, like reading from an array of random numbers (Hellyer, 1962), may be an improvement although Loess and McBurney (1965) found little difference between these two methods of interpolation for both trigrams and word triads. The experimental problem is not an easy one. Ideally, the interpolated material should not interfere and should fully occupy the subject's attention so that he does not rehearse the criterion item being retained. Realistically, the interpolated material can fail in one or both of these functions. The solutions to these problems will not be found by showing that short-term retention is the same or different for various methods of interpolation, as Loess and McBurney (1965) have done, although their work is a useful beginning. Suppose, for example, that interpolated material A results in higher short-term retention of an item than material B. Is it because material A allows a slower rate of response, with a higher level of performance because of more covert practice as the outcome? Or is it because material B is more interfering than A and produces a lowered performance level as a consequence? The research problem is untangling these two influences and learning how to control them.

REFERENCES

Averbach, E. The span of apprehension as a function of exposure duration. *J. verbal Learn. verbal Behav.*, 1963, 2, 60–64.

Baddeley, A. D. Semantic and acoustic similarity in short-term memory. *Nature, London*, 1964, 204, 1116–1117.

Baddeley, A. D. Short-term memory for word sequences as a function of acoustic, semantic and formal similarity. *Quart. J. exp. Psychol.*, 1966, 18, 362–365.

Baddeley, A. D., & Dale, H. C. A. The effect of semantic similarity on retroactive interference in long- and short-term memory. *J. verbal Learn. verbal Behav.*, 1966, 5, 417–420.

Battig, W. F. Procedural problems in paired-associate learning research. *Psychon. Monogr. Suppl.*, 1965, 1, No. 1.

Blankenship, A. B. Memory span: A review of the literature. *Psychol. Bull.*, 1938, 35, 1–25.

Briggs, G. E. Retroactive inhibition as a function of the degree of original and interpolated learning. *J. exp. Psychol.*, 1957, 53, 60–67.

Brown, J. Some tests of the decay theory of immediate memory. *Quart. J. exp. Psychol.*, 1958, 10, 12–21.

Bugelski, B. R. Presentation time, total time, and mediation in paired-associate learning. *J. exp. Psychol.*, 1962, 63, 409–412.

Bugelski, B. R., & Rickwood, J. Presentation time, total time, and mediation in paired-associate learning: Self-pacing. *J. exp. Psychol.*, 1963, 65, 616–617.

Conrad, R. Errors of immediate memory. *Brit. J. Psychol.*, 1959, 50, 349–359.

Conrad, R. Serial order intrusions in immediate memory. *Brit. J. Psychol.*, 1960, 51, 45–48.

Conrad, R. An association between memory errors and errors due to acoustic masking of speech. *Nature, London*, 1962, 193, 1314–1315.

Conrad, R. Acoustic confusions in immediate memory. *Brit. J. Psychol.*, 1964, 55, 75–84.

Conrad, R. Order error in immediate recall of sequences. *J. verbal Learn. verbal Behav.*, 1965, 4, 161–169.

Conrad, R., & Hull, A. J. Information, acoustic confusion and memory span. *Brit. J. Psychol.*, 1964, **55**, 429–432.

Crossman, E. R. F. W. Information and serial order in human immediate memory. In C. Cherry (Ed.), *Information theory*. London: Butterworth, 1961. Pp. 147–161.

Ebbinghaus, H. *Memory: A contribution to experimental psychology*. (Trans. by Ruger & Bussenius.) New York: Teachers College Press, 1913.

Estes, W. K. Statistical theory of spontaneous recovery and regression. *Psychol. Rev.*, 1955, **62**, 145–154.

Glanzer, M., & Clark, W. H. Accuracy of perceptual recall: An analysis of organization. *J. verbal Learn. verbal Behav.*, 1963, **1**, 289–299. (a)

Glanzer, M., & Clark, W. H. The verbal loop hypothesis: Binary numbers. *J. verbal Learn. verbal Behav.*, 1963, **2**, 301–309. (b)

Greenberg, Ruth, & Underwood, B. J. Retention as a function of stage of practice. *J. exp. Psychol.*, 1950, **40**, 452–457.

Groninger, L. D. Natural language mediation and covert rehearsal in short-term memory. *Psychon. Sci.*, 1966, **5**, 135–136.

Hebb, D. O. Distinctive features of learning in the higher animal. In J. F. Delafresnaye (Ed.), *Brain mechanisms and learning: A symposium*. Springfield, Ill.: Charles C Thomas, 1961. Pp. 37–46.

Hellyer, S. Supplementary report: Frequency of stimulus presentation and short-term decrement in recall. *J. exp. Psychol.*, 1962, **64**, 650.

Jahnke, J. C. Serial position effects in immediate serial recall. *J. verbal Learn. verbal Behav.*, 1963, **2**, 284–287.

Keppel, G. Problems of method in the study of short-term memory. *Psychol. Bull.*, 1965, **63**, 1–13.

Keppel, G., & Underwood, B. J. Proactive inhibition in short-term retention of single items. *J. verbal Learn. verbal Behav.*, 1962, **1**, 153–161.

Klemmer, E. T. Does recoding from binary to octal improve the perception of binary patterns? *J. exp. Psychol.*, 1964, **67**, 19–21.

Krueger, W. C. F. The effect of overlearning on retention. *J. exp. Psychol.*, 1929, **12**, 71–78.

Krueger, W. C. F. Further studies in overlearning. *J. exp. Psychol.*, 1930, **13**, 152–163.

Lindley, R. H. Effects of controlled coding cues in short-term memory. *J. exp. Psychol.*, 1963, **66**, 580–587.

Lindley, R. H. Effects of trigram-recoding cue complexity on short-term memory. *J. verbal Learn. verbal Behav.*, 1965, **4**, 274–279.

Lindley, R. H., & Nedler, S. E. Further effects of subject-generated recoding cues on short-term memory. *J. exp. Psychol.*, 1965, **69**, 324–325.

Loess, H. Proactive inhibition in short-term memory. *J. verbal Learn. verbal Behav.*, 1964, **3**, 362–368.

Loess, H., & McBurney, Judith. Short-term memory and retention-interval activity. *Proc. 73rd Annu. Conv. Amer. Psychol. Ass.*, 1965. Pp. 85–86.

McNulty, J. A. Short-term retention as a function of method of measurement, recording time, and meaningfulness of the material. *Canad. J. Psychol.*, 1965, **19**, 188–196.

Melton, A. W. Implications of short-term memory for a general theory of memory. *J. verbal Learn. verbal Behav.*, 1963, **2**, 1–21.

Miller, G. A. The magical number seven, plus or minus two: Some limits on our capacity for processing information. *Psychol. Rev.*, 1956, **63**, 81–97.

Milner, B. The memory defect in bilateral hippocampal lesions. *Psychiat. res. Rep.*, 1959, **11**, 43–52.

Montague, W. E., Adams, J. A., & Kiess, H. O. Forgetting and natural language mediation. *J. exp. Psychol.*, 1966, **72**, 829–833.

Murdock, B. B., Jr. The retention of individual items. *J. exp. Psychol.*, 1961, **62**, 618–625.

Murdock, B. B., Jr. Short-term memory and paired-associate learning. *J. verbal Learn. verbal Behav.*, 1963, **2**, 320–328.

Neimark, Edith, Greenhouse, P., Law, S., & Weinheimer, S. The effect of rehearsal-preventing task upon retention of CVC syllables. *J. verbal Learn. verbal Behav.*, 1965, **4**, 280–285.

Peterson, L. R., & Peterson, Margaret J. Short-term retention of individual verbal items. *J. exp. Psychol.*, 1959, **58**, 193–198.

Peterson, L. R., Peterson, Margaret J., & Miller, A. Short-term retention and meaningfulness. *Canad. J. Psychol.*, 1961, **15**, 143–147.

Pillsbury, W. B., & Sylvester, A. Retroactive and proactive inhibition in immediate memory. *J. exp. Psychol.*, 1940, **27**, 532–545.

Platt, J. R. Strong inference. *Science*, 1964, **146**, 347–353.

Pollack, I. Interference, rehearsal, and short-term retention of digits. *Canad. J. Psychol.*, 1963, **17**, 380–392.

Postman, L. Retention as a function of degree of overlearning. *Science*, 1962, **135**, 666–667.

Sanders, A. F. Rehearsal and recall in immediate memory. *Ergonomics*, 1961, **4**, 29–34.

Schaub, G. R., & Lindley, R. H. Effects of subject-generated recoding cues on short-term memory. *J. exp. Psychol.*, 1964, **68**, 171–175.

Sperling, G. The information available in brief visual presentations. *Psychol. Monogr.*, 1960, **74** (Whole No. 498).

Sperling, G. A model for visual memory tasks. *Hum. Factors*, 1963, **5**, 19–31.

Strong, E. K., Jr. The effect of time-interval upon recognition memory. *Psychol. Rev.*, 1913, **20**, 339–372.

Thorndike, E. L., & Lorge, I. *The teacher's word book of 30,000 words.* New York: Teachers College Press, 1944.

Underwood, B. J. Degree of learning and the measurement of forgetting. *J. verbal Learn. verbal Behav.*, 1964, **3**, 112–129.

Underwood, B. J., & Keppel, G. Retention as a function of degree of learning and letter-sequence interference. *Psychol. Monogr.*, 1963, **77** (Whole No. 567).

Waugh, Nancy C., & Norman, D. A. Primary memory. *Psychol. Rev.*, 1965, **72**, 89–104.

Wickelgren, W. A. Acoustic similarity and intrusion errors in short-term memory. *J. exp. Psychol.*, 1965, **70**, 102–108. (a)

Wickelgren, W. A. Acoustic similarity and retroactive interference in short-term memory. *J. verbal Learn. verbal Behav.*, 1965, **4**, 53–61. (b)

Wickelgren, W. A. Phonemic similarity and interference in short-term memory for single letters. *J. exp. Psychol.*, 1966, **71**, 396–404.

Wickens, D. D., Born, D. G., & Allen, C. K. Proactive inhibition and item similarity in short-term memory. *J. verbal Learn. verbal Behav.*, 1963, **2**, 440–445.

Woodworth, R. S., & Schlosberg, H. *Experimental psychology.* New York: Holt, 1954.

The last chapter dealt with the serial recall of verbal responses in STM, in which elements of an item had to be remembered in their original order. Free recall imposes no restraint on order. Virtually all the experiments on free recall use an immediate retention test. A typical paradigm has a list of words read at a reasonably fast rate. The subject must then report immediately all the words he can remember. Customarily the report is in writing so that an objective record is obtained. Why immediate recall should be a standard procedure is a bit of a mystery because length of the retention interval is one of the variables that any area of memory will usually investigate first. Being immediate recall, it would seem that these experiments are of STM. Yet this is not necessarily the case, as we shall see in the final section of this chapter.

FREE RECALL OF RANDOMLY ORDERED WORDS

The words of the list to be remembered are usually chosen so that subsets of words belong to conceptual categories or contain words which are high associates of each other. The words are scrambled randomly when the list is presented. The reason for so much interest in free recall is that a subject's performance will show a rearrangement of the random words in terms of clusters based on the conceptual categories or associations inherent in the list. In an excellent paper, Cofer (1965, p. 261) distinguishes between *category clustering* and *associative clustering:*

> The first experiments by Bousfield employed lists which contained categorized subgroups of words. For example, a list of 40 items might be composed of 10 animals, 10 weapons, 10 cities, and 10 articles of clothing. These 40 items were presented to the

subject in a random order, and the extent to which, in his recall, the subject put together the animals, the cities, and so on, represents a reorganization or clustering of categorized items. I shall refer to this procedure as *category clustering*. Jenkins and Russell (1952; see also Jenkins, Mink, & Russell, 1958) selected pairs of items from their standardization (Russell & Jenkins, 1954) or the Kent-Rosanoff Word Association Test. They took stimuli, say TABLE and MOUNTAIN, and frequent responses to the stimuli, e.g., CHAIR and HILL, respectively. Words selected in this manner were presented in a random order to subjects for recall. What I shall call *associative clustering* was found when in their recalls the subjects put together in sequence the stimuli and their responses which had been separated at list presentation.

Category and associative clustering are not independent topics, but they will be separated in discussion because they are two lines of research that converge on common themes.

Category Clustering

The Research of Bousfield. Clustering was discovered by Bousfield (1953). His list contained 60 nouns, with 15 in each of four different categories: animals, names, professions, and vegetables. As a control for frequency of word usage, the words of each category were equated in terms of the Thorndike-Lorge word count (Thorndike & Lorge, 1944), which is an estimate of the frequency per million words in ordinary printed English text. The 60 words were presented at a 3-second rate to a group of subjects, and recall was immediate. Bousfield used what he called "repetitions" as an index of clustering. A repetition is a sequence in recall of two or more items from one of the four categories of the stimulus list. The number of repetitions was defined as number of items from a category recalled together minus one. If the subject recalled DOG, CAT, and LION together, DOG and CAT would be one cluster from the animal category and CAT and LION another. Bousfield calculated the number of repetitions that could be expected by chance, and he found a significant tendency to reorganize the randomly presented words into their four conceptual categories. In a very similar study, Bousfield, Cohen, and Whitmarsh (1958) found the same result when empirically derived, taxonomic norms were used to specify the four categories rather than the experimenter's rational judgment, which was used in Bousfield's 1953 study. These norms specify the frequency with which a large number of subjects gave various responses in free association to category or concept names, and these responses were used as items of the four category sublists. The experiment compared lists of words which had a high probability in the norms of being associates of a category name with lists whose words had a low probability. For example, CARROT and PEA were high-probability associates in the vegetable category, and MELON and YAM were low-probability associates. Lists with high-probability associates of the category name had the highest level of correct recall, and the number of their repetitions was higher.

Bousfield and his associates also studied the effects of list repetition, or reinforcement as they called it, on free recall (Bousfield & Cohen, 1953). The same list of 60 nouns with four conceptual categories that had been used before (Bousfield, 1953) was presented one to five times to independent groups of subjects. The mean total recall increased from 23.9 words for one reinforcement to 37.9 words after five reinforcements. Using repetitions as the index of clustering, Bousfield and Cohen found that clustering increased steadily from one to five reinforcements, with five reinforcements having about twice the level of repetitions as one.

Bousfield and Cohen (1955) undertook another approach to the reinforcement variable. Their 1953 study used experimentally manipulated reinforcement, but the 1955 experiment used the

Thorndike-Lorge word count as an index of frequency of use in the language, and thus a kind of index of habit strength. Presumably, the more often a word appears in the written English language, the more times it has been experienced and the greater its associative strength. Two main word lists of 60 nouns were again used, and each list again had sublists for four conceptual categories. One of the main lists had words of low frequency of usage, with a mean frequency of occurrence in the language of 2.60 per million words. The other list had high-frequency words with a mean frequency of 23.87 per million. The outcome of this approach was not as decisive as manipulating reinforcement experimentally, but the results tended to the same direction. Out of the 60 words, mean total recall was 25.5 for high-frequency words and 22.2 for low-frequency words—a difference that is small but significant. Also, repetitions were greater and size of clusters larger for words with a high frequency of occurrence. Similar and confirming results of this work have been found by other investigators. Hall (1954) and Deese (1960) also studied the effects of frequency of use in the language on free recall and found a small but significant increase in mean number of words recalled as frequency increased. The impressive thing about these findings is that frequency of occurrence in the language has a so much smaller effect on free recall than does experimentally manipulated reinforcement. Probably a main reason for this result is shortcomings of the Thorndike-Lorge word count as an index of habit strength underlying probability of correct recall. Because the count is based on frequency of words in newspapers, magazines, books, etc., it is not unreasonable to consider word count as an index of experience. However, as an index of language experience it lacks completeness because it omits frequency of contact with words that are heard or spoken by individuals themselves; and this omission makes the Thorndike-Lorge count a weak, thin index at best. The frequency of contact with spoken words is unknown, although not unknowable. With modern portable tape recorders there is no reason why we cannot record a representative sample of spoken words and combine it with data on visual experience with words. Even considered by itself, the Thorndike-Lorge count probably should be redone and brought up to date because our language, being dynamic, is in a state of change. An index published in 1944 may no longer reflect correct word frequency. Another reason for the relatively strong effect of experimentally manipulated reinforcement is that a subject may be able to form complex mnemonic associations (NLMs) between two or more words as trials progress, and they could be used to benefit recall. Perhaps the increased tendency with trials to repeat combinations of words (not clusters as more narrowly defined above), that has been found by Tulving (1962) and Bousfield, Puff, and Cowan (1964), is a product of NLMs. There has been little systematic study of NLMs in free recall, but their frequent occurrence when verbal materials are used in other retention paradigms leaves little doubt that probing procedures will uncover them in free recall also. If the effects on free recall of reinforcements, defined experimentally as list repetitions, can partly be due to NLM formation, then frequency of experience as measured by the Thorndike-Lorge word count is not the same thing. Possibly the Thorndike-Lorge word count has a small effect on free recall because it lacks the benefits that NLMs bring to free recall when experience is experimentally manipulated by list repetitions.

How do Bousfield and his associates account for clustering theoretically? They see it as a concept-formation situation. The separate words of a concept category have their separate habit strengths, or "subordinate perceptions" as Bousfield calls it; and these separate words are organized under a "superordinate perception" which is a conceptual state that has strength of its own derived from the strength of individual words. The strength for the superordinate accrues with practice on the subordinate. As a result of such learning, the occurrence of a subordinate perception will activate the superordinate structure, which in turn activates the responses of other subordinates. The result is words of the same conceptual class being recalled together, which is clustering. To illustrate, the occurrence at recall of the subordinate word COW arouses the animal superordinate, which in turn increases the chances of naming DOG and CALF in the animal category and inducing a clustering phenomenon. As number of reinforcements increase for the separate words like COW, DOG, and CALF, and their separate strengths increase, the strength of the animal superordinate increases and the clustering effect increases.

Underwood's Experiment. Underwood (1964, pp. 62–65) presented four lists of words to the same group of subjects. The lists varied in interitem similarity, as Underwood called it. Table 6-1 contains the lists, and they are representative of the kind often used in free recall experiments. Lists 1 and 4 have low interitem similarity and contain unrelated words. Lists 2 and 3 have high interitem similarity, with four items in each of four concept categories. The words of lists 2 and 3 were not, of course, presented in the organized fashion shown in Table 6-1. As is the custom in free recall experiments, the words were essentially randomized, with each block of four items having one randomly assigned word from one of the four categories. The lists were presented in order 1, 2, 3, and 4; thus the subject, after receiving list 1, would have no expectation that list 2 contained categorized words (although PI influences might have been present—see Miller, 1958). Each list was presented once.

The mean number of items correctly recalled was 11.08, 14.57, 14.86, and 11.35 for lists 1 through 4, respectively. Thirty-eight percent of the recall performances on lists 2 and 3 were

Table 6-1.   Lists Used to Study Free Recall as a Function of Conceptual Similarity. From Underwood (1964)

List 1	List 2	List 3	List 4
apple	Bob	France	daisy
football	Bill	England	wall
emerald	Joe	Russia	bee
trout	John	Germany	second
copper	rabbi	blue jay	knife
theft	priest	canary	bus
hat	bishop	sparrow	geology
table	minister	robin	maple
cruiser	cow	measles	arm
trumpet	horse	mumps	hammer
doctor	horse	polio	salt
doctor	dog	polio	salt
head	cat	cancer	tent
wine	rumba	nitrogen	cobra
blue	fox-trot	oxygen	mountain
gasoline	tango	hydrogen	window
cotton	waltz	sulphur	rain

perfect, although only three percent were perfect on lists 1 and 4. On category clustering, Underwood says:

> In recall of the high-similarity lists, clustering was nearly perfect. Only five of the 37 subjects might be said not to have shown extreme clustering. The other 32 subjects in general produced recall protocols in which all four items in a category were recalled together, then another four, and so on. The subjects were not told the number of items in the list, yet it was clear in many of the protocols that the subject knew there were 16 items and four instances of each of four concepts. No subject ever gave five words from a concept. In the 74 recalls only three showed a failure to recall any word from a category. That is, these three protocols showed perfect or nearly perfect recall for the 12 units forming three categories but no recall for the fourth. In several of the protocols in which 15 items were given correctly, a blank space was left for the fourth item in the category. No subject

ever wrote down less than three items from a given category (Underwood, 1964, p. 64).

Underwood concludes that the unit of memory for the high-similarity lists is not the individual word but the category name. This is in essential agreement with Bousfield's hypothesis about higher-order concept habits governing category clustering. In some ways Underwood, in the quotation above, goes beyond Bousfield by saying that subjects not only knew the concepts but also knew that there were 4 items under each concept and a total of 16 items in all. The subjects, by exerting this more general intellectual control, were executing a kind of editing process. Underwood (1964, p. 62) calls this editor a "selector mechanism." Bousfield talks of subjects using concept behavior only, but Underwood sees the operation of other higher behavioral functions also. The notion of a central editor is controversial. Deese (1961, p. 19) believes it to be an unnecessary assumption because of his preference for a simpler explanation in terms of word associations, which will be discussed next.

Associative Clustering

Bousfield's theoretical explanation did not stand unchallenged very long. Bousfield's theory is compatible with data and modern ideas about concept formation, but the challenge came from those who assert that clustering is no more than word association. Higher mental structures like concepts are not required—only words and the other words which they elicit. If this contention is correct, clustering is explained in comparatively simple terms, which is always desirable. This section will examine the attempts to explain free recall in associational terms.

Kent-Rosanoff Free Association Norms. In a free association test, as everyone knows, a stimulus word is presented, and the subject gives the first word that comes to mind—a word which is known as the primary response for the stimulus. The associative strength of the stimulus to elicit its primary response is measured by the percentage of subjects who give the response when the stimulus is presented. The original Kent-Rosanoff Free Association Test of 100 words (Kent & Rosanoff, 1910) has been updated on a large sample of students from the University of Minnesota ($N = 1,008$) by Russell and Jenkins (1954), and it is these norms which are now in common use.

Jenkins and Russell (1952) were the first to demonstrate that a clustering effect could be predicted from free association norms. A list of 48 words was made up of 24 pairs, in which a pair was a stimulus word from the Kent-Rosanoff Free Association Test and its primary response, such as TABLE-CHAIR. The stimuli and responses of the 24 pairs were randomized. The free recall data were analyzed in terms of the clustering of the stimulus and response word of a particular pair. They defined a "forward association" as a stimulus word followed by its own response word and a "reverse association" as the response word followed by its stimulus. The mean total number of words recalled was 24, and of these 50 percent were accounted for by forward and reverse associations. Jenkins and Russell conclude that associative strength between words is a variable for clustering, and although Bousfield's theoretical interpretation is not denied, there is the implication that associations might account for clustering in Bousfield's experiments, too. Suppose a list had a military concept as the basis for a category, and SOLDIER, ARMY, and NAVY were given together in recall. According to Bousfield, the superordinate military concept would be active in promoting this cluster, but an alternate explanation is that SOLDIER often elicits ARMY in free association and ARMY in turn elicits NAVY (Russell & Jenkins, 1954). Through free association, the subjects have a good chance of performing correctly. It is not at all unreasonable that the basic associational structure of language could account for some clustering without resorting to higher mental organization, although this possibility does not deny Bousfield's interpretation. Both associative and category clustering could contribute to clustering.

Jenkins, Mink, and Russell (1958) performed a related study which used four lists of 12 pairs each from the Kent-Rosanoff norms, with the variable being the strength of a stimulus member of a pair to evoke its response term in a free association test. List 1 had a mean of 70.9 percent of common response occurrence to a stimulus, which meant that 70.9 percent of the time subjects would give the same response in free association to a stimulus word. List 1, therefore, was composed mostly of pairs like MAN-WOMAN and BREAD-BUTTER. In the same vein, lists 2, 3, and 4 had mean percents of 47.3, 29.8, and 13.8, respectively, which represent the decreasing reliability of a stimulus to elicit a common response from subjects. The 24 words of a list were randomized, and an independent group of subjects was used for each list. The mean number of responses correctly recalled was 19, 18, 17, and 14 for lists 1, 2, 3, and 4, respectively. The data were analyzed in terms of forward and reverse associations, as in their earlier study (Jenkins & Russell, 1952), and the results are presented in Figure 6-1. Forward associations are more frequent than reverse associations, as might be expected, but more important is that clustering increases as strength of the association increases. This is precisely the expectation from ideas about an associative basis for clustering.

Association Networks. The Kent-Rosanoff norms are based on the probability that one word will evoke another as a free association. Since the studies of Jenkins and Russell (1952) and Jenkins, Mink, and Russell (1958), an interest in more elaborate indices of word association has emerged. Deese's Index of Interitem As-

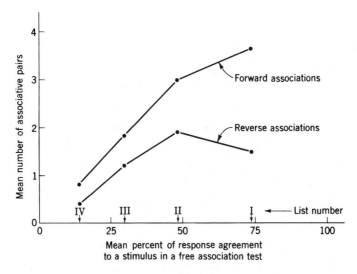

Fig. 6-1. Clustering in free recall as a function of association level of pairs in a list. Plotted from Table 2 (p. 130) in Jenkins, Mink, and Russell (1958).

sociative Strength (Deese, 1959, 1961) is based on the proba-bility that a word of a list will evoke any one of the other words of the list as an association. A revision of this index, called the Index of Associative Meaning (Deese, 1962), similarly uses the number of associates which any two words of the list have in common, except that in this case the associates need not be words of the list. Deese's approach is based on the assumption that word sets embody an elaborate network of associations, and that the simple associative links of the Kent-Rosanoff norms un-justly represent the associative bonds that actually exist. Deese (1959) was successful in predicting free recall from his Index of Interitem Associative Strength. Number of words recalled cor-related .88 with the index, and Deese concludes (p. 309) that "the likelihood of a particular item's occurring in free recall is a function of the associative strength of that item to other items in the list." Deese (1960) also found free recall to increase as length of the list increased, and he sees this as consistent with implications of his Index of Interitem Associative Strength (Deese, 1961, p. 23). Even random words would have associations among them, and the longer the list, the greater the likelihood that a particular word would have another word of the list as an associate.

But what of the Index of Interitem Associative Strength and clustering? We have seen that lists whose items are arranged in conceptual categories have a tendency to cluster in the free recall test according to the categories, and it is reasonable to expect also that these clustered items would be associates of one another to some degree. The words of a military category, like ARMY, NAVY, SOLDIER, SAILOR, etc., would tend to cluster; and they would also tend to elicit one another in a free association test and have a relatively high Index of Interitem Associative Strength. Bousfield, Steward, and Cowan (1961) made a test of this implication. They used two lists of two categories each. One list had a low Index of Interitem Associative Strength and the other a high index. The list with the high index had both a higher level of recall and a greater tendency toward clustering than the other list. This finding demonstrates that the Index of Interitem Associative Strength can predict clustering, but it does not exclude Bousfield's concept hypothesis of category clustering. Clustering may occur over and beyond that which can be accounted for by an index of association. Marshall (reported in Cofer, 1965) conducted an experiment to demonstrate this.

Marshall used a Mutual Relatedness Index which is based on *all* the associations that any two words of the list have in common. This index is essentially the same as Deese's Index of Associative Meaning (Deese, 1962), and it should be distinguished from Deese's Index of Interitem Associative Strength which only tallies the frequency that one word of a list is associated with another word of the same list. Marshall worked with six groups of subjects. Each group was presented a scrambled list of 24 words for free recall. In a list were 12 categorized pairs and 12 uncategorized pairs. The pairs of a list in a prior free association test had about the same number of associates in common and thus the same Mutual Relatedness Index. The category pairs, however, were conceptually related, while the noncategory pairs were not. There were six lists, one per group, each representing a level of the Mutual Relatedness Index. By using this thorough approach, Marshall could test whether categorized pairs tended to go together, or cluster, in recall more than uncategorized pairs with level of the Mutual Relatedness Index held constant. Each list was given four trials, with the items arranged in a new random order each time. Clustering was tabulated when a pair appeared together in recall. Figure 6-2 shows the plot of repetitions (expressed as index of repetitions called

Fig. 6-2.   RR (ratio of repetition), an index of clustering in free recall, as a function of practice trials and the Mutual Relatedness Index (MR). From Cofer (1965).

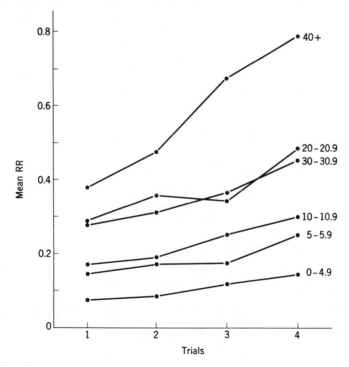

RR) as a function of trials for the six groups, with the Mutual Relatedness Index as the curve parameter. An average has been taken for both the categorized and the noncategorized pairs. Clearly, the index is a powerful determiner of clustering. Figure 6-3 is a plot of repetitions for categorized and noncategorized pairs, with the average value of the Mutual Relatedness Index the same for both curves. Theoretically, Figure 6-3 is the most interesting because it shows that conceptual categorization is a determinant of clustering in its own right. Another analysis demonstrated that categorization had its biggest effect on clustering at the lower values of the index, and that the effect tended to wash out at the higher levels. Marshall's experiment is important because it is the only study which attempts to distinguish the relative contributions of category and associative factors in clustering. Theoretically, it would have been tidier had his data

Fig. 6-3. RR, an index of clustering in free recall, as a function of practice trials and the conceptual categorization or noncategorization of words. From Cofer (1965).

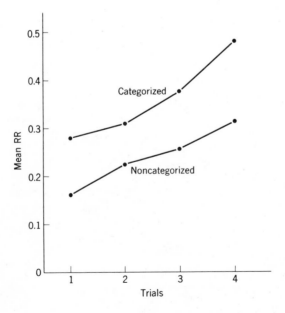

come out decisively for one or the other as a basis for clustering, but such was not the case. Both factors contribute to clustering, and so both Bousfield's conceptual hypothesis and the associative hypothesis have validity (Cofer, 1965, p. 271).

FREE RECALL OF APPROXIMATIONS TO ENGLISH TEXT

That so much of the research on free recall has been done with randomly ordered words should not turn us away from the fact that much of free recall in this world is of organized material. Randomly ordered words provide a useful way to examine hypotheses about free recall, but their use sidesteps the problem of free recall of organized word sets. One research approach has been to study the free recall of word sets with different degrees of organization, ranging from randomness to the coherent structure of conventional English language text.

The Miller-Selfridge Study

This experiment (Miller & Selfridge, 1950) investigated immediate free recall as a joint function of length of passage and eight orders of approximation to the statistical structure of English. The list of zero-order approximation to the language had randomness, and a random sample of words was drawn from the count of 30,000 words by Thorndike and Lorge (1944). These words were drawn truly at random, with no regard to their relative frequency of occurrence in the language; thus indeed, the approximation order was zero. First-order approximation required that the relative frequency of words in the language be represented; therefore words were drawn at random from conventional printed text. Approximation orders two through seven used human subjects to generate them. To have higher orders of approximation empirically correct, it would have been necessary to have data on the relative frequency of word occurrences in the language, of all word combinations of different lengths, and of the conditional probability of words and combination of words occurring after each combination of a given length. Maybe someday a computer of giant capacity that can read will digest the language and summarize its structural properties in a usable way for language description and research, but there are no data remotely like this at present. Therefore, Miller and Selfridge relied on human subjects who, through learning, have the statistical structure of the language built into them and could at least approximate the sequential dependencies in the language. Miller and Selfridge describe the generation of second-order approximations as follows:

> At the second order, for example, a common word, such as
> *he, it* or *the,* is presented to a person who is instructed to use the
> word in a sentence. The word he uses directly after the one given
> him is then noted and later presented to another person who has
> not heard the sentence given by the first person, and he, in turn,
> is asked to use that word in a sentence. The word he uses directly after the one given him is then noted and later given to
> yet another person. This procedure is repeated until the total
> sequence of words is of the desired length. Each successive pair
> of words could go together in a sentence. Each word is determined in the context of only one preceding word (Miller &
> Selfridge, 1960, p. 180).

For approximation orders 3 through 7 (sixth order was omitted) the subject saw a sequence of two or more words each time and used the sequence in a sentence. The highest order was regular language text taken from current fiction or biography. In this fashion, lists of 10, 20, 30, and 50 words were constructed for each order.

Here are examples of 10-word passages:

Zero order: byway consequence handsomely financier bent flux cavalry swiftness weather-beaten extent

First order: abilities with that beside I for waltz you the sewing

Second order: was he went to the newspaper is in deep and

Third order: tall and thin boy is a biped is the beat

Fourth order: saw the football game will end at midnight on January

Fifth order: they saw the play Saturday and sat down beside him

Seventh order: recognize her abilities in music after he scolded him before

Text: the history of California is largely that of a railroad

The words were presented orally, and free recall was immediate. Scoring was based on number of correct words correctly recalled; order of words in recall was not part of the scoring. Although a study of language organization might seem to require a consideration of word order in the scoring, this does not seem to be so. King (1960) evaluated seven ways of scoring the recall of ordinary prose passages, ranging from counting the words to judges' scaling of the entire recall sequence, and he found intercorrelations to be high. With the evidence available at the moment, a simple measure of counting words correctly recalled is about as good as a complex measure that is intuitively more reasonable. This does not mean there is no value in scoring order, as we shall see in the next section. What it does mean is that different methods of scoring recall have a high linear relationship and that about the same functional forms for recall data are expressed with any of the seven measures that King evaluated.

The results of the Miller-Selfridge experiment are given in Figure 6-4. Percentage recalled increased with order of approximation and decreased with length of list. It is interesting to see that most of the higher orders of approximation are recalled

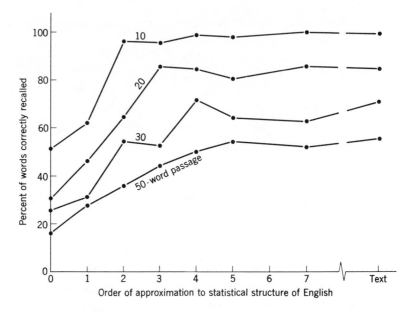

Fig. 6-4. Free recall as a function of length of passage and order of approximation of the words to statistical structure of English. From Miller and Selfridge (1950).

about as well as conventional, organized text. Miller and Selfridge suggest that material which preserves the short-range associations of the English language utilizes past learning, benefits from positive transfer, and is easy to learn and remember. Sharp (1958) and Richardson and Voss (1960) repeated the essentials of the Miller-Selfridge experiment and obtained about the same results.

The Chunk

Postman and Adams (1960), in a free recall experiment, used the zero, second-, and fourth-order approximations, and regular prose text, of 50-word length from the Miller-Selfridge experiment. One of their analyses concerned the scoring of correct sequential order. The number of items recalled in correct sequences of two or more was tallied, and the percent that these sequences were of the total recall score increased as order of approximation to the English language increased. Taking this approach as the point of departure, Tulving and Patkau (1962) interpreted these sequences as the chunk (Miller, 1956) which was discussed in Chapter 5 and is hypothesized to be the unit of STM. It will be remembered that Miller believed the span of STM to be from five to nine chunks, with an average of about seven.

Using the general procedures of Miller and Selfridge for generating word lists, Tulving and Patkau generated 24-word lists of first, third, fifth, seventh, and text order of approximation. For each of these orders, Tulving and Patkau constructed lists with only words of high frequency of occurrence (Thorndike & Lorge, 1944), or with words of both high and low frequency. As in the Miller and Selfridge experiment, the lists were presented orally and free recall was immediate. They defined the chunk as

> . . . any group of one or more items which occur in a subject's recall in the same sequence as the input list. For example, if the stimulus list consists of a sequence A, B, C, D, . . . V, W, X, and the subject recalls T, U, V, A, B, D, E, F, R, K, in this order, we assume that the ten items the subject recalled are organized into five adopted chunks: TUV, AB, DEF, R, and K (Tulving & Patkau, 1962, p. 90).

Tulving and Patkau found that number of words correctly recalled increased with the order of approximation, which is consistent with previous work, but as a new finding they discovered that number of chunks was essentially invariant regardless of the order of approximation and the frequency of word occurrence. For all conditions, the mean number of chunks was 5 to 6, which is consistent with Miller's hypothesis about the chunk and the capacity of STM. Because amount recalled was greater for the higher orders of approximation, and with number of chunks invariant, it follows that chunks are larger as order of approximation increases. Miller and Selfridge hypothesized that the increase in recall with increase in order of approximation is a function of the short-range associations which the subject can muster from his past language learning, and Tulving and Patkau have shown that about six of these sequences can be accommodated at a time. McNulty (1966) reports data which support the findings and conclusions of Tulving and Patkau.

DISCUSSION

Free recall studies have used an immediate retention test, and so it might be presumed that the memory traces reside in STM. Yet this presumption may be wrong, at least in part. In Chapter 5 on STM and serial recall we saw that the order of elements had to be preserved in memory and, in the absence of recoding into mediators and a bond with LTM, it was reasonable to assume that the order variable involved new learning and was in a special STM compartment. Free recall, however, lacks the requirement for preservation of order, and so there are ample opportunities for the material to enter LTM directly. To what extent might this conjecture be true? There are three basic circumstances of free recall that have been discussed in this chapter, and each of these need examination for its relations with STM and LTM.

The first case is recall of a randomly ordered list of words explained by association principles based on norms of the Kent-Rosanoff type, and more complex association networks represented by measures like the Index of Interitem Associative Strength. The explanatory power of these approaches was seen to be considerable, and it is fair to say that the associations reside wholly in LTM. The association between two words, or the multiple associations among words in a series, is the product of a life-time of verbal learning, and it is a strong habit connection in LTM. The position can be taken that the working of the associative bonds is fully "automatic," although it is not unreasonable to speculate the operation of some conscious control in which the subject is aware of the associations in a list and is able to verbalize them. Or a subject may, under some circumstances, sidestep the free association relationships inherent in the list and use idiosyncratic NLMs between words. New studies are needed which use verbal reports and relate the working of these mechanisms to the content of free recall. Regardless of the mechanisms for the free recall of randomly ordered words, they would all seem based on well-learned response relationships, and there is no need to invoke STM even though recall is immediate.

The second case is one in which conceptual behavior enters to determine free recall. Bousfield (1953) hypothesized this explanation in his pioneering work, and Underwood (1964) and Marshall (reported in Cofer, 1965) concur, although Marshall has evidence that association variables operate, too. In the conceptual case we can assume that the presentation of a list with words in well-defined concept categories keys the higher-order concept memory traces that are in LTM from past concept learning. The subjects may not be consciously aware of these concept categories and be able to verbalize them, although possibly they may if anyone were to ask them. But, whether the subjects are aware or not, the concepts in LTM can become the unit of memory (Underwood, 1964, p. 64) and govern free recall. Underwood (1964) goes somewhat further and suggests that concepts also exercise an editorial role and screen the responses to limit them to conceptual categories of the list. Presumably, as the subject readies a response for evocation, it is referenced to the traces of the concept categories and rejected if it fails to conform. If it conforms, it is given. The use of an internal standard against which to compare will be discussed in Chapter 10 as the basis for response recognition, and eventually it may become useful for understanding free recall also. The rejection and acceptance of responses is a common part of our everyday responding, but we customarily ignore these facets of responding in our records of laboratory behavior. When someone says "It's Sarah! No! I mean Rachel!" he is rejecting Sarah as the wrong response and replacing it with Rachel, which conforms to a standard of correctness. In the same fashion, reference standards are operating in the free recall of categorized words. The reference standard is a big difference between free associational and conceptual explanations of free recall. Free association is a straight-through, or open-loop, model in which responses occur freely according to their strength of association and without comparison to a reference. Free association norms do not seem to explain screening in which the response is fed back and compared to a standard in a closed-loop paradigm. Chapter 10 will discuss closed-loop paradigms in more detail.

The third case is the free recall of approximations to English language text, and it is the only one of the three cases in which the material seems to be stored in STM. Free association and concept mechanisms appear to have little value for this case. Free associations are not helpful when words are parts of meaningful sentences, which they usually are for these experiments. Free associations are helpful for randomly ordered single words because one word unit can suggest another on the list and possibly aid recall. But when the material has an approximation to English of a higher order, the perceptual unit is a subgroup of words that can be a fragment of a sentence. A free association to this fragment would probably be a word series to complete the sentence. Words to complete the suggested sentence would probably not help because they would not be words of the list whose occurrence would aid the subject's recall score. And, of course, there are no categories represented in the word list; therefore conceptual machanisms would be of no value. What the subject appears to do is to use the quasi-sentences as units, or chunks, without appreciable resort to concepts or free associations, and store the chunks in STM until recall is required. The defining of a chunk is always a problem, but if the approaches of Tulving and Patkau (1962) and McNulty (1966) are accepted, their free recall data nicely fit Miller's theory and other data on the capacity of STM.

In summary, research on free recall is something of a curiosity in the experimental psychology of memory, but this remark is not intended in a derogatory way. The research has been good and important. However, the interest in organizational factors (e.g., clustering) has been an overriding one, and most of the variables that have traditionally occupied investigators of other areas of memory have been ignored. Substantive empirical data are lacking on such variables as length of the retention interval and intralist and interlist PI and RI effects as they relate to the interference theory of forgetting. Miller (1958) has presented preliminary findings on negative and positive transfer in free recall, and Postman and Phillips (1965) have made a start on interference issues. But the primary laws of retention for free recall remain to be worked out.

REFERENCES

Bousfield, W. A. The occurrence of clustering in the recall of randomly arranged associates. *J. gen. Psychol.*, 1953, **49**, 229–240.

Bousfield, W. A., & Cohen, B. H. The effects of reinforcement on the occurrence of clustering in the recall of randomly arranged associates. *J. Psychol.*, 1953, **36**, 67–81.

Bousfield, W. A., & Cohen, B. H. The occurrence of clustering in the recall of randomly arranged words of different frequencies-of-usage. *J. gen. Psychol.*, 1955, **52**, 83–95.

Bousfield, W. A., Cohen, B. H., & Whitmarsh, G. A. Associative clustering in the recall of words of different taxonomic frequencies of occurrence. *Psychol. Rep.*, 1958, **4**, 39–44.

Bousfield, W. A., Puff, C. R., & Cowan, T. M. The development of constancies in sequential organization during repeated free recall. *J. verbal Learn. verbal Behav.*, 1964, **3**, 489–495.

Bousfield, W. A., Steward, J. R., & Cowan, T. M. The use of free associational norms for the prediction of clustering. Technical Report No. 36, Univer. of Connecticut, Contract Nonr-631(00), Office of Naval Research, 1961.

Cofer, C. N. On some factors in the organizational characteristics of free recall. *Amer. Psychologist*, 1965, **20**, 261–272.

Deese, J. Influence of inter-item associative strength upon immediate free recall. *Psychol. Rep.*, 1959, **5**, 305–312.

Deese, J. Frequency of usage and number of words in free recall: The role of association. *Psychol. Rep.*, 1960, **7**, 337–344.

Deese, J. From the isolated verbal unit to connected discourse. In C. N. Cofer (Ed.), *Verbal learning and verbal behavior.* New York: McGraw-Hill, 1961. Pp. 11–31.

Deese, J. On the structure of associative meaning. *Psychol. Rev.*, 1962, **69**, 161–175.

Hall, J. F. Learning as a function of word-frequency. *Amer. J. Psychol.*, 1954, **67**, 138–140.

Jenkins, J. J., Mink, W. D., & Russell, W. A. Associative clustering as a function of verbal association strength. *Psychol. Rep.*, 1958, **4**, 127–136.

Jenkins, J. J., & Russell, W. A. Associative clustering during recall. *J. abnorm. soc. Psychol.*, 1952, **47**, 818–821.

Kent, G. H., & Rosanoff, A. J. A study of association in insanity. *Amer. J. Insanity*, 1910, **67**, 37–96.

King, D. J. On the accuracy of written recall: A scaling and factor analytic study. *Psychol. Rec.*, 1960, **10**, 113–122.

McNulty, J. A. The measurement of "adopted chunks" in free recall learning. *Psychon. Sci.*, 1966, **4**, 71–72.

Miller, G. A. The magical number seven, plus or minus two: Some limits of our capacity for processing information. *Psychol. Rev.*, 1956, **63**, 81–97.

Miller, G. A. Free recall of redundant strings of letters. *J. exp. Psychol.*, 1958, **56**, 485–491.

Miller, G. A., & Selfridge, J. A. Verbal context and the recall of meaningful material. *Amer. J. Psychol.*, 1950, **63**, 176–185.

Postman, L., & Adams, Pauline A. Studies in incidental learning: VII. The effects of contextual determination. *J. exp. Psychol.*, 1960, **59**, 153–164.

Postman, L., & Phillips, L. W. Short-term temporal changes in free recall. *Quart. J. exp. Psychol.*, 1965, **17**, 132–138.

Richardson, Patricia, & Voss, J. F. Replication report: Verbal context and the recall of meaningful material. *J. exp. Psychol.*, 1960, **60**, 417–418.

Russell, W. A., & Jenkins, J. J. The complete Minnesota norms for responses to 100 words from the Kent-Rosanoff Word Association Test. Technical Report No. 11, Univer. of Minnesota, Contract N8onr-66216, Office of Naval Research, 1954.

Sharp, H. C. Effect of contextual constraint upon recall of verbal passages. *Amer. J. Psychol.*, 1958, **71**, 568–572.

Thorndike, E. L., & Lorge, I. *The teacher's word book of 30,000 words.* New York: Teachers College Press, 1944.

Tulving, E. Subjective organization in free recall of "unrelated" words. *Psychol. Rev.*, 1962, **69**, 344–354.

Tulving, E., & Patkau, J. E. Concurrent effects of contextual constraint and word frequency on immediate recall and learning of verbal material. *Canad. J. Psychol.*, 1962, **16**, 83–95.

Underwood, B. J. The representativeness of rote verbal learning. In A. W. Melton (Ed.), *Categories of human learning.* New York: Academic, 1964. Pp. 47–78.

We saw in Chapter 5 that interference is the best explanation of forgetting in STM (short-term memory). The reason that interference principles were invoked so capably to guide STM research and explain it (e.g., Keppel & Underwood, 1962) was that the interference theory of forgetting has had a laboratory substrate built in studies of PI (proactive inhibition) and RI (retroactive inhibition) (Chapter 4), and in studies of verbal forgetting over the relatively long term (hours, days, months, etc.), which are to be discussed in this chapter. Mediational and conceptual behavior will also be covered here because they involve verbal processes and because they have been studied as LTM (long-term memory) phenomena. What will not be covered is the "curve of forgetting" which abounds in introductory textbooks. To say that processes operate in time and cause forgetting is trite. The search for these curves was motivated by an expectation to find THE forgetting function—a line of thinking which is archaic. When the variables for behavior become better known, there will be a family of retention functions depending upon the configuration of variables operating, and our understanding of these functions will evolve naturally as the experimental study of memory matures.

TESTS OF THE INTERFERENCE THEORY OF FORGETTING

Chapter 5 said that interference is a preeminent explanatory mechanism for verbal STM, and that trace decay has no status for explaining loss over the retention interval. The same is true for verbal LTM, although the interference explanation is not without its problems. That this chapter is richly involved with implications of the interference theory of forgetting has its scientific justification.

Effects of Events in the Retention Interval

The laboratory RI experiment which experimentally manipulates the events that are learned in the retention interval is the parallel of the LTM experiments in this section. In the usual forgetting experiment, in which the retention interval is measured at least in hours, the subject is allowed to leave the laboratory and conduct his normal affairs. The retention interval is unstructured under these circumstances, and it is difficult to gain experimental control of the events which are potentially interfering.

One research possibility is to try to give structure to events in the retention interval, even though it is difficult to do so. We could assume that inactivation of the organism with low temperature or drugs represents a state of neutrality which mostly removes the organism from interfering events without inducing organic change. Animals could be subjected to treatments such as these in the retention interval. We are understandably reluctant to use such potentially dangerous methods on human subjects, although it is not outside the realm of possibility if proper medical safeguards are employed. Human beings have not been used in experiments of this sort, although animals have (Hunter, 1932; Russell & Hunter, 1937). More innocuous methods have been used with human beings. Sleeping subjects would seem removed from most interfering experiences, and their retention has been compared with that of waking subjects who have gone about their regular activities during the retention interval (e.g., Jenkins & Dallenbach, 1924). If the interference theory is correct, sleeping should produce better retention than waking. Another approach, which has been given limited trial, has been to keep subjects in the laboratory for relatively long periods of time under severe sensory restriction throughout both sleeping and waking periods (Grissom, Suedfeld, & Vernon, 1962). Neither of these procedures for human beings has been tested as thoroughly as it might be. Some of the experiments are old, but nevertheless they are conceptually important enough to be discussed here.

The Jenkins-Dallenbach Study. This is a classic study (Jenkins & Dallenbach, 1924) that has found its way into many textbooks and whose general findings have been supported by other experiments (Spight, 1928; Van Ormer, 1932; Newman, 1939). Two subjects were used, and at each session they learned a serial list of 10 nonsense syllables to a criterion of one correct repetition of the list. The experimental variable was whether the retention interval was spent sleeping or waking. Retention intervals of 1, 2, 4, and 8 hours were used, and each subject had eight different lists for each of the intervals under both sleeping and waking conditions. With the exception of two or three waking sessions which each subject missed, the two subjects contributed 16 retention scores for each point of the sleeping and waking retention curves. Free recall was used. The subjects slept in the laboratory so that control over the sleeping behavior was maintained.

The results are shown in Figure 7-1. For both subjects, recall was higher when the retention interval was spent in sleeping and the likelihood of encountering interfering events was reduced. More than twice as many syllables were recalled after sleeping than after waking by both subjects. The results are in nice harmony with the interference theory of forgetting, and the authors conclude that ". . . forgetting is not so much a matter of the decay of old impressions and associations as it is a matter of the interference, inhibition, or obliteration of the old by the new" (Jenkins & Dallenbach, 1924, p. 612).

Sensory Deprivation. Recent years have seen a brisk interest in sensory deprivation, which involves study of restriction in the amount of general environmental stimuli which bombard us massively in several sensory modalities all the time (Scott, 1957;

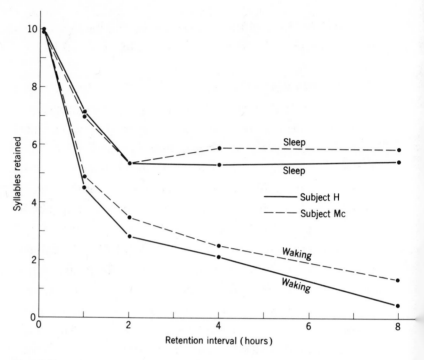

Fig. 7-1. Retention of nonsense syllables over intervals of sleeping or waking for two subjects H and Mc. From Jenkins and Dallenbach (1924).

Wheaton, 1959; Vernon, 1963). Explorers and shipwrecked sailors who have been isolated in impoverished, uniform environments for long periods of time report that they sometimes lapsed into mental instability and had auditory and visual hallucinations. These informal observations were given systematic laboratory investigation at McGill University and later in other laboratories. Research on sensory deprivation has accelerated in recent years because of interest in behavioral changes that might take place in astronauts in the sensory uniformity of outer space, and in military men in isolated outposts or under the sea. It was within the context of research on isolation that Grissom, Suedfeld, and Vernon (1962) made a contribution to the interference theory of forgetting. They used isolation with minimal stimulation as the means of controlling interpolated activities, just as Jenkins and Dallenbach (1924) and others had used sleep. According to interference theory, subjects who spend their retention interval in an isolation chamber should remember more than subjects who were allowed normal activity outside the laboratory.

The subjects were male university students who were presented a 182-word prose passage orally and then were given an immediate retention test to provide a measure of how much was learned. After the immediate test control subjects were dismissed from the laboratory, but experimental subjects were placed in individual, soundproof, dark rooms and restricted to bed. Food, water, and urinal tubes were at the bedside. A subject was required to keep total silence. A recall test was given all subjects after 24 hours. The control subjects forgot 12.6 percent of the material that they had known on the immediate recall test, but experimental subjects actually had a minor improvement of 1.8 percent over the retention interval. A shortcoming of an experiment of this kind could be that confined subjects had time on their hands for rehearsal, but the authors were alert to this possibility and took steps to prevent it. The subjects were not told there would be a recall test; therefore they had no reason to rehearse. As a check, all subjects were interviewed and only one subject, of the experimental group, admitted to rehearsal in anticipation of a possible recall.

All in all, the experiment is a small but good one, and it conforms to expectations for the interference theory of forgetting. Forgetting was eliminated by reducing the possibility of interfering activity in the retention interval.

Animal Research. The Jenkins and Dallenbach study sparked animal research on retention that used ways other than sleep to control activity during the retention interval. We are free to do most anything we please with animals, and there are possibilities for important dividends for the interference theory of forgetting.

As it has turned out, the research freedom we have with animals has not given us large benefits for laws and theory of memory. The attempts have been interesting, however, and are worthy of discussion.

Hunter (1932) taught cockroaches a dark-avoidance response. The insects of the control group spent the retention interval in their normal living quarters, but the experimental group was subjected to cold in which the temperature was low enough (2 to 6°C) to keep them quiescent. Periods of 2 and 4 hours cold were studied, and the effect was to lower recall relative to the control subjects, which is contrary to the interference theory of forgetting. Hunter, however, did not conclude against interference theory but rather believed that cold probably induced organic change rather than an organically neutral state. In a later study with rats, Russell and Hunter (1937) used Sodium Amytal and kept the experimental animals anesthetized during most of the retention interval. No difference between experimental and control animals was found, and it is hard to say why. Sodium Amytal may not be a neutral agent for the organic basis of memory.

The only animal experiment that is fully consistent with the human studies in the Jenkins-Dallenbach vein is a cockroach experiment by Minami and Dallenbach (1946). Cold or drugs were not used to restrict activities in the retention interval, so that the criticism of organic change is avoided. Minami and Dallenbach capitalized on the fact that a cockroach is quiescent when in contact with surrounding materials. During the retention interval a cockroach of the experimental group was placed in a small box which completely surrounded it with soft tissue paper and kept it immobile. Control group subjects were returned to their living cages during the retention interval. As in Hunter's cockroach experiment, a dark-avoidance response was used. Retention intervals were 1, 2, 3, 8, and 24 hours. The best retention was found for the experimental group with the restricted activity.

Effects of Prior Language Habits

Underwood's Analysis.   Underwood (1957) wrote a classic paper on forgetting which, along with the paper by Peterson and Peterson (1959) on STM, was the catalyst that stimulated a modern interest in memory research. Prior to Underwood's analysis, the tests of the interference hypothesis of forgetting had concentrated on RI, as had the laboratory studies of interference per se. This was consistent with the reasonable assumption that forgetting over the retention interval is a function of events in the interval. No one denies this, but the thrust of Underwood's analysis was to show the interfering power of learning prior to the learning and recall of criterion material and to emphasize that PI can be a more potent influence than RI, at least when retention intervals are of moderate duration like 24 hours or so. With relatively long intervals RI can become strong relative to PI because the chances of interfering events increase.

Underwood presented empirical data from several sources which showed that recall of a verbal list was inversely related to number of prior lists which had been learned in the laboratory in the same or other experiments. In general, the lists were dissimilar. From these data, Underwood was led to the larger observation that amount of verbal material which an adult subject has learned outside the laboratory and prior to the learning of a criterion verbal list can be large relative to that which he will learn in the retention interval that follows, and the chances of PI affecting retention can be greater than RI. This position hardly seems earthshaking because it is wholly consonant with interference theory. But the impact was strong because PI and RI were placed in a new perspective, and PI emerged with a significance that it never had before. From Underwood's thinking came a major series of experiments on retention and extraexperimental interference.

The Underwood-Postman Hypothesis of Extraexperimental Sources of Interference in Forgetting. In Chapter 4 the extinction hypothesis for PI said that the learning of a verbal list interfered with previously learned verbal responses and partly extinguished them. Some spontaneous recovery of the extinguished items in the retention interval occurs, and their conflict with the list at recall produces the decrement which we call forgetting. This hypothesis, along with Underwood's (1957) analysis, led Underwood and Postman (1960) to test the hypothesis that verbal lists learned in the laboratory conflict with responses which have been previously acquired throughout a lifetime of normal language learning, and the recovery of these extinguished responses can produce forgetting. Their approach was to construct verbal lists with different prospects of interference with normal language sequences in the extraexperimental verbal environment. If the hypothesis is correct, and if operations for interference can be realized, forgetting should correspond to the amount of interference that has occurred. Empirical verification of the Underwood-Postman hypothesis would be a handsome dividend for the interference theory of forgetting. Beyond that, it would weaken the annoying criticism that interference may be an explanation of forgetting by analogy. Mentioned in Chapter 5 was the possibility that a forgetting decrement in a standard learn-recall sequence may only parallel the decrement found by interference operations in the laboratory and not necessarily occur for the same reasons. As Underwood and Postman (1960, p. 74) point out, when formal operations for interference are lacking and forgetting is observed over an unstructured retention interval, an interference theorist must *assume* the presence of interference. An important finding would be the identification of sources of extraexperimental interference. Experiments like those of Jenkins and Dallenbach (1924) gave some comfort along these lines within an RI paradigm.

Underwood and Postman (1960) distinguished *letter-sequence interference* and *unit-sequence interference* as two sources of extraexperimental interference. Their definitions deserve direct quotation. Of letter-sequence interference, they say:

> One source of interference is believed to come from well-established letter-sequence habits. By well-established habits we simply mean habits that are developed through the normal course of learning the language. It may be thought of as producing intraunit interference or between-letter interference. As an extreme illustration, a low-association value consonant syllable such as JQB may be considered. If this syllable were in a list which the subject has to learn, it is assumed that: (a) Previously learned letter-sequence habits will make this particular sequence difficult to learn since the previously established habits will have to be extinguished. For example, Q never follows J in the language, but all the vowels do. These habits, we presume, must be extinguished or inhibited before the syllable can be learned. (b) With the passage of time following learning of the syllable, these older habits will recover and interfere at the time of the retention test. In addition, it is quite likely that the previously established letter habits will be used during the retention interval to augment the interference resulting from recovery (Underwood & Postman, 1960, p. 74).

They go on to define unit-sequence interference:

> The second potential source of interference will be referred to as unit-sequence interference. By the *unit* we mean a word or sequence of letters appearing in a list as an independent unit. Each syllable in a list of nonsense syllables is a unit, as is each word in a list of words. The interference we are referring to,

then, is the interference falling on sequential associations between units. Conceptually, it may be thought of initially in
exactly the same way as the interference between letters within
a unit. As an illustration, assume that the word *over* is a unit in
a serial list. Assume further that, due to long existing language
habits, there is a strong tendency for the *over* to elicit *there*. We
presume that this association will have to be extinguished before
a new association can be established, but that with the passage
of time the original association will recover to interfere with retention. In addition, since the sequence *over-there* will probably
occur (be said, or heard) during a retention interval, the recovery process of the interfering association will be augmented by
its use (Underwood & Postman, 1960, p. 75).

Underwood and Postman constructed four lists for serial
learning. Two lists had words which defined two levels of unit-
sequence interference. List Hi-W had words which occur with
high frequency in the language (Thorndike & Lorge, 1944),
like AGE, END, and HIM. According to the hypothesis, it would be
assumed that END rarely if ever follows AGE in the language, and
the requirement to learn these words serially so that the subject
must respond with END when AGE appears would require the extinction of words which normally follow AGE in the language.
Extraexperimental interference should be high for the Hi-W list
and retention low. A Lo-W list had low-frequency words like
ADO, COB, and DOE which are infrequently used and which would
have relatively few associations of appreciable strength to be extinguished in the serial learning of the experimental list. Extraexperimental interference for the Lo-W list should be low and
retention high. The third and fourth lists defined two levels of
letter-sequence interference. The third list, called Hi-T, had trigrams that occurred with high frequency in the language, like
ATI, EST, and HAN. Because these letter sequences commonly
occur, interference should be low for them. A fourth list was
Lo-T, and it had low-frequency trigrams like ARP, COF, and DOP.

Retention for the Hi-T list should be better than for the Lo-T list. Retention intervals were 30 seconds and one week. The 30-second interval was an immediate retention test to provide an index of amount learned and be a baseline from which the forgetting over one week was measured. The four lists and the two intervals required eight independent groups of subjects. The criterion of original learning was one perfect repetition of the list, and the subjects had both to spell and pronounce an item.

The prediction for retention after one week was that Lo-W would be better than Hi-W and Hi-T better than Lo-T. The results are shown in Figure 7-2. There were minor differences in the level of original attainment as seen by the performance level at the 30-second interval, but if the reader will perceptually adjust the one-week values for these differences, he will see there is little difference between groups after one week. Statistical

Fig. 7-2. Retention of words (W) and trigrams (T) that occur with low (Lo) and high (Hi) frequency in the English language. From Underwood and Postman (1960).

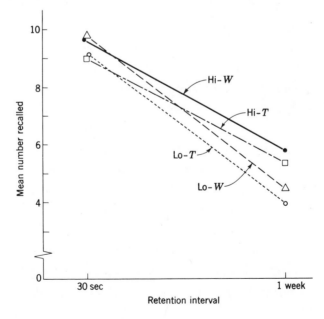

analysis found no significant difference in amount of retention loss. A number of other analyses were carried out on other performance measures. Some of them had small trends which tended as the hypothesis indicated, but all things considered, the outcome was discouraging for the hypothesis.

The most comprehensive test of the Underwood-Postman hypothesis was by Underwood and Keppel (1963). Lists of nine letter pairs were learned by the anticipation method. They used an LA (low-association) list of pairs like *M-K*, *A-G*, and *X-V*, in which the response term had a low probability of being given in free association when the stimulus letter was presented (Underwood & Schulz, 1960). According to the hypothesis, the learning of a low-association letter would entail the extinction of higher-frequency letter associations, and spontaneous recovery of the extinguished associations in the retention interval should produce forgetting. The other list that was used was an HA (high-association) list in which response terms had high probability of occurrence when their respective stimulus terms were presented— examples being *Z-X*, *E-K*, and *R-N*. Lower retention was predicted for the LA list than for the HA list because the learning of low associations would come into greater conflict with established letter-sequence habits. Each list had six degrees of learning and two retention intervals associated with it. For each list, each combination of degree of learning, and each retention interval, there was a separate group of subjects, so that there were 24 groups in all. The six degrees of learning were 2, 4, 6, 10, 15, and 25 anticipation trials following an initial study trial. The retention intervals were one and seven days.

The results are presented in Figure 7-3. The curve marked "Learning" is the combined performance curves of the two 25-trial groups for each list to illustrate the acquisition functions. The other two curves for each list are the recall data. They demonstrate the well-known facts that forgetting (1) increases

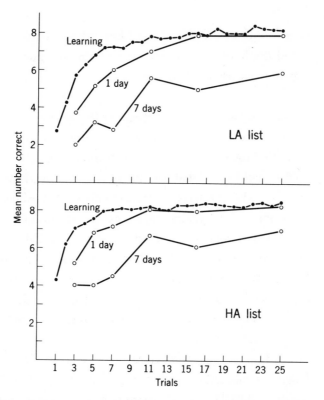

Fig. 7-3. The retention of low-association (LA) and high-association (HA) lists of letter pairs over intervals of one and seven days after 2, 4, 6, 10, 15, and 25 trials of original learning. The curves marked "Learning" are the acquisition functions for those subjects who were given 25 trials of original learning. From Underwood and Keppel (1963).

as length of the retention interval increases and (2) decreases as level of original learning increases (Krueger, 1929, 1930; Postman, 1962b). There is a slight tendency for the HA list to be recalled better at both the one- and the seven-day intervals, which might be taken as evidence for the hypothesis. But the level of the original learning curve for the HA list is higher, and this could be the reason. Underwood and Keppel corrected their data for these differences, and the outcome was no effect at recall for the two kinds of lists. These data, and those of Underwood and Postman (1960), are not the only failures of the hypothesis. Postman (1961, 1962a, 1964) and Ekstrand and Underwood (1965) tested the hypothesis in several contexts, and none of their findings were clearly positive.

Critique of the Underwood-Postman Hypothesis.   Does failure to support the hypothesis about extraexperimental interference mean that the interference theory of forgetting is threatened? The failure *could* mean that the theory is in trouble, but it is wise to first ask whether tests of the hypothesis have been adequate. Were there shortcomings in the experimental approaches or uncontrolled variables that could have attenuated the tests? We do not reject the law of falling bodies because a leaf does not conform to the time that the law defines for an object to fall. Further experimental analysis would show the leaf to be at variance with the law only because of atmospheric resistance, which is not a variable in the law.

A big variable that might have been overlooked is natural language mediation, and the experiment by Underwood and Keppel (1963) is a good illustration of it. We have discussed in previous chapters how subjects freely impose NLMs on pairs being learned. In Chapter 5 NLMs were shown to be a powerful variable in STM experiments. The next section of this chapter will demonstrate a corresponding power for NLMs in LTM also. The paired letters which Underwood and Keppel used seem an easy possibility for NLM formation. Any of the two letters would be a likely source for an association about the initials of a friend, a company, a word, or a sentence. Associations of this sort are easily achieved with word pairs, and it seems even easier with letter pairs. The damage that NLMs could do to the hypothesis under test is to force a sidestepping of interference between laboratory and extraexperimental responses. According to the hypothesis, the learning of the pair X-V from the LA list should result in forgetting because V is a relatively rare associate of X

and would conflict with well-established language habits. However, Roman numeral 15 is an easy association for *X-V*. If the subjects used 15 or similar associations with any regularity, there would be no interference of the kind that would result in extinction of outside responses, at least not of the kind that Underwood and Keppel sought. The problem for the subject in original learning is not associating *V* with *X* but encoding *XV* as 15, and the problem at recall is not simply remembering that *V* goes with *X* but recalling 15 and decoding it to retrieve *V*. And if NLM formation is taking place with about the same frequency in both the LA and HA lists, and NLMs serve as a potent variable for retention as we know they do, both lists should be recalled at about the same level (which was the case). This is all conjectural, but at the same time reasonable from our knowledge of NLMs. Whether NLMs were operating in a similar fashion in the serial learning that was used by Underwood and Postman (1960) is not clear. Jensen and Rohwer (1963) were unsuccessful in their attempts to facilitate serial learning by teaching mentally retarded subjects sentence mediators for successive item pairs, although they were very successful with paired associates. Their failure should not necessarily be taken to mean that mediation is absent in serial learning for, as Jensen and Rohwer comment (1963, p. 351), we know next to nothing about mediators and how they might operate for serial sequences. However, considering the widespread occurrence of NLMs in paired-associate learning, it would be surprising to find NLMs absent in serial learning. The presence of NLMs does not, of course, negate the interference theory of forgetting, but it places in doubt the tests of extraexperimental interference that have been made. With NLMs operating the issue now becomes one of extraexperimental influences on complex verbal associations, and this is a more difficult research question.

Another criticism can be leveled. The basic premise of the

Underwood-Postman hypothesis is that forgetting depends upon
the compatibility of the to-be-learned response with established
language sequences. Learning the response DOG to the stimulus
OVER will interfere with the established response THERE because
OVER THERE is a strongly connected sequence in the English language. The word THERE will undergo experimental extinction
when DOG is learned, and its recovery will cause some forgetting
of DOG, according to the hypothesis. These conditions of interference which Underwood and Postman specified are probably
not true because there is no dimension of similarity specified for
the interference. Without a similarity specification, the hypothesis
says that only one response can exist for a stimulus, and if another is learned, the original one must be displaced through extinction. This is wrong, of course, because most words have multiple associations in which different responses exist compatibly
together for the same stimulus word. What is needed is a similarity principle for interference, like the transfer-retroaction surface
in Chapter 4. If this had been done, the selection of experimental
materials and possibly the experimental outcome would have
been much different. The term DOG would no longer be a suitable
response for the stimulus OVER. Instead, we would look for a
word whose similarity to THERE would produce interference. This
variant of the Underwood-Postman approach deserves a try because verification of extraexperimental sources of interference is
important for the interference theory of forgetting.

MEDIATION

Natural Language Mediation

Chapter 5 discussed the potent role of NLMs for verbal STM,
and all this research is very recent. Being current, there is not

very much of it to discuss, but what there is of it is impressive. The work on NLMs in verbal LTM is no more plentiful, but its roots reach further back in psychology (Reed, 1918). Overall, whether STM or LTM, the role of NLMs for memory processes is just beginning to unfold.

The Study by Montague, Adams, and Kiess. Using suggestions in the earlier literature and exploratory work of their own as points of departure, Montague, Adams, and Kiess (1966) conducted an experiment on NLMs and long-term retention. Their procedure in acquisition used a slide projector to give the subject a single presentation of a CVC pair like XAZ-BIK. The subject studied the pair and wrote down his NLM if he had one. At recall the subject saw only the stimulus member of the pair and attempted to recall in writing the response as well as the NLM that went with it. The recall of an NLM was an important part of the experiment because an NLM is a response, and it can be forgotten, just like the response term of the pair. One purpose of the study was to understand how retention of a response term was related to retention of its NLM. The experimental variables were high and low meaningfulness (Noble, 1961) and presentation times of 15 and 30 seconds. The stimulus and response members of a pair were both from the same high or low range of meaningfulness values and randomly paired with each other. It was assumed that more NLMs would be formed for high- than for low-meaningfulness CVCs because they are more similar to common words, and that more NLMs would occur at the longer presentation time. The two levels of meaningfulness and two presentation times defined four independent groups of subjects, and each group had a list of 96 pairs. The retention interval was 24 hours.

Table 7-1 shows the mean number of NLMs that was formed in acquisition. There was a generous number of NLMs formed, and the mean number of NLMs increased as both meaningfulness and presentation time increased.

Table 7-1.   In a List of 96 Paired CVCs, the Mean Number of Natural Language Mediators (NLMs) Used in Acquisition. From Montague, Adams, and Kiess (1966)

		Meaningfulness		
		Low	High	$\overline{X}$
Presentation	15	31.1	59.4	45.2
time (sec)	30	50.5	74.7	62.6
	$\overline{X}$	40.8	67.1	

Table 7-2 shows the recall data broken down into NLM and Rote categories. If there was no NLM reported in acquisition, the item was categorized "Rote." If a pair had an NLM in acquisition and the NLM was recalled in substantially its original form, it was categorized as "Same or similar" for Table 7-2. And if an item had an NLM in acquisition but had either a markedly different version of it or no NLM at all at recall, the pair was assigned to the "Not the same" category. In effect, the items in the "Not the same" category had their NLMs forgotten. By this method of categorization, it was possible to see how recall of the response terms of the pair related to rote learning and whether or not NLMs were correctly recalled. The row proportions in Table 7-2 show that recall increased as both presentation time and meaningfulness increased. The effects of categories as represented by the column proportions are of the most importance for the role of NLMs. For rote learning the proportion correct was only 0.058, and when NLMs were used in original learning and then forgotten, the chances of correct recall were even less (0.018).

But when pairs had NLMs which were correctly remembered, the proportion correct rose dramatically to 0.726.

Table 7-2. Proportion Correct Recalls in Each NLM Category for Each Group. The Proportion Is Based on the Ratio Given, Which Is Number Correct over Number of Items in a Category for a Group. The Groups Are Designated as L and H for Low and High Meaningfulness, and 15 and 30 for Length of the Presentation Time in Seconds. From Montague, Adams, and Kiess (1966)

| | *NLM Category* | | | |
Group	*Same or similar*	*Not the same*	*Rote*	*Group total*
L–15	83:182	6:752	57:1,946	146:2,880
	0.456	0.008	0.029	0.051
L–30	154:337	5:1,178	72:1,365	231:2,880
	0.457	0.004	0.053	0.080
H–15	339:421	32:1,361	93:1,098	464:2,880
	0.805	0.024	0.085	0.161
H–30	666:770	41:1,472	73:638	780:2,880
	0.865	0.028	0.114	0.271
Category total for all groups	1,242:1,710	84:4,763	295:5,047	1,621:11,520
	0.726	0.018	0.058	0.141
				(All items, all groups)

These data make the important point that NLMs are a powerful variable for high retention providing they are correctly recalled. The pairs with forgotten NLMs in the "Not the same" category have a trivial level of recall and poorer than rote learning, which was itself low. It seems reasonable to assume that in rote learning a subject used the available presentation time to repeat an item covertly and strengthen it. Similarly, when the subject formed an NLM, he also covertly repeated the whole stimulus-NLM-response complex over and over to himself as long as time allowed. Thus, when the NLM was forgotten, the response could not be recalled because the stimulus had an associative tie with the response via the NLM and had no capability for arousing the response directly.

The authors discuss their findings in the same vein as Groninger (1966). The occurrence of an NLM represents positive transfer from past language learning to the new verbal material and, being well-learned and dissimilar to other language sequences, produces a resistance to interfering forgetting processes. An NLM formed is hardly a guarantee that retention will be high because out of the 6,473 NLMs that occurred in acquisition, only 1,710 were remembered. As yet we know nothing about the kinds of mediators that tend to be well remembered, or the operations that can ensure the correct recall of a mediator. Because this study shows that correct recall of an NLM is very important for correct recall of the response, a prime research topic for the future is conditions for strengthening NLMs to increase the likelihood of their recall.

Chapter 4 said that the use of retrospective reports after list learning as a means of documenting an NLM for each pair was useful but had methodological problems if one wishes to assume that the NLM was an intrinsic part of the association process for the pair. Chief among the criticisms of this procedure was that the NLM is an epiphenomenon and is formed at the time of the questioning. Learning is basically a rote development of the habit connection, and the NLM plays no part in the basic learning. The Montague, Adams, and Kiess study meets this criticism somewhat by having the subject write his NLM when a pair is being shown in acquisition when the association process is taking place, making it more reasonable to assume that the NLM plays a fundamental role in the act of learning itself. Of course, a critic might contend that the subject repeats the pair to himself one or more times in a rote fashion while the pair is displayed, after which an NLM occurs to him and he writes it down. Thus, an NLM is an epiphenomenon, and its presence would not be expected to have anything to do with retention at all. Montague, Adams, and Kiess, however, demonstrated this to be unlikely. The formation and the remembering of an NLM were powerful factors in retention, strongly suggesting the NLM to be an integral part of the associative process and not an epiphenomenon.

Concepts

To exhibit concept behavior is to categorize members of a stimulus class correctly, even in the face of irrelevant and secondary features of the stimuli. We can designate a triangle whether it is large or small or of any color, and when we do, we have the concept of "triangularity." A theoretical interpretation of concept behavior is in terms of a common mediating response (Osgood, 1953, Ch. 15; Hunt, 1962, Ch. 3) which is learned to the universe of stimuli that constitute the concept class. In concept learning, a subject is reinforced for responding correctly to stimuli which have the proper relations and qualities present, and when learning has been accomplished, the subject has the capability for responding correctly to any member of the stimulus class because the members all evoke a common mediating response. The mediator may be a verbal response in which the subject says "Triangle" to himself when each positive instance of triangularity appears, and he then proceeds to make a correct overt response (identification, sorting, naming, etc.) on the basis of it. The mediator does not have to be verbal, however. A kind of concept behavior has been observed in animals (e.g., Fields, 1932; Andrew & Harlow, 1948).

Ever since an experiment by Reed (1946), there has been a widespread belief in experimental psychology that the forgetting of conceptual responses is very small relative to rote-learned materials, and the findings of Oseas and Underwood (1952) and Lloyd (1960) have not done violence to this generalization. The following section will focus on Reed's prototypic study to illustrate some of the problems that can be encountered.

Reed's Experiment.   Reed (1946) used paired associates and the anticipation method to study concept learning and retention. The stimulus member of a pair was four words, and the response member was a CVC trigram. For example, the animal concept would be represented by items like:

	Stimulus			*Response*
horn	leaf	monkey	debt	kun
fame	ought	tiger	saucer	kun
	etc.			

The animal term is the only element these two stimuli have in common. Out of a list of 42 stimuli, there were seven which had animal terms in common, and subjects learned to say "Kun" whenever one of them appeared. Six different concepts of seven instances each were randomized in the list. The stimulus term was presented on a card. If the subject gave the correct response, the experimenter said "Right," and if the subject failed to respond or gave the wrong response, the experimenter prompted him and gave the correct response term. After every third trial the experimenter interviewed the subject and asked what each response term suggested to him, which was the way of distinguishing rote and concept learning. The subject could either be learning an item conceptually and see the relationship, say, between all animal cards and "Kun," or he could be learning by rote, and the response might be associated with the first word of the stimulus term. The criterion of original learning was one errorless trial. Retention intervals were either one, three, or six weeks, and there was an independent group of subjects for each interval.

Reed sorted his data into "consistent" and "inconsistent" concepts. The consistent concepts were those which, according to interview data, represented straightforward cases of genuine concept learning. Inconsistent concepts were cases of rote learning. As might be expected, consistent items were learned more rapidly than inconsistent ones. Once the subject obtained a concept relationship, he could respond correctly to all stimuli in the concept category. Inconsistent items, on the other hand, had to be learned one at a time in the more laborious rote fashion. Figure 7-4 gives the retention findings. The top two curves are Reed's, and the third curve represents the classic rote learning data of Ebbinghaus (1913). The retention of Reed's material was virtually perfect even at the six weeks' interval, but Ebbinghaus found that severe losses developed quickly. From these findings has come the generalization in psychology that concepts

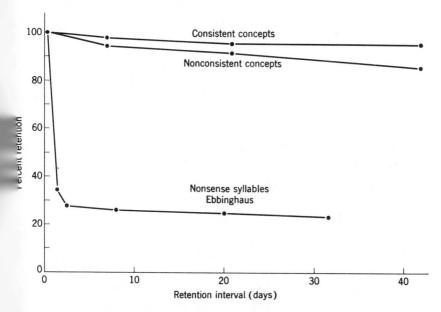

Fig. 7-4.   Retention of concepts over intervals of one, three, and six weeks compared with Ebbinghaus's data on the retention of serially learned nonsense syllables. From Reed (1946).

are retained better than rote-learned items. What confidence can we place in this generalization?

Critique of Reed (1946). First, the statement that concepts are better retained than rote-learned items is only slightly justified if we look at Reed's data in Figure 7-4 because his retention curves for consistent and inconsistent concepts are both very high and very similar. More recently, Lloyd (1960) found essentially the same thing when he compared the retention of concept and rote materials over a one-week interval. One possible reason is that inconsistent items were mediated by NLMs, and consistent items had concept mediators. Reed (p. 83) reports the various NLM devices that were used in learning the inconsistent items, and since NLMs benefit retention (Montague, Adams, & Kiess, 1966), it is not surprising that both consistent and inconsistent concepts had high retention. Reed, then, was not comparing conceptually mediated and nonmediated rote materials, but rather materials mediated in two different ways.

Secondly, the comparison with Ebbinghaus's findings is dubious. Jensen and Rohwer (1963) had difficulty in establishing mediation for serial learning, which is what Ebbinghaus used; therefore the Ebbinghaus-Reed comparison may indeed be rote versus mediated. On the other hand, the comparison may be invalid on the procedural ground that Ebbinghaus was his own subject and learned many, many lists in a monumental, solo effort. Underwood (1957) demonstrated that verbal lists learned prior to the learning and recall of a criterion list create a PI effect that decreases retention as number of prior lists increase. The Ebbinghaus retention data would certainly suffer this effect. Reed, however, used independent groups of subjects at each retention interval; thus his data are methodologically clean in this respect. Certainly the absence of PI would be one reason why Reed's functions are so high relative to the Ebbinghaus curve.

Thirdly, we must ask if concepts are somehow apart from the interference principles that govern the forgetting of rote materials. That this is not so was shown by Richardson (1956) who demonstrated that concepts are amenable to interference just like other response classes. He used an *AB-AC-AB* paradigm for RI and had subjects learn conflicting concept responses to the stimuli of a list. Verbal stimuli, being multidimensional, can often be represented by more than one concept. In *AB* learning Richardson presented his subjects a list of 16 stimulus words, with each subset of four words representing a concept. For example, a subject had to learn that the stimulus words DERBY and POT of the *AB* list were members of a stimulus class whose objects were all black, irrespective of other properties. The subject had to supply his own response when a stimulus word was presented. The experimenter said "Right" and "Wrong" after each response, and the subject had to discover that "Black" was the correct response for DERBY and POT and the other two stimulus words of the black category. The *AC* learning was the same except that a new concept response had to be learned to the same stimulus words. For DERBY and POT, the subject now had to learn that these words were members of a stimulus class in which all members had round shape. Amount of *AB* and *AC* learning were the experimental variables, with *AB* recall occurring after 24 hours. The results showed that as amount of *AC* learning increased, retention decreased. The worth of Richardson's findings is showing that concept mediators are subject to the laws of interference like any other response class, and that the interference theory of forgetting predicts forgetting for concepts as well.

Lastly, a reason that retention is so high in concept retention studies may simply be the nature of stimulus lists and the fact that stimuli can be grouped according to classes, in which a single response is correct for all members of the class. Assume in the Richardson experiment that a subject forgets one of the four concepts required for a list, so that retention measured in terms of *concepts* is 75 percent. Suppose he forgot that "Black" was one of the defining categories and was the correct response for four of the stimuli, and so when the stimulus word DERBY appeared at recall, the best strategy would be for the subject to guess. By guessing he would, in effect, be giving a high-strength free association, and he might say something like "Hat." The experimenter would say "Wrong." A bit later on the stimulus word POT from the same class would appear, and the subject would guess again. "Black" would be a likely free association for POT, and this, of course, is the correct response. The experimenter would say "Right," and the subject should now get the next two members of the "Black" stimulus class correct when they subsequently appear. In this example that borrows from Richardson's methods, the proportion of concepts retained is 75 percent. But only one error was made in classifying a "black" stimulus before the category name was relearned; thus the proportion correct in terms of number of stimuli correctly classified was 94 percent for the list of 16. The retention figure of 75 percent is closer to the empirical truth, however, because it reflects the forgetting of the concept behavior that is under scrutiny. The 94-percent value is artificial in the sense that it arises from the special nature of the experimental task at recall which allows relearning from early instances of a forgotten concept class and all examples of the class to be correct thereafter. Therefore, because of the very high 94-percent figure, we have assumed that concept retention is abnormally high and that special variables or processes must be operating. However, if we had asked how many concepts were remembered, rather than how many responses were given correctly to the different stimuli, we most likely would have come away with different sentiments about the retention of concept behavior.

CONCLUSIONS

Overview.   Studies of long-term retention gave early stimulation to the interference theory of forgetting, and this chapter has given no reason to think that interference is inappropriate as an explanation. Trace decay theory has no evidence for or against it in the long-term realm. The failure of the Underwood-Postman hypothesis about extraexperimental sources of interference could be interpreted as weakening for the interference theory, but we have seen the failure to be due most likely to an absence of NLMs in conceptualization of the hypothesis and shortcomings in specifying the conditions of interference. The strong data in behalf of the interference hypothesis are, then, from old studies which use an RI paradigm and attempt to control interfering activities in the retention interval (e.g., Jenkins & Dallenbach, 1924). These studies are old, but not necessarily poor. Nevertheless, they could stand replication and extension with modern ideas, materials, and experimental design.

A significant research area is NLMs and forgetting. Montague, Adams, and Kiess (1966) found very high recall of criterion responses whose NLMs were recalled correctly. In fact, the recall efficiency was about 12 times that of rote learning. A next research step is to devise methods that would increase the number and strength of NLMs in the hope of increasing their correct recall. Research should also be directed toward kinds of NLMs in relation to kinds of materials to be learned to determine the most effective types of NLMs. In enlarging our understanding of NLMs, we would be deliberately specifying a response complex that will be difficult to enter meaningfully into a design which would test the interference theory of forgetting. Difficult, yes, but not impossible, and it should turn our attention away from simple serial- and paired-associate schemes and toward more complex language behavior. Concept behavior, like NLMs, is another focus that will turn our attention toward more complex behavior in our continuing tests of forgetting theory.

Methodology.   Chapter 5 closed with a methodological note on the control of level of original learning and PI in STM. Most of those remarks apply in principle to LTM studies also. Level of learning is a well-documented variable for retention, and any experiment which seeks to compare retention for two or more values of a variable in acquisition, like meaningfulness or distribution of practice, must ensure their equal level of original learning so that retention measures clearly reflect the effects of the variables and are not confounded with different levels of original learning (Underwood, 1964). Chapter 5 discussed the difficulty that NLMs introduce for controlling level of learning in STM, and LTM is no exception.

The control of PI involves the same issues that relate to STM, and it requires that learning of lists prior to the experimental list be eliminated or that number of prior lists be taken as a systematic variable and entered in the experimental design. In other words, control or measure. A large PI effect was suggested for the Ebbinghaus retention function in Figure 7-4, and undoubtedly it is one of the factors which for so long has led us to believe that the retention of concepts is superior to retention of rote items. Certainly the Jenkins and Dallenbach data in Figure 7-1 were similarly contaminated because the subjects learned and recalled a number of lists throughout the course of the experiment, although there is no reason to believe that their conclusions about sleeping and waking are wrong. The experimental designs of the past that had each subject perform in several experimental conditions gave a PI effect that for a long time caused us to overestimate the amount of forgetting (Underwood, 1957). Using an independent group of subjects for each treatment condition now seems a wiser move.

REFERENCES

Andrew, G., & Harlow, H. F. Performance of macaque monkeys on a test of the concept of generalized triangularity. *Comp. Psychol. Monogr.*, 1948, **19**, No. 3.

Ebbinghaus, H. *Memory: A contribution to experimental psychology.* (Trans. by Ruger & Bussenius.) New York: Teachers College Press, 1913.

Ekstrand, B. R., & Underwood, B. J. Free learning and recall as a function of unit-sequence and letter-sequence interference. *J. verbal Learn. verbal Behav.*, 1965, **4**, 390–396.

Fields, P. E. Studies in concept formation: I. The development of the concept of triangularity by the white rat. *Comp. Psychol. Monogr.*, 1932, **9**, No. 2.

Grissom, R. J., Suedfeld, P., & Vernon, J. Memory for verbal material: Effects of sensory deprivation. *Science*, 1962, **138**, 429–430.

Groninger, L. D. Natural language mediation and covert rehearsal in short-term memory. *Psychon. Sci.*, 1966, **5**, 135–136.

Hunt, E. B. *Concept learning.* New York: Wiley, 1962.

Hunter, W. S. The effect of inactivity produced by cold upon learning and retention in the cockroach, Blatella germanica. *J. genet. Psychol.*, 1932, **41**, 253–266.

Jenkins, J. G., & Dallenbach, K. M. Obliviscence during sleep and waking. *Amer. J. Psychol.*, 1924, **35**, 605–612.

Jensen, A. R., & Rohwer, W. D., Jr. Verbal mediation in paired-associate and serial learning. *J. verbal Learn. verbal Behav.*, 1963, **1**, 346–352.

Keppel, G., & Underwood, B. J. Proactive inhibition in short-term retention of single items. *J. verbal Learn. verbal Behav.*, 1962, **1**, 153–161.

Krueger, W. C. F. The effect of overlearning on retention. *J. exp. Psychol.*, 1929, **12**, 71–78.

Krueger, W. C. F. Further studies in overlearning. *J. exp. Psychol.*, 1930, **13**, 152–163.

Lloyd, K. E. Retention of responses to stimulus classes and specific stimuli. *J. exp. Psychol.*, 1960, **59**, 54–59.

Minami, H., & Dallenbach, K. M. The effect of activity upon learning and retention in the cockroach. *Amer. J. Psychol.*, 1946, **59**, 1–58.

Montague, W. E., Adams, J. A., & Kiess, H. O. Forgetting and natural language mediation. *J. exp. Psychol.*, 1966, **72**, 829–833.

Newman, E. B. Forgetting of meaningful material during sleep and waking. *Amer. J. Psychol.*, 1939, **52**, 65–71.

Noble, C. E. Measurements of association value (*a*), rated associations (*a'*), and scaled meaningfulness (*m'*) for the 2100 CVC combinations of the English alphabet. *Psychol. Rep.*, 1961, **8**, 487–521.

Oseas, L., & Underwood, B. J. Studies of distributed practice: V. Learning and retention of concepts. *J. exp. Psychol.*, 1952, **43**, 143–148.

Osgood, C. E. *Method and theory in experimental psychology.* New York: Oxford, 1953.

Peterson, L. R., & Peterson, Margaret J. Short-term retention of individual verbal items. *J. exp. Psychol.*, 1959, **58**, 193–198.

Postman, L. Extra-experimental interference and the retention of words. *J. exp. Psychol.*, 1961, **61**, 97–110.

Postman, L. The effects of language habits on the acquisition and retention of verbal associations. *J. exp. Psychol.*, 1962, **64**, 7–19. (a)

Postman, L. Retention as a function of degree of overlearning. *Science*, 1962, **135**, 666–667. (b)

Postman, L. Acquisition and retention of consistent associative responses. *J. exp. Psychol.*, 1964, **67**, 183–190.

Reed, H. B. Associative aids: I. Their relation to learning, retention, and other associations. *Psychol. Rev.*, 1918, **25**, 128–155.

Reed, H. B. Factors influencing the learning and retention of concepts: I. The influence of set. *J. exp. Psychol.*, 1946, **36**, 71–87.

Richardson, J. Retention of concepts as a function of the degree of original and interpolated learning. *J. exp. Psychol.*, 1956, **51**, 358–364.

Russell, R. W., & Hunter, W. S. The effects of inactivity produced by sodium amytal on the retention of the maze habit in the albino rat. *J. exp. Psychol.*, 1937, **20**, 426–436.

Scott, T. H. Literature review of the intellectual effects of perceptual isolation. Defence Research Board, Department of National Defence, Canada, Report No. HR 66, July, 1957.

Spight, J. B. Day and night intervals and the distribution of practice. *J. exp. Psychol.*, 1928, **11**, 397–398.

Thorndike, E. L., & Lorge, I. *The teacher's word book of 30,000 words.* New York: Teachers College Press, 1944.

Underwood, B. J. Interference and forgetting. *Psychol. Rev.*, 1957, **64**, 49–60.

Underwood, B. J. Degree of learning and the measurement of forgetting. *J. verbal Learn. verbal Behav.*, 1964, **3**, 112–129.

Underwood, B. J., & Keppel, G. Retention as a function of degree of learning and letter-sequence interference. *Psychol. Monogr.*, 1963, **77** (Whole No. 567).

Underwood, B. J., & Postman, L. Extraexperimental sources of interference in forgetting. *Psychol. Rev.*, 1960, **67**, 73–95.

Van Ormer, E. B. Retention after intervals of sleep and waking. *Arch. Psychol.*, 1932 (Whole No. 137).

Vernon, J. A. *Inside the black room.* New York: Potter, 1963.

Wheaton, J. L. Fact and fancy in sensory deprivation studies. *USAF Air Univer. Sch. Aviat. Med.* Review 5–59, Brooks Air Force Base, Texas, August, 1959.

Most experimental data on memory, and theory derived from it, come from studies of verbal behavior. This is not a poor state of scientific affairs because, as we have seen in previous chapters, a considerable understanding is being built. However, there has also been a research effort of lesser vigor on the retention of motor behavior, and it has given us tentative generalizations and raised interesting issues.

There is good cause to branch out from our studies of verbal retention. We are charged with the scientific responsibility of discovering the generality of our laws of memory, and this means gathering retention data on other response classes and asking whether the verbal-based principles apply. Certainly there is no necessity for the laws of verbal memory to apply without restriction to other response classes.

Our understanding of motor retention is underdeveloped, and not solely because of the modest research effort that has been given it. A main reason for its conceptual impoverishment is that motor research has had a strong alliance with applied psychology and more often has asked questions about practical problems than about basic laws and theory. Some of the early motor retention research was on the forgetting of typewriting skills. Since World War II, financial support has often come from military sources which have had a practical interest in the retention of complex motor responses like those involved in aircraft control. Recently, complex motor responses of the kind used for control of space vehicles have been studied (e.g., Naylor, Briggs, & Reed, 1962). These studies give useful empirical data, but too often the investigators are satisfied with answers to immediate questions and fail to press on and ask about variables and mechanisms that make up basic laws and theory. The applied approach is valuable for the short run because it solves the pressing matters of the moment, but it can be problem-specific and fail to reach out for generalizations that will encompass the next practical problem which has a different configuration of variables. The result can be a laborious experiment for each new applied problem that comes along because the influences of the basic variables are not understood well enough. Basic law and theory, by contrast, have general power because they explain how the basic constituent variables determine the particular configuration of events that is at hand. The same basic laws of nuclear physics help us solve the quite different practical problems of nuclear engines for peace and atomic bombs for war because they have a power that transcends the seeming uniqueness of the particular problem. This viewpoint does not mean that solutions to applied problems should wait on general laws because these laws might take centuries to mature, but it does mean that we should work steadily on basic science because of the great power it can give us. In the meantime, applied experiments can fill the immediate needs of our practical lives whenever basic science fails in providing the necessary principles. A difference between motor and verbal retention research is that the verbal work has been impelled toward basic laws and theory from the start, but motor behavior has often been driven by practical motivations. This chapter, therefore, tends toward more low-order generalizations and unanswered problems than previous chapters.

THE MOTOR DOMAIN

Definition of Motor Behavior

Motor behavior is bodily movement, and motor learning is the study of variables that determine the acquisition of new motor movements. Speech is the motor behavior involved in the production of sounds, and it is comprised of lip, tongue, and jaw movements, and the muscular control of vocal cords. The learning of speech could be studied as the learning of new movements for the evocation of different sounds, particularly in very young children. Verbal learning, on the other hand, is the acquisition of new symbolic relations, not new motor movements. The adult subject has long known how to form letters and words at the motor level, but a verbal learning task requires him to associate new symbolic sequences which are represented overtly in the well-learned, sound-producing movements we call "speech."

Even though the emphasis of this chapter will be on the retention of motor movements, it is not always possible to study motor behavior in a pure sense because several response classes are often operating. The interpretation of perceptual displays can precede the making of a motor movement in some tasks, and retention can be a complex function of the forgetting of both motor and perceptual responses. Verbal responses can exist in a behavioral compound with motor responses, such as a subject saying to himself, "I must move the control to the right when the green light comes on." How to identify and measure nonmotor response classes that coexist with motor responses is a tough methodological problem. Some limited evidence is available on the interaction of verbal and motor response classes, but in general we know little about heterogeneous response compounds.

Types of Motor Tasks

Motor activities can assume endless form and variety, but the two prominent types are continuous and discrete. Continuous tasks require that a finely graded response sequence be learned. The sequence can be brief and simple or long and complex. Tracking is a long, continuous, motor response sequence, and it is commonly used in studies of motor retention because it is the response activity for vehicular control and is important to applied psychologists. Discrete motor tasks are also common in jobs of applied interest, and they usually require the subject to press a series of buttons or throw a series of switches. Because the bulk of research on motor retention has been with tracking and discrete tasks, the properties of these two classes of tasks should be explained in more detail.

Tracking Tasks.   Tracking is a paced activity (time function) that requires continuous error nulling (Adams, 1961). Tracking tasks customarily use visual displays, and the subject's job is to watch the display and manipulate his control in a continual effort to eliminate the error which he sees. Input and output are the two basic quantities of any tracking task. The stimulus to the system is often called the "input," and it is a fundamental quantity that produces the error which the subject tries to correct with the output generated by his control. Pursuit tracking and compensatory tracking are the two basic kinds of tracking tasks. In *pursuit tracking* the subject sees both the input and output quantities represented on the display, and his task is to null the error by keeping the input and output indicators in alignment. Driving a car down the road is a pursuit tracking task. The road is the visual input which defines the tracking problem, and the driver moves the steering wheel and positions the vehicle (output) to keep error tolerances within the limits defined by legal and safety requirements. Error in automobile position is a joint function of input and output. Changes in the road create error, as can the driver's response to them. In steering a space vehicle to rendezvous with a satellite, the astronaut might have a cathode-ray tube display with one blip representing the satellite and a second blip his vehicle. Manipulation of the steering control to keep the two blips in alignment would hold the vehicle on proper course for rendezvous. *Compensatory tracking* uses a more abstract display which has neither input nor output displayed directly, but only the error discrepancy between them. Although hard to visualize, driving an automobile as a compensatory tracking task would display neither the road nor the car's position on it but only error in the car's position with respect to proper position on the road. The driver would have a display with a fixed-reference indicator and an error indicator, and deviation of the error indicator from the fixed reference would be the error quantity to be nulled. The astronaut's tracking task could be structured either as pursuit or compensatory tracking because the design engineer has free choice in ways of displaying the input and output values, or transforms them. Electronically it is a simple matter to take the error difference between input and output and present it to the astronaut as a compensatory tracking task, or the two could be presented separately as a pursuit tracking task. Whether pursuit or compensatory, it is common for complex vehicles to require multidimensional tracking tasks in which several dimensions of the system must be kept aligned simultaneously by manipulating multidimensional controls. The astronaut not only must accomplish rendezvous but also attend and track other instrument displays which show vehicle orientation and speed. He may have one multidimensional control for all these functions, or two or three separate controls to manipulate simultaneously.

Whether done in a tracking system in the real world or as a laboratory task, tracking performance is scored as a function of the continuous error. Commonly used error measures are integrated error or cumulative time that the error is nulled (time on target).

Discrete Tasks. A tracking task is paced, which means that the input is programmed continuously with respect to time and changes independently of the subject's response. A discrete task is often self-paced. The task elements are stationary on the display, and the speed of response is determined by the subject. A discrete task can have a number of units in which, for example, the subject might have to press a series of buttons. Starting your car at night is a multiple-unit discrete task. You fasten the seat belt, insert the key, turn on the ignition, activate the light switch, turn on the heater, set the gearshift to REVERSE, and depress the accelerator. The discrete task is then ended, the car begins to move, and the tracking task of guiding the vehicle begins. The responses of a discrete task are not discrete in any absolute sense because each requires some continuous movement. However, the self-paced and step-by-step properties of discrete tasks clearly set them off from continuous tracking. A later section will show how the different behavioral properties of continuous and discrete tasks make a big difference for retention.

Discrete tasks are scored in two ways. Speed in completing the response sequence is commonly used. When multiple units are involved, the subject can omit units or respond in the wrong order; thus number of correct responses is another useful performance measure.

MOTOR INTERFERENCE

Retroactive Inhibition

Interference for motor behavior has received only minor attention, and so we are on weak ground for predictions about the interference theory of forgetting. A substantial portion of the basic work on motor interference was done by Lewis at the University of Iowa. Using an RI design, Lewis (1947) was the first to demonstrate unmistakable interference for motor behavior.

The conditions for motor interference are analogous to those for verbal learning. Interference in verbal behavior occurs when responses B and C are successively learned to the same stimulus A, and amount of interference is dependent upon the similarity of the two responses. Similarity of motor responses has not been

defined and explored, but there is evidence that interference requires antagonistic motor responses *B* and *C* to be learned to the
same stimulus *A*. An antagonistic motor movement is defined as
one opposite in direction to another. For example, in an RI
design, a stimulus light might define the movement of a control
to the right for original learning. Interpolated learning would
require the subject to move his control to the left when the same
stimulus light comes on. A return to the original learning condition in the retention test will show a decrement in performance.
Movements that are opposite in direction are about all we know
of the similarity conditions for motor interference. As with verbal
learning, it should be possible to define and manipulate the similarity of motor responses and, ideally, specify a motor transfer and
retroaction surface. This kind of parametric research for motor
behavior is yet to be done.

Two comprehensive and related experiments by Lewis and
his associates illustrate the conditions of motor interference and
the characteristics of data that are obtained (Lewis, McAllister,
& Adams, 1951; McAllister & Lewis, 1951). An RI design was
used, and amount of original and interpolated learning were experimental variables. The motor task employed a Modified Mashburn Apparatus, named after N. C. Mashburn, who invented it in
the 1930s as a selection device for military pilots. Later, in
World War II, the task was profitably used for pilot selection
and was known as the Complex Coordination Test (Melton,
1947). Lewis and Shepard (1950) modified the task for laboratory
work on interference. The Mashburn device was three dimen-
sional, and it had pseudo-aircraft properties—a two-dimensional stick about the size of an airplane's for manipulation by
the hand and a one-dimensional rudder bar for foot operation.
A visual display in front of the seated subject presented a set of
three lights as a stimulus in each problem. The controls had to be
moved in an amount defined by the lights. A correct amount of

movement of the stick and the rudder in each dimension produced a "match," and when it occurred, a new set of three lights came on to define the next problem for response. The number of matches on a trial was the performance score. To give some idea of learning progress, a typical subject would make about 12 matches on his first 2-minute trial and increase to about 35 matches on trial 50. In original learning the task had a particular direction of control movement required in each dimension to complete a match for a set of three lights. For interpolated learning the apparatus was changed so that an antagonistic movement was required to complete a match for the same set of lights. All combinations of 10, 30, and 50 trials of original learning, and 10, 20, 30, and 50 trials of interpolated learning, were used. Interpolated learning was followed by 20 relearning trials with the original task configuration. An independent group of subjects was used for each combination. Trial length was 2 minutes.

Figure 8-1 shows the results. The measure of interference was decrement in performance from the last trial of original learning to the first trial of relearning. Ideally, each experimental group should have had its own control group, but in another study performance on the Modified Mashburn Apparatus had no forgetting over a five-day period with no interpolated practice of antagonistic movements (Lewis, McAllister, & Adams, 1951, pp. 251–252); so no control groups were deemed necessary. The data deserve comparison with Briggs's corresponding verbal work in Chapter 4 (Figure 4-9). As with Briggs's findings, RI increased as amount of interpolated learning increased. However, Briggs found an increased resistance to interference as amount of original learning increased. But Figure 8-1 shows that just the opposite is true for motor behavior. The curve parameter is number of original learning trials. Notice that decrement *increases* as amount of original training increases. The same ordering and

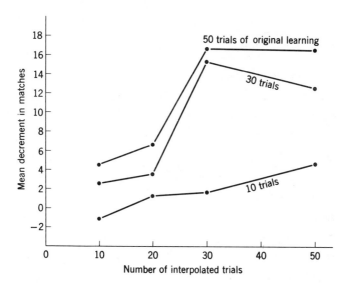

Fig. 8-1. Performance on the Modified Mashburn Apparatus as a function of amount of interpolated learning and amount of original learning shown as the curve parameter. Plotted from values in Table III (p. 253) in Lewis, McAllister, and Adams (1951).

trend of curves shown in Figure 8-1 are found when decrement is plotted as a percentage of performance level at the end of original learning. Increasing the amount of original learning strengthens a verbal response and reduces its susceptibility to interference, but a motor response acquires a heightened sensitivity to interference as original learning increases. We would be on unsure ground to use the interference theory of forgetting for a prediction about motor retention if our knowledge of interference were drawn from studies of verbal behavior. Borrowing principles from verbal behavior is tempting, because relative to motor behavior the area of verbal learning is thoroughly researched, but it is beset with hazards. The findings in Figure 8-1 strongly suggest that the laws of verbal and motor interference are not the same, which means that a prediction about motor retention from the laws of verbal interference is a dubious undertaking at our present stage of knowledge.

Proactive Inhibition

Duncan and Underwood (1953) have conducted the only motor retention experiment with a PI design. The task was self-paced and discrete, with six visual-motor paired associates. The subject had to learn to move a lever into six radially arrayed slots in response to six colored lights as stimuli. For example, a green light might come on, and the subject would be required to push the lever in a slot directly in front of him and perpendicular to his body. When this movement was completed, the green light would automatically change to another color, say red, and require the subject to remove his lever from the slot for green and place it in a slot angled at 45 degrees. Whenever the response was made initially to the correct slot, a correct response was recorded, and number of correct responses on a 20-second trial was the performance measure.

Tasks I and II were learned successively, followed by the recall of task II 24 hours later. Level of learning on task I and similarity between tasks I and II were the experimental variables related to recall. Amount of practice on task I was either 10, 40, 80, or 180 trials for an experimental group. Each of four main groups for amount of practice were divided into three subgroups for the practice of one of three levels of similarity on task II. Similarity was defined as the number of light-slot pairings that were the same from task I to task II.

The results were negative. The subgroups did not differ significantly among themselves, nor was there difference between a subgroup and a control group that did not have prior learning of another task. It is difficult to generalize about motor PI on the basis of this one study, and certainly it is premature to contend that motor behavior is not susceptible to PI. One possible reason for the results is that none of the three levels of task II similarity were interfering. All subgroups had positive transfer present in the learning of task II, and in the absence of interference effects at recall for the experimental treatments, it can be questioned whether the basic conditions of interference for PI were met.

SHORT–TERM RETENTION

Chapter 5 discussed extensive research efforts in verbal STM (a short-term memory), but regrettably only two motor experiments on short-term retention are of corresponding theoretical importance (Adams & Dijkstra, 1966; Posner & Konick, 1966).

The Adams-Dijkstra Experiment.   The principal line of interest in motor retention before the experiment by Adams and Dijkstra (1966) was long-term retention because this was the topic of most value to applied psychology, but the rapid rise of basic research on verbal STM was a goad for work on short-term motor recall. The major question that motivated the Adams-Dijkstra study was whether motor and verbal behavior follow the same laws. Are there circumstances of very rapid forgetting in motor retention as in some verbal STM situations? As we shall see in the next section on long-term motor retention, well-practiced continuous motor responses are retained at uncommonly high levels, and this might be a feature of motor behavior that is different from the comparatively large forgetting found for verbal responses. Second, how does the practice variable affect short-term motor retention? Hellyer (1962), whose findings are pictured in Figure 5-2, is among those who have found that increases in amount of practice decreased forgetting in verbal STM, and it is important to ask if motor responses are the same function of practice.

Adams and Dijkstra used a simple linear motor response. The apparatus was a metal bar with two freely sliding elements.

One slide was the experimenter's. It had a setscrew to lock the slide in place for defining the length of response which the subject was to make on a trial. The other slide had a knob on the top for fingertip grasping and was used by the subject. The subject was seated, and a curtain screened the apparatus from him so that responses were based on motor, not a combination of motor and visual, cues. A trial was the reinforcement and recall of a response. At the start of a trial, the experimenter locked his slide in position. The subject moved his slide from the starting position to the experimenter's fixed slide and then back to the starting position. This action defined a reinforced response, in the sense that the subject was informed of the response that was required of him. If the experimental condition called for multiple reinforcements, the subject repeated this movement the required number of times. After the reinforced response(s) was completed, the retention interval began and the subject waited quietly with his hand on his slide at the starting position. During the retention interval the experimenter moved his slide out of the way, and at the end of the interval, the experimenter instructed the subject to recall the response that he had just made before the retention interval. Deviation of the recalled movement in millimeters from the length of the originally learned response was the retention score. In a complex experimental design, each subject had the same number of reinforcements for seven movements of different length on seven trials. Each movement length had a different retention interval associated with it. Values of the retention intervals ranged from 5 to 120 seconds. Independent groups of subjects had either 1, 6, or 15 reinforcements.

The results are given in Figure 8-2. The response measure is absolute error in millimeters, which meant that all error deviations from the correct response length were treated alike regardless of whether they were too long or too short. Error for each retention interval was averaged over the seven response lengths

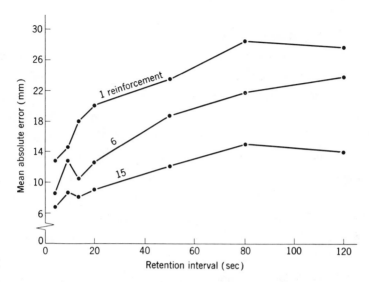

Fig. 8-2. Short-term retention of a simple linear motor response as a function of time and number of reinforced repetitions of the response, which is the curve parameter. From Adams and Dijkstra (1966).

in the complex design. The results conform nicely to those of Hellyer in Figure 5-2, except that the curves go in the opposite direction because Hellyer used percent correct as the measure, and Adams and Dijkstra used error. There is rapid forgetting over seconds, and forgetting is an inverse function of number of reinforcements. The seven trials were not a significant variable. In a closely related experiment, Posner and Konick (1966) confirmed these findings. They had subjects move a concealed lever. Retention intervals were 0, 10, 20, and 30 seconds. The retention interval was filled with either neutral rest, recording of digit pairs, addition of digit pairs, or classification of digit pairs into high or low or odd or even. Retention decreased significantly from 0 to 30 seconds. The activity interpolated in the retention interval was not a significant variable, and neither was trials.

Theoretical Considerations. What possibilities exist for explanation of this rapid forgetting of motor responses? The first possibility to dispense with is that the motor responses studied by Adams and Dijkstra had a strong verbal component so that the retention functions mainly represent the forgetting of verbal responses. If true, this could account for the similarity of Figures 8-2 and 5-2. Certainly it is conceivable that subjects might have used verbal cues to aid their remembering like, "That was a long movement which I made that time and will have to recall in a moment." However, the seven response lengths which Adams and Dijkstra used had successive differences of only 4 centimeters, and it is unlikely that subjects had verbal labels which could accurately discriminate differences so small. Posner and Konick (1966, p. 83) interviewed their subjects after the experiment and obtained reports of crude labels such as long or short, but found insufficient verbal detail to account for the observed accuracy of motor recall. Secondly, the empty retention interval was a rich opportunity for covert verbal rehearsal. Response strength should have been strengthened as the retention interval increased, and forgetting should have decreased, but just the opposite effect was found. And thirdly, Posner and Konick found that interpolation of different kinds of verbal-decision tasks had no effect on motor retention, which probably would not have been the case had the task been fundamentally a verbal one. We must conclude that the responses were primarily motor and that very rapid forgetting is a striking property of them.

In Chapter 5 the experiments by Keppel and Underwood (1962) and Loess (1964) forced the interpretation of rapid forgetting in verbal STM as a PI effect, and reinforcement in Hellyer's experiment was seen as strengthening the responses against effects of interference. The data of Adams and Dijkstra have the same descriptive features as Hellyer's, and so at one level of analysis follow the same empirical laws, but do the findings have the same underlying theoretical explanation? It is compelling to think so, because the curves of Hellyer, and Adams and Dijkstra, are the same functions of the same variables. However, there is no empirical necessity for the two sets of data to have a common theoretical explanation. For the same explanation to hold, it is necessary to show that the same operations which define the explanation prevail for both sets of data, which, for Hellyer's findings, are those of interference. Do we have cause to believe that interference is operating for the motor retention functions? The answer seems to be "No," although we know far less about motor than verbal interference, and we should be cautious about delivering a final pronouncement. Nevertheless, there are two reasons why these motor findings do not seem amenable to an interference explanation. First, as we saw earlier in this chapter, motor interference is induced by the learning of responses antagonistic to the criterion motor responses being remembered. What potential was there for antagonistic responses that might lead to PI and RI in the Adams-Dijkstra experiment? None, apparently. The verbal studies of Keppel and Underwood (1962) and Loess (1964) demonstrated that number of prior learn-recall sequences (PI) was a strong variable for retention loss in verbal STM situations, which is another way of saying that retention loss is an increasing function of trials. Neither the experiments of Adams and Dijkstra nor of Posner and Konick found trials a significant effect. This is not an unreasonable expectation, given our limited understanding of motor interference. Prior trials had responses of the same class, only of a different length, and there is no reason, as far as we know, to consider them antagonistic and interfering. Second, there was no reason to expect RI. Adams and Dijkstra merely had the subjects sit and wait during the retention interval, and Posner and Konick had their subjects perform simple verbal tasks. None of these operations are conducive to motor interference.

If interference fails as an explanation, does the theory of trace decay apply? With interference reasonably excluded, trace decay theory is the only remaining explanation. It is an explanation by exclusion, but the exclusion of alternative hypotheses is one approach to hypothesis verification. The trace decay explanation is offered with considerable caution, however, because interference is the strong theory of verbal forgetting, and it complicates memory theory to suggest that motor and verbal responses are governed by different mechanisms. Needed are more experiments that explicitly manipulate interference variables in motor retention paradigms so that a stronger understanding of interference theory emerges. Until then, there are preliminary reasons for entertaining a trace decay explanation of short-term motor forgetting.

LONG–TERM RETENTION

Retention of Continuous Responses

We all know from personal experience that the forgetting of continuous motor skills like ice-skating and riding a bicycle is trivial over long retention intervals of weeks, months, and years. These anecdotal observations are supported by controlled laboratory investigations. The high retention of continuous tracking responses has been found for the pursuit rotor (Bell, 1950), two-dimensional compensatory tracking (Battig, Nagel, Voss, & Brogden, 1957), three-dimensional compensatory tracking (Ammons et al., 1958; Fleishman & Parker, 1962), one-dimensional pursuit tracking (Melton, 1964), and the multidimensional tracking control of an aircraft simulator (Mengelkoch, Adams, and Gainer, 1958). The very high retention shown in these experiments is a research challenge because the long-term retention of well-learned verbal responses (as well-learned is defined in laboratory studies) is so much poorer than of continuous motor responses. Underwood (1957) considers that 15 to 25 percent forgetting over 24 hours is normal expectation for a verbal list, but this much forgetting for continuous motor responses is unlikely over a year or two. The findings of all these motor retention experiments that study continuous responses (usually tracking) have much in common; therefore only one study will be presented in detail.

The Fleishman-Parker Experiment. Using a three-dimensional compensatory tracking task and retention intervals up to 24 months, Fleishman and Parker (1962) report findings that are consistent with all the experiments over the last 50 years or so that have found high retention of continuous motor skills. Their experimental task had some of the display and response characteristics of certain aircraft control tasks. Two dimensions of the task had their stimuli presented on a cathode-ray tube. A programmed target dot was continually displaced in both the horizontal and vertical dimensions of the tube, and the seated subject manipulated a control stick in two dimensions to keep the dot centered on the display. Beneath the cathode-ray tube was a voltmeter whose needle had programmed displacements from center, and the subject tried to keep the needle centered by foot control of a rudder bar. All three stimulus dimensions varied continuously and simultaneously, so that the subject's task was a complex, three-dimensional coordination. Integrated error was the measure of performance. The more the dot and the needle were kept centered, the less the error deviation, and the better the performance. Extensive original training (17 daily sessions) was given all subjects. At the end of original training the subjects were divided into three groups with retention intervals of 9, 14, or 24 months.

Figure 8-3 has the results. The acquisition curve is for all three groups combined because they all had common treatment at this stage of the experiment. The task was undoubtedly diffi-

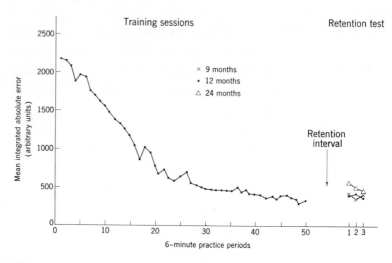

Fig. 8-3. Retention of a well-learned skill on a three-dimensional compensatory tracking task. These data, with retention intervals from 9 to 24 months, are a good example of the high retention of continuous motor responses. From Fleishman and Parker (1962).

cult, but the extensive training brought the acquisition curve near its asymptote. Retention was almost perfect, although the 24-month group had slightly more forgetting than the other two groups. A detailed minute-by-minute analysis of the retention and relearning data revealed that virtually all the retention loss was recaptured after the first minute or so. Fleishman and Parker state the inescapable conclusion that retention of their complex skill is extremely high, and the small losses are recovered very rapidly in relearning.

The Challenge of Continuous Motor Responses and Their Very High Retention. Experimental psychologists have not worried enough about continuous motor responses and why they are retained so much better than verbal responses. There is good scientific cause to puzzle the problem because large discrepancies of this kind can represent the action of special variables or mechanisms of significance for memory theory. On the other hand, the design and uses of continuous motor tasks may contain uncontrolled variables which operate in behalf of high retention, and if these variables could be defined and controlled, the retention of verbal and motor responses might be the same. The following are four possible reasons why continuous motor skills are retained so well. There is no particular evidence for any of them; therefore the four can be considered as hypotheses for future research.

1. Continuous motor responses may be greatly overlearned relative to the amount of learning that is ordinarily given verbal responses in retention studies. In human learning the fundamental operation for learning is knowledge of results. The subject is informed of response error, or some function of it. As a learning operation, knowledge of results can be equated with reinforcement because it is the stimulus event in association with response which produces the rather stable change that we call "habit." Consider a pursuit tracking task like the pursuit rotor in which the length of a practice trial might be about 30 seconds. We can presume that the subject makes a corrective movement, sees the error discrepancy between his stylus tip and target (knowledge of results), experiences a habit increment from this error information, makes the next corrective response, and so on. Over a series of practice trials the subject receives a large, indefinite number of these reinforcing operations, and the outcome is acquisition of the pursuit tracking skill. When retention is called for, we can expect it to be high because so many reinforcements were given. In comparison, the word pairs of a list in the usual verbal retention experiment have relatively few reinforcements, and forgetting should be much greater. A test of this overlearning hypothesis will require a task that is predominantly motor and allows control over number of reinforcements. A task like that of Adams and Dijkstra (1966) could satisfy these requirements.

2. If the interference theory of forgetting has validity for motor behavior, and this has yet to be proved, the unstructured,

everyday motor activities that occur before the learning of the criterion motor response (PI), or during the retention interval (RI), may have little likelihood of interfering with the highly specific skills that are learned with a laboratory motor task. Tests (e.g., Underwood & Postman, 1960) for extraexperimental sources of interference for verbal responses have not been successful so far (Chapter 7), but the line of thinking is important and eventual verification of interference theory by this approach would seem necessary to secure the theory. We need tests of the Underwood-Postman hypothesis for motor behavior too, and from them may come clarification of why so little forgetting occurs. Earlier in this chapter the possibility was discussed that interference theory is inappropriate for motor responses and that trace decay may be the explanation. Explicit tests of interference theory for motor retention would work toward clarifying this basic theoretical issue.

3. Chapter 2 said that the domain of forgetting research was determinants of effects on habit over the retention interval. Is it possible that well-learned continuous motor responses have traces which are relatively resistant to forgetting processes, and that initial motor movements at recall fully reinstate kinesthetic cues which are such an important part of the motor response complex and on which full expression of the response depends? Gagne (1941) found retention of maze running in rats to decrease over intervals of 3 to 28 days, but when Ehrenfreund and Allen (1964, 1966) took special pains to maintain the cue complex, they found perfect retention of maze running after 27 days. Other response classes, such as verbal ones, may lack the condition of full cue reinstatement; and retention is poor, not because of effects on habit, but because too much of the arousing cue complex is absent.

4. Method of measurement may be a factor in the high re-

tention of continuous motor skills. Many response errors may occur at recall, but if of short duration, they make relatively little contribution to the total error score integrated over a relatively long trial period. When an analogous type of error occurs in verbal learning, the recording of a full error may result, and it does not take very many of them to result in a low retention score.

Retention of Discrete Responses

The generalization that motor skills are retained better than verbal ones is true, as we have seen in the last section, but it is not always emphasized that this generalization applies only to continuous motor activities. When motor responses are discrete, the forgetting can be large and similar to that found for verbal responses. Neumann and Ammons (1957) report an experiment that is representative of those on the retention of discrete responses. The subject sat in front of a large board with inner and outer circles of switches set in the OFF position. There were eight switches in each circle. The subject turned the inner switches ON in clockwise order and had to learn which outer switch matched each inner switch. When a correct match occurred, a buzzer sounded. The task was paced, with only 3 seconds to make a match, and one complete circuit of the eight switches was a trial. Retention intervals were 1 minute, 20 minutes, 2 days, 7 weeks, and 1 year. Original learning and relearning were to a criterion of two successive errorless trials.

The results of the Neumann-Ammons study are shown in Figure 8-4. Forgetting occurred in as little as 20 minutes, and by one year it was complete. The rapid forgetting of discrete motor responses has been obtained in several other experiments (Duncan & Underwood, 1952; Mengelkoch, Adams, & Gainer, 1958;

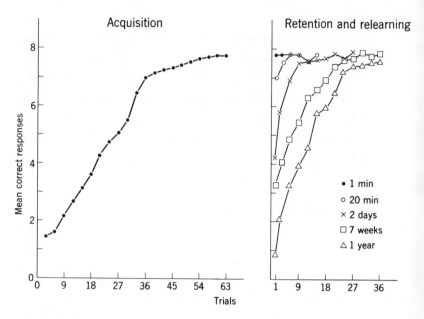

Fig. 8-4. Acquisition, and retention and relearning for intervals of 1 minute to 1 year, for a discrete motor task. The criterion of performance was two successive errorless trials, and for this plot, based on a common number of trials, a subject was given a perfect score of 8 after he had attained the criterion. From Neumann and Ammons (1957).

Ammons et al., 1958; Adams & Hufford, 1962). Ammons et al. (1958) found less forgetting for greater amounts of original learning of a discrete task, which is consistent with verbal studies.

Apparently one reason for the rapid forgetting of discrete motor responses is that they are behaviorally complex and have a verbal component in them, at least at certain stages of training. Neumann and Ammons (1957) interviewed their subjects and found that 44 percent of them had used verbal cues in designating the location of the switches. Trumbo, Ulrich, and Noble (1965) manipulated verbal cues by pretraining the subject in verbal responses that described the target path of a one-dimensional pursuit tracking task that he was to practice subsequently. The pretraining was learning a list of numbers that corresponded to positions on the display through which the target would cycle repeatedly, and it was hypothesized that giving the subject a relevant verbal cue system would aid his tracking performance. A 31-day retention interval followed verbal pretraining and training on the tracking task. It was found that verbal pretraining had a positive effect on performance at the early trials of original training, but no effect at either the end of original training trials or the retention test. The research of Trumbo and his associates is a proper beginning toward identifying motor tasks with a verbal component and gaining control over the verbal behavior in them. The role of verbal responses for motor behavior has been discussed speculatively since research on motor skills began, but investigated rather little, and we probably shall not achieve good prediction of motor retention until we understand it.

A verbal component of discrete motor responses is one likely explanation for the rapid forgetting of these responses, and degree of learning is another. Great overlearning was discussed as a reason why continuous motor skills are retained so well. Discrete motor responses, like verbal responses, may be poorly retained because their level of learning is low.

METHODOLOGY

Chapter 2 said that the scientific study of memory is investigation of habit's fate over the retention interval. This means the control of nonhabit variables so that effects on habit are not clouded at recall. Massing of practice in original learning is a common instance of failure to consider this problem in studies of motor retention (Adams, 1964, p. 190). Massed practice of a motor task frequently results in spontaneous gain, or reminiscence, over the retention interval which operates counter to forgetting. The net result of these opposing factors is little retention loss, or even increase in performance over the retention interval if the massing is great enough. The research of Purdy and Lockhart (1962), Ryan (1962), and Eysenck (1960) is an example of this shortcoming. Widely distributed practice in original learning is a necessary control to minimize the contamination of reminiscence.

Chapters 5 and 7 discussed the control of level of learning as an important methodological problem for verbal STM and LTM, and the matter is equally important for studies of motor retention. Underwood (1964) and Keppel (1965) have thoroughly discussed these matters for verbal retention, and their papers deserve to be read for their corresponding relevance to motor retention. An experiment that asks, for example, about the effects of different levels of meaningfulness on verbal retention must equate each type of material for associative strength in original learning. Otherwise, retention loss will be a joint function of meaningfulness and associative strength, and the effects on retention of meaningfulness alone will be obscured. The problem of equating for associative strength when there are different conditions of original training has not come up for motor retention, perhaps because motor retention is less well developed as a research area. But the issue is the same as for verbal retention and deserves the same attention.

Two recent motor retention experiments are examples of failure to handle this problem. Trumbo, Noble, Cross, and Ulrich (1965) studied the regularity of target action in a one-dimensional pursuit task on retention. Four types of target courses were used, ranging from complete randomness in its moment-to-moment position to complete repetitiveness. All groups were given a constant number of original training trials, and retention intervals were one week, one month, or five months. The four target courses differed markedly in difficulty, and so all groups had large differences in performance level at the end of original training. As the authors admit (Trumbo, Noble, Cross, & Ulrich, 1965, p. 256), there is no meaningful way to compare retention losses because of inequities in associative strength. It would have been better if all the groups had been brought to a common performance level in original training so that equal associative strength could have been reasonably assumed for the different task conditions. Melton (1964) reports an experiment based on an interesting idea, but which has the same methodological problem. In an attempt to extend verbal interference theory to motor behavior, Melton hypothesized that the learning of incompatible control-display relationships, in which response movements are the reverse of those expected from general cultural experience with everyday motor tasks, would bring some extinction of the expected response. Spontaneous recovery of the extinguished response in the retention interval should produce competition with the criterion response at recall and lower retention. Comparison was with a control condition that used an expected, compatible control-display relationship. The task was a one-dimensional pursuit tracking task, with random and nonrandom target paths as experimental variables in addition to compatible and incompatible control-display relationships. A constant number of trials was given in original learning, and retention intervals were 5 minutes, 1 day, and 1 week. Here again, no meaningful comparison of retention losses was possible. All groups had different performance levels in original learning, so that retention loss for each was a confounded function of associative strength and the experimental variables. For the future we can hope that the area of verbal retention cross-fertilizes research on motor retention so that its methodological sophistication, richly bred over a long history, can be brought to bear.

REFERENCES

Adams, J. A. Human tracking behavior. *Psychol. Bull.*, 1961, **58**, 55–79.

Adams, J. A. Motor skills. *Annu. Rev. Psychol.*, 1964, **15**, 181–202.

Adams, J. A., & Dijkstra, S. Short-term memory for motor responses. *J. exp. Psychol.*, 1966, **71**, 314–318.

Adams, J. A., & Hufford, L. E. Contributions of a part-task trainer to the learning and relearning of a time-shared flight maneuver. *Hum. Factors*, 1962, **4**, 159–170.

Ammons, R. B., Farr, R. G., Bloch, Edith, Neumann, Eva, Dey, M., Marion, R., & Ammons C. H. Long-term retention of perceptual-motor skills. *J. exp. Psychol.*, 1958, **55**, 318–328.

Battig, W. F., Nagel, E. H., Voss, J. F., & Brogden, W. F. Transfer and retention of bidimensional compensatory tracking after extended practice. *Amer. J. Psychol.*, 1957, **70**, 75–80.

Bell, H. M. Retention of pursuit rotor skill after one year. *J. exp. Psychol.*, 1950, **40**, 648–649.

Duncan, C. P., & Underwood, B. J. Retention of transfer in motor learning after 24 hours and after 14 months as a function of degree of first-task learning and inter-task similarity. *USAF Wright Air Development Center Tech. Rep. 52–224*, Dayton Ohio, October, 1952.

Duncan, C. P., & Underwood, B. J. Retention of transfer in motor learning after twenty-four hours and after fourteen months. *J. exp. Psychol.*, 1953, **46**, 445–452.

Ehrenfreund, D., & Allen, J. Perfect retention of an instrumental response. *Psychon. Sci.*, 1964, **1**, 347–348.

Ehrenfreund, D., & Allen, J. Role of $r_g - s_g$ in forgetting. *Psychon. Sci.*, 1966, **5**, 281–282.

Eysenck, S. B. G. Retention of a well-developed motor skill after one year. *J. gen. Psychol.*, 1960, **63**, 267–273.

Fleishman, E. A., & Parker, J. F., Jr. Factors in the retention and relearning of perceptual-motor skill. *J. exp. Psychol.*, 1962, **64**, 215–226.

Gagne, R. M. The retention of a conditioned operant response. *J. exp. Psychol.*, 1941, **29**, 296–305.

Hellyer, S. Supplementary report: Frequency of stimulus presentation and short-term decrement in recall. *J. exp. Psychol.*, 1962, **64**, 650.

Keppel, G. Problems of method in the study of short-term memory. *Psychol. Bull.*, 1965, **63**, 1–13.

Keppel, G., & Underwood, B. J. Proactive inhibition in short-term retention of single items. *J. verbal Learn. verbal Behav.*, 1962, **1**, 153–161.

Lewis, D. Positive and negative transfer in motor learning. *Amer. Psychologist*, 1947, **2**, 423. (Abstract)

Lewis, D., McAllister, Dorothy E., & Adams, J. A. Facilitation and interference in performance on the Modified Mashburn Apparatus: I. The effects of varying the amount of original learning. *J. exp. Psychol.*, 1951, **41**, 247–260.

Lewis, D., & Shepard, A. H. Devices for studying associative interference in psychomotor performance: I. The Modified Mashburn Apparatus. *J. Psychol.*, 1950, **29**, 35–46.

Loess, H. Proactive inhibition in short-term memory. *J. verbal Learn. verbal Behav.*, 1964, **3**, 362–368.

McAllister, Dorothy E., & Lewis, D. Facilitation and interference in performance on the Modified Mashburn Apparatus: II. The effects of varying the amount of interpolated learning. *J. exp. Psychol.*, 1951, **41**, 356–363.

Melton, A. W. (Ed.) Apparatus tests. *AAF Aviat. Psychol. Program res. Rep.* 4, Washington, 1947.

Melton, A. W. Retention of tracking skills. Final report, U.S. Army Medical Research and Development Command, Contract No. DA-49-007-MD-1020, September, 1964.

Mengelkoch, R. F., Adams, J. A., & Gainer, C. A. The forgetting of instrument flying skills as a function of the level of initial proficiency. *USN Train. Devices Cent., Hum. Engng. tech. Rep.* NAVTRADEVCEN 71-16-18, Port Washington, New York, September, 1958.

Naylor, J. C., Briggs, G. E., & Reed, W. G. The effects of task organization, training time, and retention interval on the retention of skill. *USAF 6570th AMRL tech. docum. Rep.* AMRL-TDR-62-107, Wright-Patterson Air Force Base, Dayton, Ohio, September, 1962.

Neumann, Eva, & Ammons, R. B. Acquisition and long-term retention of a simple serial perceptual-motor task. *J. exp. Psychol.*, 1957, **53**, 159–161.

Posner, M. I., & Konick, A.F. Short-term retention of visual and kinesthetic information. *Organiz. Behav. and hum. Perf.*, 1966, **1**, 71–
86.

Purdy, B. J., & Lockhart, A. Retention and relearning of gross motor
skills after long periods of no practice. *Res. Quart. Amer. Ass.
Hlth. Phys. Educ. Recr.*, 1962, **33**, 194–201.

Ryan, E. D. Retention of stabilometer and pursuit rotor skills. *Res.
Quart. Amer. Ass. Hlth. Phys. Educ. Recr.*, 1962, **33**, 593–598.

Trumbo, D., Noble, M., Cross, K., & Ulrich, L. Task predictability in
the organization, acquisition, and retention of tracking skill. *J.
exp. Psychol.*, 1965, **70**, 252–263.

Trumbo, D., Ulrich, L., & Noble, M. E. Verbal coding and display
coding in the acquisition and retention of tracking skill. *J. appl.
Psychol.*, 1965, **49**, 368–375.

Underwood, B. J. Interference and forgetting. *Psychol. Rev.*, 1957, **64**,
49–60.

Underwood, B. J. Degree of learning and the measurement of forgetting. *J. verbal Learn. verbal Behav.*, 1964, **3**, 112–119.

Underwood, B. J., & Postman, L. Extraexperimental sources of interference in forgetting. *Psychol. Rev.*, 1960, **67**, 73–95.

Recognition Memory 9

C hapter 2 defined the recall and recognition tests for measuring retention, but it will do no harm to restate the definitions, briefly. For recall, the subject attempts to repeat and duplicate a response which he learned earlier. Recognition is the identification of stimuli or responses that have occurred before. In deference to psychology's emphasis so far, this chapter is about the recognition of stimuli, not responses. Chapter 10 will express regrets that response recognition has not been studied more, and will define an importance for it.

METHODS OF RECOGNITION TESTING

In broad outline, the laboratory method of stimulus recognition is to expose a subject to a series of stimuli and then later, in a recognition test of retention, have him attempt to identify the stimuli that were presented earlier. The recognition test has "old" stimuli along with "new" ones of the same class that were not presented before, and the task is to select the old ones. The measure of performance is customarily the percentage of old stimuli correctly identified.

There are two main ways of designing a recognition test. One, which will be called the "method of single stimuli," has old and new items mixed. The subject's task is to designate each one as old or new. The stimuli can be presented singly to the subject, or they can all be presented together, as on a printed page. Whatever the means of presentation, each stimulus is separately examined and designated as old or new. The difficulty with this procedure is that a subject's criterion or response bias can distort the results. In the extreme case a subject can get them all correct or all wrong. By using a relaxed criterion of correctness that resolves all uncertainties in favor of old stimuli, all stimuli are identified as old, all old stimuli are correctly identified, but many new stimuli are falsely identified as old. Conversely, probability correct can be zero by using a strict criterion which identifies all stimuli as new. The response bias can vary between these extremes and, moreover, can change during the recognition test. As long as it can be demonstrated that subjects have no response bias, and have no tendency to give a disproportionate number of old or new responses, the method of single stimuli is satisfactory. Recent developments in decision theory (e.g., Swets, 1964) have been brought to bear on recognition in an attempt to quantify response bias (Egan, 1958; Murdock, 1965). This work arises from psychophysical problems, like the discrimination of a signal in random noise. In this case a subject reports whether or not he thinks a signal is present, just as in a recognition test he must report whether a stimulus is old or new. Some of the research based on decision theory has used five- and seven-point rating scales, and a subject indicates his degree of confidence in his judgment about the stimulus. The use of ratings in recognition experiments is not new (Strong, 1912, 1913).

The other way of designing a recognition test is the "method of multiple stimuli," which uses a multiple-choice test item. The item of the test is two or more stimuli presented together, only one of which is the old stimulus. The subject examines all the stimuli of the set and then chooses the one he thinks is old. Shepard and Chang (1963, p. 93) contend that this method has an advantage over the method of single stimuli because response bias operates equally for all stimulus alternatives in the test item. Thus, the discrimination between alternatives and the choice is unaffected. The method of multiple stimuli has been used frequently in several tests (e.g., Postman, Jenkins, & Postman, 1948; Deese, 1956; Postman & Rau, 1957; Shepard & Chang, 1963; Ellis & Muller, 1964; Clark, 1965; Teghtsoonian, 1965).

BASIC DATA

Recognition and Retention

A striking thing is the impressively high level of retention obtained by using the recognition method. This does not mean that correct recognition is *always* high, but there are conditions which produce extremely high retention which vastly exceeds anything that might be found by using recall. The best example is a series of experiments by Shepard (1967) that deserve examination in detail.

Shepard's Experiments. Three separate experiments investigated the recognition of words, sentences, and pictures. The words and sentences were presented on cards, and the subject went through the deck at his own pace. The method of multiple stimuli was used in an immediate recognition test. At the end of this inspection series, cards with stimulus pairs were presented. One stimulus of a pair was from the deck just inspected and was old, and the other was new. The procedure for pictures was just the same, except that they were shown by a stripfilm projector which the subject advanced at his own pace. There were 540 stimuli and 60 test pairs for the words. The sentences and pictures both had 612 stimuli and 68 test pairs.

Retention was remarkable. The median percent correct in the test was 90 for words, 88.2 for sentences, and 98.5 for pictures. Out of the 34 subjects in the pictures group, 9 had perfect performance. Not only is retention extremely high; a subject's capacity to store perceptual data is very large also.

Shepard's findings should not suggest that the capability for recognition is not forgotten. Relatively short retention intervals of 5 to 20 minutes (Clark, 1965), or 1 to 5 hours (Arnoult, 1956) do not influence recognition accuracy, but longer intervals definitely do. In a minor experiment with only a few subjects, Shepard

(1967) tested pictures for recognition after retention intervals of 2 hours, 3, 7, and 120 days and found median percents retained of 100.0, 93.0, 92.0, and 57.0, respectively. Using the method
of multiple stimuli for the recognition test, Bahrick and Bahrick
(1964) had four abstract stimulus patterns and their three-digit
number associates that were either easy or difficult to discriminate
from one another, and retention intervals of 2 hours, 2 days, and
2 weeks. After 2 hours, the groups with difficult recognition tasks
had percent correct in the 67 to 75 percent range, and the groups
with easy tasks were in the 82 to 84 percent range. But, after 2
weeks, correct recognition fell to 32 to 36 percent for the difficult
groups and to 57 to 64 percent for the easy groups. Strong (1913)
gave one exposure to each of 20 meaningful words and then
tested retention by the method of single stimuli after intervals
from 15 seconds to 42 days. Strong seems to have been the first to
use judgments of confidence in having seen the stimulus before
(essentially a rating scale). Of those stimuli which subjects rated
with 100 percent confidence, percent correct dropped from 84.3
at 15 seconds to zero at 42 days. These experiments have obvious
differences in materials and procedures, but this is less important
than the substantial forgetting that occurs in all of them when
intervals are long enough. Even so, it is hard to set aside the extremely high retention found by Shepard in an immediate recognition test. As with the high retention of continuous motor skills,
a challenge exists to uncover the reasons for so little forgetting.

Number of Stimulus Alternatives

Whether the method of single or multiple stimuli is used, number of alternatives from which old stimuli must be discriminated
is a primary determiner of performance. Davis, Sutherland, and
Judd (1961) showed their subjects lists of 15 letters or numbers,
and then gave them a recognition test by the method of single

stimuli. The original list of 15 was imbedded in a larger list of 30, 60, or 90 items of the same type. Calculations from data which they presented (their Table 1, p. 424) revealed that tests with 30, 60, and 90 items produced percent correct of 70, 56, and 50 for letter stimuli and 63, 50, and 40 for number stimuli, respectively. Strong (1912) obtained a similar result when popular advertisements were used as stimuli.

Using the method of multiple stimuli, Postman (1950) reports a region of indifference before number of alternatives have an effect. After reading a list of syllables five times, Postman gave multiple-choice test items that had either 2, 4, 7, or 10 syllables, one of which was a correct syllable. The test items with 2, 4, and 7 alternatives had about the same mean number correct, but significantly poorer performance resulted when the number of alternatives was 10.

The point of this section is that there is no absolute level of recognition per se; it is a function of the test conditions. Any law is a function of the ways of defining and measuring the variables that enter it, and in this sense the observation is trite, but the potency of number of alternatives in the test makes the comments seem worth saying.

Familiarity

Number of learning trials is a positive variable for recall, and analogous operations should benefit recognition. This factor has been called "familiarity" in the realm of recognition. Frequency of stimulation is the operational definition of familiarity. Noble (1953, 1954, 1963) says that familiarity is a learned stimulus attribute, and he distinguishes it from meaningfulness m which is defined as the number of associations for a word in a fixed period of time (Noble, 1952, 1963). Although a meaningful word is intuitively more familiar, and indeed the correlation between meaningfulness and familiarity is high, Noble makes a good argument for some independence of the two (Noble, 1953). Certainly a stimulus can be experienced many times and have few or no associations for it. Riley and Phillips (1959) and Schulz and Thysell (1965) have confirmed empirically that familiarity operations have no appreciable effect on meaningfulness. Thus, in not being a direct influence on the responses which a word can elicit, familiarity can be conceived as an associative strength variable for the stimulus *qua* stimulus, and we should expect recognition to be a positive function of it. The more times you experience a stimulus, the more readily you recognize it.

Noble (1954) manipulated familiarity experimentally. Artificial, disyllabic words were used as stimuli, and Noble exposed them with a slide projector from zero to 25 times. Subjects then rated the words on a five-point scale for familiarity (Noble, 1953), and judged familiarity was found to be an increasing, negatively accelerated function of stimulation frequency. Noble's lowest scale position was defined as "You have never seen or heard the word used in your life" (Noble, 1953, p. 90). If Arnoult's reasoning (Arnoult, 1956, p. 273) is accepted that any rating higher than this represents some degree of recognition, Noble's familiarity function can be interpreted as a relationship between frequency of stimulation and recognition. Arnoult (1956) conducted an experiment very similar to Noble's, except that he used meaningless shapes as stimuli. His results were about the same.

There are two experiments (Gorman, 1961; Shepard, 1967) which are curiously contradictory to the work of Noble and Arnoult, and they used the Thorndike-Lorge (1944) word count as a measure of visual experience. The Thorndike-Lorge count shows the frequency of words in the written language; therefore it is a measure of visual experience with words and essentially conforms to Noble's definition of familiarity. The approaches of Noble and Arnoult are unquestionably the best because they provide experimental control over the amount of experience, but words from the Thorndike-Lorge listing define a fair prediction for the familiarity hypothesis and present another chance to test it. Part of Gorman's experiment (1961) was exposure to words of high and low frequency in the Thorndike-Lorge tabulation, followed by a recognition test. Contrary to a prediction from Noble's familiarity hypothesis that high-frequency words should have a higher level of recognition, just the opposite occurred. High-frequency words were less well recognized than comparatively rare words. Shepard (1967) reports the same finding. In his experiment on word recognition Shepard used both high- and low-frequency words from the Thorndike-Lorge list. Low-frequency words were recognized 92.5 percent of the time, but high-frequency words were only 84.4 percent correct. Both Gorman and Shepard lean toward an interference explanation and conjecture that relatively rare words are less amenable to the interfering effects of other words in the series. This hypothesis could be true, although we know so little at present about the laws of interference for recognition that interference cannot be used meaningfully to explain recognition. Until explanatory principles are found, we must accept data like these on an empirical basis and wait for research to reconcile the findings of Gorman and Shepard with those of Noble and Arnoult.

RECOGNITION AND RECALL COMPARED

The Accepted Superiority of Recognition over Recall

A generalization of long standing in psychology textbooks is that recognition gives higher performance than recall. The generalization has justification because virtually all experiments (until recently, at least) that have compared recall and recognition have found a superiority for recognition, sometimes by a factor of about 3 (MacDougall, 1904; Myers, 1914; Achilles, 1920; Postman, Jenkins, & Postman, 1948; Postman, 1952; Luh, 1922; Postman & Rau, 1957; Bruce & Cofer, 1965). Luh's experiment (1922) is often used to portray these facts in textbooks, and it would be profitable to examine Luh's experiment and then look at Postman and Rau's (1957) modern version of it.

Luh's Experiment and the Postman-Rau Study. The motivation for Luh's experiment was the research of Ballard (1913) which found a reminiscence effect for poetry over the retention interval. Ballard's failure to report the negatively accelerated decay function of forgetting found by Ebbinghaus (1913) led Luh to ask whether method of measuring retention and degree of learning were not the two variables responsible for Ballard's results. Ballard had used the method of written reproduction, in which a subject attempts written recall of the material in its proper order, and a 20 to 40 percent degree of learning, which were departures from the procedures of earlier experiments. Luh studied both method of measuring retention and degree of learning, but it is Luh's work on measurement methodology that has held the interest of so many textbook writers for so long. It is also the aspect of his work which holds our interest here.

In the part of his experiment on methods of measurement, Luh required the serial learning of 12 nonsense syllables to a criterion of one errorless repetition of the list. Retention intervals were 20 minutes, 1 hour, 4 hours, 1 day, and 2 days. All subjects served in all experimental conditions. In original learning all subjects learned by the anticipation method, but the retention test was either recall and relearning by the anticipation method; written reproduction, in which the syllables were to be written in their proper order; reconstruction, in which the syllables were on cards and the order of items in the series had to be reassembled; or recognition, in which the 12 syllables had to be selected out of 24 within 90 seconds. The procedures for recall deserve comment. With the anticipation method the subjects simply recalled and relearned, and that ended the session. However, measures for the other three methods were collected successively in the same session as indices of the same retention capability. The subject was first tested for retention by written reproduction, followed by recognition, and finally reconstruction.

Luh's results are shown in Figure 9-1. The superiority of recognition over recall by the anticipation method is large and dramatic. The other methods of measuring retention depicted in Figure 9-1 have slipped from favor over the years, so that only the recall and recognition functions are of current interest.

Luh's experimental design was good enough for his time, but it is lacking by modern standards. Postman and Rau (1957, pp. 220–221) do a good job of criticizing Luh's design, and their observations deserve restating. One flaw was that Luh obtained three of his retention measures in the same retention session, and

Fig. 9-1.   Retention curves for five measures of performance. From Luh (1922).

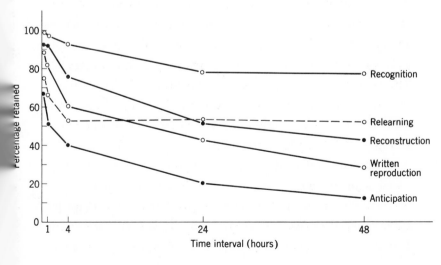

there is a strong chance that one influenced another. A second flaw, which has persisted in experiments until very recent years, was use of the same subjects in all experimental conditions. Certainly there are legitimate uses of the same subjects in different experimental treatments, but learning experiments tend not to be of this type because there is likelihood that participation in one treatment will affect performance in another. Underwood (1957) convincingly demonstrated that PI created by the prior learning of other verbal lists is a strong determinant of forgetting. We now know that a proper design for experiments on verbal retention must use independent groups of subjects.

Because a knowledge of retention as a function of method of measurement is important for psychology, Postman and Rau (1957) ran a major experiment that remedied the shortcomings of Luh's design. Serial learning was used for a 12-item list, and original learning was carried to a criterion of one errorless trial. Two kinds of verbal materials were used—nonsense syllables and meaningful words. Three retention intervals of 20 minutes, 1 day, and 2 days were used. Method of measurement was limited to three measures of contemporary interest: recall and relearning by the anticipation method, free recall, and recognition. Two kinds of material, three retention intervals, and three measures gave 18 experimental conditions; and an independent group of subjects was used for each one. The results are shown in Figure 9-2. The most interesting aspect of Figure 9-2 is that Luh's finding of the superiority of recognition over recall by the anticipation method is confirmed, despite the weaknesses of his experiment. In Figure 9-2 virtually no forgetting is shown by the recognition measure. The anticipation curve in Figure 9-2 should be compared with its counterpart in Figure 9-1. Anticipation has the poorest performance in both experiments, but Luh's anticipation curve plunged to near zero after two days whereas Postman and Rau have their anticipation curves in the 60 to 70 percent region.

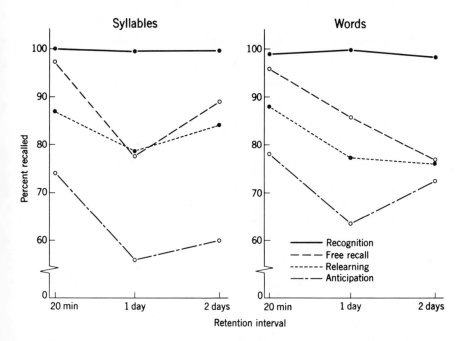

Fig. 9-2. Postman and Rau's extension of Luh's study—retention functions for four measures of performance. From Postman and Rau (1957).

This is evidence for the strong PI effect emphasized by Underwood (1957). Luh had all subjects serve in all conditions; therefore a subject usually would have learned and recalled several lists prior to any particular list and would have generated PI to lower his level of recall. Postman and Rau used independent groups of subjects that had no prior list learning, and recall by the anticipation method is much higher as a result.

When Recognition Is Not Superior to Recall

We have seen that recognition is a decreasing function of number of alternative stimuli in the retention test, which suggests that the superiority of recognition over recall is not absolute but can be lessened, and even upset, if the number of alternatives is large enough. Empirical data bear out this possibility. Earlier, the experiment by Davis, Sutherland, and Judd (1961) was discussed with respect to recognition and number of alternatives. Another feature of their study was a comparison of recall and recognition. It will be remembered that they investigated the recognition of 15 numbers or letters from among 30, 60, or 90 alternatives and, in addition, that they included recall of the 15. Recall was 41 percent for letters and 45 percent for numbers. When the 15 had to be chosen from among 30 stimuli, recognition was 70 percent for letters and 63 percent for numbers, which demonstrates the well-established superiority of recognition over recall. But when number of alternatives was 90 in the recognition test, percent correct fell to 50 for letters and 40 for numbers—values which are not much different from those for recall.

Another variable which demolishes the difference between recognition and recall is the discriminability among alternatives that determines the ease with which an old stimulus can be selected from among the new ones. Bahrick and Bahrick (1964) used abstract patterns as stimuli and three-digit numbers as responses which were learned as associates to the stimuli. After learning, retention was tested by recall and the anticipation method, or by recognition in which the old stimulus and its response had to be chosen from among four stimuli and their responses. Two levels of similarity were used, defined in terms of judged correspondence between the four stimuli and responses. Retention intervals of two hours, two days, and two weeks were used. The easy (dissimilar) recognition test produced performance superior to recall at all retention intervals. The difficult recognition test, with the similar alternatives, however, produced performance that was poorer than recall in all comparisons but one. Closely related findings from an STM experiment are reported by Bruce and Cofer (1965).

Thus, number and discriminability of alternatives are two

variables that can eliminate the superiority of recognition over recall, and undoubtedly there are more. That the superiority of recognition over recall can be abolished should not subtract from the very high retention and capacity that can be produced by the recognition method when number of alternatives is small. Recall can yield nothing like the vast capacity for recognizing hundreds of stimuli, as Shepard (1967) has found.

RECOGNITION AND INTERFERENCE

In Chapter 4 we saw a large amount of information about interference for verbal recall, and although the relationships were not fully detailed, they stand tall and impressive when compared with the scanty findings on interference and recognition. In the absence of substantive knowledge about interference, we are handicapped in making decisions about theories of forgetting and in deciding, say, whether trace decay or interference applies as a basic explanation for forgetting when recognition is the measure of performance. The best that can be done in this section is to discuss the few relevant experiments and indicate the trend of research so far.

Proactive Inhibition

There is very little research on recognition and PI to mention, and what there is of it is conflicting. Peixotto (1947) used nonsense syllables with a study trial followed by an immediate recognition test. This learn-test procedure was repeated with a different set of syllables each day for five days. A learn-test sequence repeated on successive days has close resemblance to the PI experiment by Greenberg and Underwood (1950) that used a recall measure. Peixotto found a distinct PI effect, with a significant drop in correct recognition from the first to the final day, which is consistent with the Greenberg and Underwood result.

Shepard and Chang (1963) studied the recognition of three-digit numbers over a long series. According to PI considerations, recognition should decrease as the series progresses because the number of prior learn-test sequences steadily increases. However, in three experiments they failed to find any such decrement (Shepard & Chang, 1963, Figure 1, p. 96). In an earlier experiment Shepard and Teghtsoonian (1961) found some evidence for PI, but use of the method of single stimuli resulted in uncontrolled response bias, and they considered it less than a good approach (see remarks by Shepard & Chang, 1963, p. 93).

With only the experiments of Peixotto and of Shepard and Chang for guidance, it is difficult to say much about PI. There is no reason to doubt the validity of either investigation; thus differences in outcome seem a function of methods and procedures. If so, future research will resolve the differences. When future researchers get around to it, they can improve on the experimental design used by Peixotto and by Shepard and Chang which assumes that a study trial experience is sufficient for original learning. Neither of these studies had a measure of performance in original learning. Equal and sufficient learning is assumed for all items, but this is a rash assumption. In neither were control groups used as a basis for measuring PI. Some of the RI experiments in the next section show greater sensitivity to this matter.

Retroactive Inhibition

Somewhat more work on recognition and RI has been done, but most of the studies are old and none are tied to the modern ideas about interference which were discussed in Chapter 4. One of the early experiments was by Gibson (1934), who used five-letter nonsense words in an RI design and found a small amount of decrement in a recognition test. But McKinney (1935) conducted the most comprehensive of the older experiments. He performed three RI experiments with the same general design, two with advertisements as stimuli and one with nonsense syllables. In the first experiment, original learning for an experimental group was the presentation of 10 advertisements for 3 seconds each, and it was immediately followed by a recognition test in which a subject tried to identify the 10 advertisements from among a set of 30. The recognition test at this point was given to establish level of performance at the end of original learning, which is a very desirable procedure. Interpolated learning was the same except that a different set of advertisements was used. Following interpolated learning, a recognition test for the originally learned items was given. A control group received the same treatment except that the period of interpolated learning was spent in a neutral activity of counting the number of times the digit 5 appeared on a sheet of random numbers. The second experiment was essentially a replication of the first, and the third experiment was the same design except that nonsense syllables were used.

McKinney found that neither of the first two experiments revealed significant RI. In the first experiment the control group at the retention test correctly recognized 83.9 percent of the stimuli that it had correct at the end of original learning, and the experimental group recognized 81.1 percent. In the second experiment the control group was 100 percent correct and the experimental group 93.1 percent correct. The results of the third experiment were more heartening for a demonstration of RI. The control group correctly recognized 90.6 percent, but the experimental group had only 77.4 percent correct. McKinney's findings are hardly strong evidence for RI when the recognition method is used, but they represent a worthwhile beginning.

Postman (1952) compared recognition and recall in an RI design. Discussion here will be limited to two experimental groups and their respective control groups from a larger study which Postman reported. One experimental group and its control used recall, and another experimental group and its control used the recognition method. Original learning for all four groups was four presentations of a list of 24 nonsense syllables. The syllables were presented at a 2-second rate, and the subjects were instructed to study and learn them. Immediately after original learning, level of performance was tested as a means of assessing the equivalence of an experimental group and its respective control. The recall group and its control were given a free recall test in which they were required to write down as many of the syllables as they could. The recognition group and its control were given a multiple-choice test of items with four syllables each, one of which was in the original series. Interpolated learning followed the same procedure, with the experimental groups given a second list of nonsense syllables and the control groups resting. In the retention test the recall group and its control again had a free recall test of the original list, and the recognition group and its control had the multiple-choice test. Postman's results showed the recall group and its control to be about equivalent at the end of original learning, with a mean recall of 8.6 and 8.0, respectively. In the retention test, however, the control group had very high retention with a mean of 7.4, but the recall group showed RI with a lower mean of only 6.3—a difference that was statistically significant. Recognition was superior to recall. At the end of original learning the recognition group had a mean of 21.6 items correct. Its control had 21.5. At the retention test the recognition group had a mean of 19.4, and its control had 21.0—a significant difference that indicated RI for recognition also. The RI for recognition was small, however, as McKinney found.

Any recognition experiment (e.g., Shepard & Teghtsoonian, 1963; Shepard, 1967) is intrinsically an RI design because

other stimulus events usually intervene between the original presentation of a stimulus and its later recognition test. By proper
experimental design, different numbers of events can be made to
intervene, and the experiment becomes essentially one of amount
of interpolated learning. Shepard and Chang (1963, Figure 2,
p. 97, Experiment III), found that recognition for three-digit
numbers was perfect when there were no intervening items, but
that it dropped to about 60 percent with 12 intervening items.
Intervening events are not always so devastating in a recognition
experiment of this general kind. As discussed earlier in this chapter, Shepard (1967) gave hundreds of words, sentences, and
pictures in a series for study and followed the presentation with
an immediate recognition test for a sample of them. Sentences
showed the lowest recognition level with 88.2 percent correct. Words were next with 90 percent, and pictures were
98.5. There may be RI operating in these experiments, but it
certainly is not a very significant amount considering the hundreds of stimuli intervening between the study opportunity for
an item and its recognition test. There are obvious differences
between this experiment of Shepard and that of Shepard and
Chang which had a substantial decrement in recognition due to
intervening items. Shepard and Chang intermingled learning and
recognition testing, but Shepard presented continuous study opportunities for the hundreds of stimuli, followed by recognition
tests. And Shepard and Chang used numbers which might be
more interfering than the words, sentences, and pictures that
Shepard used. These differences will be clarified someday, but
it is interesting to see that an experiment like Shepard's with an
apparently high potential for RI actually exhibits so little of it.
The RI-recognition experiments of more conventional format by
McKinney (1935) and Postman (1952) also show little RI. These
conventional RI-recognition experiments, incidentally, in using

control groups and in assessing performance level after original and interpolated learning, are of better design for the study of interference than a standard recognition experiment like Shepard and Chang's (1963) which has RI (and PI, too) as an incidental outcome. Equal and sufficient learning is unrealistically assumed for all items, and control groups are lacking as a baseline for soundly computing interference decrements. For these reasons, the standard recognition experiment is probably not the best way to study interference, although interference is undoubtedly operating in it.

Interference and Number of Alternatives. Earlier it was discussed that retention measured by the recognition method was a decreasing function of number of alternatives in the test, and there is a suggestion that this may be an interference effect. Postman (1950) and Davis, Sutherland, and Judd (1961) have held this view, and aspects of Peixotto's findings (1947) tend to support it. She used a test booklet in which each of the first three pages had 10 criterion nonsense syllables. One minute was allowed for the study of each page. The fourth page was the recognition test, and on it were 120 nonsense syllables arranged in five columns of 24 items each. Each column had six of the criterion syllables assigned randomly to it. The subject's task was the usual one of selecting the criterion syllables from among the others. The learn and test procedure was repeated for five days, using a different set of syllables each day. Of interest was a within-session decrement as a function of column in the recognition test. Each day there was a steady decline in correct recognition from the first to the fifth column. This decrement could be interpreted as an RI effect within a session, because the later a criterion item appeared on the test page, the greater the number of items that intervened between the original learning of an item and its test.

THEORIES OF RECOGNITION

The research on recognition and memory is not impressive, and it lacks the direction that research on recall shows in which basic questions like interference versus trace decay, and whether or not STM-LTM compartments are implied by the data, are explored continually. That most of the preceding eight chapters were given over to recall is indicative of the imbalance that exists.

Recognition, frankly, does not seem to be getting anywhere conceptually. Perhaps a reason is the popular hypothesis that recognition and recall are indicants of the same underlying memory state (e.g., Postman, Jenkins, & Postman, 1948; Bahrick, 1965), with recognition being the more sensitive measure and having a higher performance level than recall because it has a lower threshold. On the assumption that recall and recognition mirror the same memory state, investigators might have thought that the measure of retention does not make much difference and, feeling a freedom of choice, tended strongly toward recall. This hypothesis (and that is all it is) may be true, and recognition and recall may indeed be sides of the same memory state. On the other hand, the hypothesis may be false. No one has ever seriously challenged the hypothesis empirically, which is surprising because a decision about it lies at the very center of our understanding about the laws of memory. If the hypothesis is false, and different mechanisms are required for recall and recognition, our scientific picture of memory is complicated with two basic habit mechanisms. The implications are quite different from STM and LTM, which are two stages of a single trace. Rather, two habit mechanisms mean two fundamentally different traces, each perhaps having an STM and LTM compartment. The issue is expressed here as two hypotheses for recognition. One will be called the "memory trace hypothesis" because it is the same memory trace that was defined as the determinant of recall in Chapter 2. With respect to recognition, it holds that recognition and recall are products of the same underlying memory trace. The other is the "perceptual trace hypothesis" which contends that recognition of stimuli is based on an S perceptual trace from the environmental stimulus. In not explaining recall, it implies that memory trace as a separate state is required for recall.

The S perceptual trace is specifically designated with the S for environmental stimulus to distinguish it from the R perceptual trace from response-produced stimuli and the SR perceptual trace from joint actions of environmental and response-produced stimuli. Only the S perceptual trace is of interest in this chapter on the recognition of environmental stimuli. Chapter 10 will define a theoretical place for R and SR perceptual traces.

Memory Trace Hypothesis

The memory trace hypothesis says that the same memory trace is the basis for both recall and recognition and, furthermore, that recognition is the more sensitive of the two indicants. It is a point of view that has arisen from research by psychologists who are interested in learning (e.g., Postman, Jenkins, & Postman, 1948; Bahrick, 1965), and it reflects a desire for parsimony. Parsimony, however, may be empirically unjustified—it is a goal to be attained through research, if the goal exists at all.

The hypothesis of a memory trace with dual function comes from two types of experiments. One is the experiment in which a recognition test shows a higher level of retention than recall (e.g., Postman & Rau, 1957). The other is one in which recall and recognition are administered successively in the retention test. When recognition follows recall, performance is higher and many responses become correct which were missed in recall

(Postman, Jenkins, & Postman, 1948; Brown, 1965). The recognition measure produces a high performance measure in both cases because it is more sensitive, according to the hypothesis.

Perceptual Trace Hypothesis

A basic premise of the perceptual trace hypothesis is that exposure to an environmental stimulus establishes an *S* perceptual trace of some stability. Noble's concept of familiarity (1953, 1954, 1963) as a stimulus attribute whose strength was defined by frequency of stimulus occurrences and independent of responses learned to the stimulus, can be taken as a statement of *S* perceptual trace, although Noble never called it that. As far as memory is concerned, the *S* perceptual trace is reactivated by the original stimulus at the recognition test and causes the subject to identify it as old. A capability for recalling a response associated with the stimulus need not be present for the identification response to occur, although it may be in some cases. If so, the recall of the response is assumed to be based on a different memory state which is being called the "memory trace."

Particularly in the early literature, the *S* perceptual trace was called an "image." This label has the connotation of a conscious, recognizable event that can be seen by the introspective mind turned inward upon itself (so to speak). The connotation of consciousness is unfortunate because "image," in this narrow sense, is not a necessary implication of the *S* perceptual trace. As a general concept the *S* perceptual trace can be considered a stimulus representation of unknown accuracy, either "conscious" or "unconscious."

The notion of the image, or *S* perceptual trace, goes back to antiquity (Gomulicki, 1953), and has assumed many forms over the centuries. Woods (1915), writing at a time when introspectionist psychology still had currency, listed many of the theories of recognition of her day, and the image played a central role in a number of them. By 1932 Bartlett saw recognition theories reduced to four main ones, of which the image played a part in two (Bartlett, 1932, pp. 191–192). The other two theories dealt with feelings of "familiarity" and "knowledge" that induced the recognition of an old stimulus. The image is far from an old-fashioned idea, however. Very recent articles and books have made use of the image or something very similar to it (e.g., Clark, 1965; Holt, 1964; Teghtsoonian, 1965; Mowrer, 1960, pp. 164–175; Sheffield, 1961). Mowrer gives an image the status of a conditioned sensation (a kind of perceptual habit) which is strengthened by a reinforcement process whose defining operations are unknown as yet. For Mowrer the impingement of any stimulus, either of internal or external origin, can result in a learned internal representation. The image from an impressionable visual scene could be conscious in which case the subject reports that he "sees" it, or it could be unconscious like the proprioceptive stimulation from a leg movement. Images, according to Mowrer, can occur in any sense modality (Mowrer, 1960, p. 174). In calling an image a conditioned sensation, Mowrer is giving his hypothesis the ring of learning theory, but the hypothesis has about the same heuristic value as corresponding ideas from perception.

Sheffield (1961) holds a learning-theory position very similar to Mowrer's. He also believes that sensations can be conditioned, although he calls the learned product "sensory responses." He says:

> An important assumption is that of the existence of sensory responses which are completely central in locus and which need not have any motor components. Such sensory responses are assumed to be subject to the learning principle of association by contiguity and are assumed to have cue properties as well as response properties. That is, a sensory response can not only be

connected to a cue, but also is a cue to which other responses can be connected (Sheffield, 1961, p. 14).

Critique of Memory and Perceptual Trace Hypotheses

That recall and recognition are based on a common memory trace, but that recognition has a lower threshold and is more sensitive, is a hypothesis with little to support it today even though it could conceivably be true. The hypothesis is based on the premise that more items will be recognized than recalled, but this is not always true. There remains the uncomfortable fact that recognition is not so superior to recall when the number of alternatives in the recognition test is large or the discriminability of alternatives is low (Davis, Sutherland, & Judd, 1961; Bahrick & Bahrick, 1964; Bruce & Cofer, 1965). About the only discriminating research idea in the hypothesis, which is untested, is that items which can be recognized but not recalled have less associative strength than items which can be both recognized and recalled. Recognition, being more sensitive according to the hypothesis, should reflect a lower level of associative strength. A prediction is that a recognition test should show more forgetting for verbal items that are recognized but not recalled at the final stage of original learning than for items which are both recalled and recognized in original learning. Of course, any demonstration that items can be recalled but not recognized would throw the hypothesis out because the least sensitive measure would be showing the most sensitivity.

A factor that seems behind the memory-trace hypothesis is that the experiments on which it was based used verbal materials that permitted both recall and recognition responses at the retention test. It is easy to see how one might assume that the same memory state lies behind both response modes. Yet the occurrence of both modes hardly proves one memory state. An

S perceptual trace as a basis for recognition can be formed when the word is sensed during learning, and a reinforced response can be the basis of the memory trace and a recall potential, making it reasonable to assume that two traces are formed rather than one. Because investigators of recognition continue to use experimental materials like words, in which the strong likelihood of S perceptual and memory traces coexisting is always present, we lack the means of discriminating the theoretical issue of one versus two memory states. Perception psychologists have been closer to situations in which only the S perceptual trace is laid down, although they too have had confounded situations in which S perceptual and memory traces are formed concurrently. The seemingly meaningless forms and shapes that are often their stimuli might uncritically be considered nonverbal and be taken as the basis for a pure S perceptual trace. This assumption is false in many cases. The human being has the ubiquitous capability for attaching verbal symbols to stimuli that impinge on him. A subject might be shown a seemingly meaningless shape in a recognition experiment and, if asked, might say that it reminds him of a soaring eagle. The recall of these responses can be a variable for recognition, presumably because the responses are recognized when they occur (see Chapter 10) and the subject then identifies the stimuli that elicited them. Verbal responses such as these are in the subject's covert verbal environment, and their intervention between the stimulus and the identification response in the recognition test gives them the status of mediators. Verbal mediators in a laboratory experiment of shape recognition can be from the natural language (NLMs) and represent transfer from general learning outside the laboratory (Vanderplas & Garvin, 1959), or they can be deliberately taught in the laboratory (e.g., Ellis, 1965, Ch. 6; Ellis & Muller, 1964) as responses to stimuli which later occur in the recognition test. The laboratory learning of verbal mediators has flown under the banner of stimulus predifferentiation or verbal pretraining (e.g., Miller & Dollard, 1941; Arnoult, 1957). Among these experiments one must distinguish between studies which ask how verbal mediators influence stimulus recognition and those which inquire if verbal mediators for stimuli affect motor behavior (e.g., McAllister, 1953; Goss, 1955). Stimulus recognition and mediation are the only interest here.

Thus, perception psychology, with its focus on recognition, can have the same difficulty as learning psychology, with its emphasis on recall, in deciding the theoretical issue of one versus two traces. Too often the recognition act for shapes and forms has the recall of a verbal response present and has a recall and recognition potential present just as words do, and either one or two traces can explain the findings. Nevertheless, form and shape stimuli offer more hope than word stimuli for clarifying this issue because their level of verbal mediation can be controlled. By having the verbal encoding absent, it should be possible in shape identification experiments to observe recognition solely as a function of the S perceptual trace.

Both Deese (1956) and Clark (1965) document verbal encoding of the "nonsense" (no apparent likeness to shapes of the real world) shapes which they used in their recognition experiments, but they also found recognition when verbal encoding was essentially absent. Both found very high recognition with low verbal encoding (Deese, 1956, Figure 2; Clark, 1965, Table 4), and it is reasonable to infer that much of this high recognition was in the absence of memory traces and the recall of verbal mediators; it represents recognition based on a pure S perceptual trace, or an "uncoded image," as Clark called it (p. 594). On preliminary evidence like this, a pure S perceptual trace can be reasonably assumed to explain recognition in which memory traces and a capability for response recall are missing. Subjectively it would certainly seem that one could be exposed to a stimulus without ever learning a response to it, learn only an S perceptual trace, and have a capability for recognizing it with no recall of responses whatsoever. We are all familiar with the recognition of faces and scenes where there is no apparent recall of verbal responses that accompanies the act of recognition. Embarrassment will be created for the memory trace hypothesis to the extent that we get at situations of this kind experimentally because they are evidence for a memory state that exists in the absence of a recall capability.

CONCLUSIONS

Neither the memory nor the perceptual trace hypothesis alone can bear the weight of recognition facts. There is enough preliminary empirical evidence to indicate the existence of two traces, and this is opting for two kinds of habit—a perceptual trace that grants the power of recognition and a memory trace that governs recall by being the associative agent that fires the response when its stimulus is presented. And both traces operate in recognition when the stimuli have verbal mediators.

Although issues about recall and recognition have orbited around memory, it is interesting to see that one learning theorist (who is more interested in conditions of habit formation than of habit retention) is alert to the possibility that recall and recognition can abide by different laws. Estes (1960, Footnote, pp. 220–221) says that his all-or-none hypothesis (learning can occur in one trial) must be tested separately for recognition and recall, and there is no necessity for findings on recall to bear on recognition. Later, Estes (1964, pp. 23–24) stated the suggestion again in response to criticisms from Postman (1963, p. 300). Postman said that a dual-habit conception lacks parsimony and would greatly complicate learning theory. Estes (1964, p. 24) returned the controversy to the empirical arena when he observed that lack of parsimony may be inherent in the organism and implied that research, not debate, will resolve the matter. Our understanding would be accelerated if both learning and memory theorists attempted to solve this problem.

Suppose the final decision is that S perceptual and memory traces are both needed for learning and memory theory. Each would be subject to its own laws of interference, and we cannot test the interference theory of forgetting very well until we work out these laws. Memory traces for recalled verbal responses would presumably follow the laws of interference in Chapter 4, for example. The S perceptual traces, on the other hand, may follow quite different laws (the PI-RI research on recognition is too scanty to say this with confidence). And when we are dealing with the commonplace case of stimuli with verbal mediators attached, we are obliged to consider the action of both sets of interference laws. Learning and memory theory will not be the only beneficiaries of research on these topics. Applied psychology stands to gain also. Psychometricians may come to better understand the behavior found in multiple-choice tests (recognition) and essay examinations (recall). The independent paths of experimental and differential psychology have existed too long (e.g., Cronbach, 1957).

REFERENCES

Achilles, Edith M. Experimental studies in recall and recognition. *Arch. Psychol.*, 1920, **6** (44), 1–80.

Arnoult, M. D. Familiarity and recognition of nonsense shapes. *J. exp. Psychol.*, 1956, **51**, 269–276.

Arnoult, M. D. Stimulus predifferentiation: Some generalizations and hypotheses. *Psychol. Bull.*, 1957, **54**, 339–350.

Bahrick, H. P. The ebb of retention. *Psychol. Rev.*, 1965, **72**, 60–73.

Bahrick, H. P., & Bahrick, Phyllis O. A re-examination of the inter-relations among measures of retention. *Quart. J. exp. Psychol.*, 1964, **16**, 318–324.

Ballard, P. B. Obliviscence and reminiscence. *Brit. J. Psychol. monogr. Suppl.*, 1913, **1**, No. 2.

Bartlett, F. C. *Remembering: A study in experimental and social psychology.* London: Cambridge Univer. Press, 1932.

Brown, J. A comparison of recognition and recall by a multiple-response method. *J. verbal Learn. verbal Behav.*, 1965, **4**, 401–408.

Bruce, D., & Cofer, C. N. A comparison of recognition and recall in short-term memory. *Proc. 73rd Annu. Conv. Amer. Psychol. Ass.*, 1965. Pp. 81–82.

Clark, H. J. Recognition memory for random shapes as a function of complexity, association value, and delay. *J. exp. Psychol.*, 1965, **69**, 590–595.

Cronbach, L. J. The two disciplines of scientific psychology. *Amer. Psychologist*, 1957, **12**, 671–684.

Davis, R., Sutherland, N. S., & Judd, B. R. Information content in recognition and recall. *J. exp. Psychol.*, 1961, **61**, 422–429.

Deese, J. Complexity of contour in the recognition of visual form. *USAF Wright Air Development Center Tech. Rep.* 56–60, Dayton, Ohio, February, 1956.

Ebbinghaus, H. *Memory: A contribution to experimental psychology.* (Trans. by Ruger & Bussenius.) New York: Teachers College Press, 1913.

Egan, J. P. Recognition memory and the operating characteristic. *USAF CRC tech. Note* AFCRC-TN-58-51, Washington, June 15, 1958.

Ellis, H. *The transfer of learning.* New York: Macmillan, 1965.

Ellis, H. C., & Muller, D. G. Transfer in perceptual learning following stimulus predifferentiation. *J. exp. Psychol.*, 1964, **68**, 388–395.

Estes, W. K. Learning theory and the new "mental chemistry." *Psychol. Rev.*, 1960, **67**, 207–223.

Estes, W. K. All-or-none processes in learning and retention. *Amer. Psychologist*, 1964, **19**, 16–25.

Gibson, J. J. Retroaction and method of recognition. *J. gen. Psychol.*, 1934, **10**, 234–236.

Gomulicki, B. R. The development and present status of the trace theory of memory. *Brit. J. Psychol. monogr. Suppl.*, 1953, No. 29.

Gorman, A. M. Recognition memory for nouns as a function of abstractness and frequency. *J. exp. Psychol.*, 1961, **61**, 23–29.

Goss, A. E. A stimulus-response analysis of the interaction of cue-producing and instrumental responses. *Psychol. Rev.*, 1955, **62**, 20–31.

Greenberg, Ruth, & Underwood, B. J. Retention as a function of stage of practice. *J. exp. Psychol.*, 1950, **40**, 452-457.

Holt, R. R. Imagery: The return of the ostracized. *Amer. Psychologist*, 1964, **19**, 254–264.

Luh, C. W. The conditions of retention. *Psychol. Monogr.*, 1922, **31**, (Whole No. 142).

McAllister, Dorothy E. The effects of various kinds of relevant verbal pre-training on subsequent motor performance. *J. exp. Psychol.*, 1953, **46**, 329–336.

MacDougall, R. Recognition and recall. *J. Phil.*, 1904, **11**, 229–233.

McKinney, F. Retroactive inhibition and recognition memory. *J. exp. Psychol.*, 1935, **18**, 585–598.

Miller, N. E., & Dollard, J. *Social learning and imitation.* New Haven: Yale Univer. Press, 1941.

Mowrer, O. H. *Learning theory and the symbolic processes.* New York: Wiley, 1960.

Murdock, B. B., Jr. Signal-detection theory and short-term memory. *J. exp. Psychol.*, 1965, **70**, 443–447.

Myers, G. C. A comparative study of recognition and recall. *Psychol. Rev.*, 1914, **21**, 442–456.

Noble, C. E. An analysis of meaning. *Psychol. Rev.*, 1952, **59**, 421–430.

Noble, C. E. The meaning-familiarity relationship. *Psychol. Rev.*, 1953, **60**, 89–98.

Noble, C. E. The familiarity-frequency relationship. *J. exp. Psychol.*, 1954, **47**, 13–16.

Noble, C. E. Meaningfulness and familiarity. In C. N. Cofer & Barbara S. Musgrave (Eds.), *Verbal behavior and learning.* New York: McGraw-Hill, 1963. Pp. 76–119.

Peixotto, Helen E. Proactive inhibition in the recognition of nonsense syllables. *J. exp. Psychol.*, 1947, **37**, 81–91.

Postman, L. Choice behavior and the process of recognition. *Amer. J. Psychol.*, 1950, **63**, 576–583.

Postman, L. Retroactive inhibition in recall and recognition. *J. exp. Psychol.*, 1952, **44**, 165–169.

Postman, L. One trial learning. In C. N. Cofer & Barbara S. Musgrave (Eds.), *Verbal behavior and learning.* New York: McGraw-Hill, 1963. Pp. 295–321.

Postman, L., Jenkins, W. O., & Postman, Dorothy L. An experimental comparison of active recall and recognition. *Amer. J. Psychol.*, 1948, **61**, 511–519.

Postman, L., & Rau, Lucy. Retention as a function of the method of measurement. *Univer. of California Publ. Psychol.*, Berkeley, 1957, **8**, 217–270.

Riley, D. A., & Phillips, L. W. The effects of syllable familiarization on rote learning association value, and reminiscence. *J. exp. Psychol.*, 1959, **57**, 372–379.

Schulz, R. W., & Thysell, R. The effect of familiarization on meaningfulness. *J. verbal Learn. verbal Behav.*, 1965, **4**, 409–413.

Sheffield, F. D. Theoretical considerations in the learning of complex sequential tasks from demonstration and practice. In A. A. Lumsdaine (Ed.), *Student response in programmed instruction.* Washington: National Academy of Sciences–National Research Council. Publication 943, 1961. Pp. 13–32.

Shepard, R. N. Recognition memory for words, sentences, and pictures. *J. verbal Learn. verbal Behav.*, 1967, **6**, 156–163.

Shepard, R. N., & Chang, J. Forced-choice tests of recognition memory under steady-state conditions. *J. verbal Learn. verbal Behav.*, 1963, **2**, 93–101.

Shepard, R. N., & Teghtsoonian, Martha. Retention of information under conditions approaching a steady state. *J. exp. Psychol.*, 1961, **62**, 302–309.

Strong, E. K., Jr. The effect of length of series upon recognition memory. *Psychol. Rev.*, 1912, **19**, 447–462.

Strong, E. K., Jr. The effect of time interval upon recognition memory. *Psychol. Rev.*, 1913, **20**, 339–372.

Swets, J. A. (Ed.) *Signal detection and recognition by human observers.* New York: Wiley, 1964.

Teghtsoonian, R. The influence of number of alternatives on learning and performance in a recognition task. *Canad. J. Psychol.*, 1965, **19**, 31–41.

Thorndike, E. L., & Lorge, I. *The teacher's word book of 30,000 words.* New York: Teachers College Press, 1944.

Underwood, B. J. Interference and forgetting. *Psychol. Rev.*, 1957, **64**, 49–60.

Vanderplas, J. M., & Garvin, E. A. The association value of random shapes. *J. exp. Psychol.*, 1959, **57**, 147–154.

Woods, Elizabeth L. An experimental analysis of the process of recognizing. *Amer. J. Psychol.*, 1915, **26**, 313–387.

Some Theory and Concluding Remarks 10

The examination of the experimental literature on human memory is finished, and it is time to sum up. There are endless unanswered questions, but this is the state of things, and a dynamic scientific scene will always have gaps. For psychology, a young science, the gaps are frequent, but the frequency is less important than deciding which gaps to attack first. There are priority problems whose answers might carry us a bit farther than other problems, although certainly the order of priorities is controversial. What clearly has low priority and is not controversial are low-order empirical laws which will be answered by the steady effort of laboratory investigators in the normal course of their work—effects on retention of amount and type of material, length of the retention interval, amount of practice, individual differences, and so forth. This chapter will not deal with routine but necessary laws such as these that will be found with enough time and effort. Instead, this chapter will express a conviction about priority questions whose answers might better define fundamental matters on which other research must stand.

The discussion will be limited mainly to the verbal recall paradigm, without intending to diminish the significance of motor recall or perceptual learning for stimulus recognition. Verbal recall, as a charted region in the psychology of learning, contains the substance for critical remarks.

A REVISED CONCEPTION OF VERBAL LEARNING

For the most part, investigators of memory have taken a broad, uncritical view of *habit formation* and have centered their concern on *habit changes* over the retention interval. Considerable scientific distance can be traveled with this emphasis, but it seems likely that the theory of habit formation is tied conceptually to the changes in habit that we call forgetting. By thinking

more about learning we might better understand forgetting. This
section outlines a feedback theory of verbal learning that combines the memory trace, or the conventional notion of habit which
bonds stimulus and response, with the perceptual trace from response-produced stimuli.

The Conventional Model for Verbal Recall

The term "model" will be used in a loose fashion, and not in the
sense of a mathematical model of learning. The schema discussed
in this section is called the "recall model" because recall is its
only emphasis, and it will be distinguished from a feedback
model that uses recognition and recall.

The model that is most common in the phychology of learning had its strong beginnings in animal-operant situations. In
this conventional model a response must be learned to a stimulus
so that when the stimulus is presented, the response will occur.
The stimulus may have responses of varying strength attached to
it from preexperimental learning, and the new response to be
learned may or may not be one of them. Learning occurs as the
experimental situation reinforces the subject by informing him
of the correctness of his response on a trial. The result of reinforcement is an increment of habit, or memory trace as we have
been calling it. Moreover, withdrawal of reinforcement results in
the performance decline that is called "experimental extinction."
The exact conditions under which habit is formed, and the specific nature of reinforcing operations, are an eminent mystery
for experimental psychology and the cause for one of our most
distinguished theoretical controversies. There have been theories
of habit formation, and many experimental tests of them, but
none are scientifically secure. The result is our pragmatic, contemporary position of *empirical reinforcement*. The position of
empirical reinforcement says that there are verifiable empirical

operations which can reasonably be presumed to determine habit strength and that these are discovered through empirical investigation. An empirical hunting exercise for reinforcers should be contrasted to a sound theory of habit formation which would allow the *prediction* of operations that result in an increment of habit strength. Empirical reinforcement requires systematic observation to determine, for example, that a rat will learn to press a bar for food pellets but not rocks. It is in this pragmatic way that reinforcement has been used throughout this book, and it has become a convention in experimental psychology to use the term reinforcement in this way.

Reinforcement operations at the human level are often called "knowledge of results." Knowledge of results is customarily expressed as a function of response error in achieving the defined goal of the task. In verbal paired-associates learning by the anticipation method, the stimulus member of the word pair is presented, and the subject attempts to recall the response. After his response, or failure to respond, the subject is shown the correct response by the apparatus (e.g., memory drum); and the discrepancy between the correct response and the response he made, or failed to make, is his knowledge of results. Repeated application of knowledge of results over the series of practice trials results in increased probability of correct responding when the stimulus member alone is presented, and formation of habit strength for the pair is assumed. For a motor tracking task like the Rotary Pursuit Test, in which the subject attempts to keep a hand-held stylus in contact with a rotating target, the visual indication of moment-to-moment discrepancy between stylus tip and target is continuous knowledge of results about the adequacy of his movements. Repeated practice trials increase proficiency in the continuous following response that the task demands. Students who wish to read more thoroughly on the topic of knowledge of results for human learning should see Thorndike (1931),

Postman (1947), Bilodeau (1966), and Adams (1964, 1968). For more theoretically oriented discussions of habit and its definitions, see Spence (1951, 1956) and Kimble (1961).

Empirical reinforcement defines the way that a memory trace is formed between a stimulus and a response, but the conventional model presents further considerations for how reinforcement induces the reliable occurrence of a response. The principal consideration is the *habit family hierarchy* which assumes that at the start of learning there usually are a number of responses associated with the stimulus from past learning and that each of these responses has its own habit strength. The response which the experimenter wants associated with the stimulus may or may not be a member of the hierarchy, but it is the only response reinforced. Those responses in the hierarchy whose initial habit strengths are greater than the correct response will occur as errors. They are never reinforced and undergo weakening through experimental extinction, while the correct response is always reinforced and strengthened. Eventually the correct response becomes dominant in the hierarchy and occurs with increasing reliability from then on. Consider as an example the paired-associate learning by the anticipation method of the word pair DOG-RAT. Assume that through past experience the three strongest associates in the language for the stimulus term DOG are CAT, BARK, and FUR. By the anticipation method the stimulus occurs, and the subject must give the response before the correct response is shown as knowledge of results, usually 2 seconds later. In the early trials, CAT, BARK, and FUR occur as errors because they are the strongest responses associated with DOG, but they are never reinforced and eventually undergo experimental extinction. However, RAT is always reinforced and steadily builds habit strength. Eventually RAT becomes stronger than CAT, BARK, and FUR, dominates the hierarchy, and occurs with regularity thereafter.

There is nothing wholly wrong with the conventional model of verbal recall. Predictions can be based on it, but the questions for psychology are whether the predictions are accurate enough and whether behavioral phenomena exist which cannot be deduced from the model. Accepting the limitations of empirical reinforcement as a pragmatic definition of habit, it is the contention that the recall model fails in explaining important behavioral phenomena and needs revision. There is little in the way of systematic documentation for the areas of failure, but here are three of them and certainly there are more. The absence of documentation is less a fault than it seems because most of the phenomena are commonplace and well known.

1. Omission behavior. The failure of the correct response to occur when its stimulus is presented does not sound like a problem for the conventional model, and at one level of analysis it is not. Response failure can be a matter of inadequate habit strength, assuming all else, like motivation, is equal. Unquestionably, inadequate habit strength is a major variable for omitted responses, but is it a sufficient variable for the phenomenon? Is it not reasonable to assume that some of the subjects some of the time have a response available and on the verge of occurrence but withhold it because they are not sure of its correctness? Subjects report that they sometimes withhold responses at recall for various reasons, and this is why they are often encouraged by permissive instructions to be relaxed in their response criterion and guess so that a number of otherwise inhibited responses will occur for observation and measurement. That instructions can tease out some of the inhibited responses is of less interest than how subjects "know" about the correctness or incorrectness of a response and can act on the basis of this knowledge.

2. Error-rejection behavior. A common occurrence in paired-associate learning by the anticipation method is response correction at the time the stimulus term is showing alone and before the response term appears. Suppose the word pair is DOG-CUP. When DOG is displayed alone, and the subject is supposed to respond with the word CUP, he might say, "CAT. No! I mean CUP!" The subject makes an overt error and quickly corrects it, although conceivably he could come up with another error. Here, in this example, the subject could get credit for his correct response if he gave it in time, but the occurrence of a correct response on time hardly does justice to the actual complexity of the behavior. Error rejection is common in everyday life. We all recognize errors in our everyday speech—wrong words, mispronounced words, etc.—and correct them without any external knowledge of results to inform us what the correct response should have been. In the absence of external information, how does a subject recognize that a response is wrong and deserving of correction? The conventional recall model would say that an error cannot be replaced quickly by the correct response in the absence of a reinforcer. According to the habit family hierarchy notion, the error CAT must be followed by the seeing of CUP as knowledge of results, and the seeing of the error would produce some extinction of it. On the *next* trial CUP would have a chance of replacing CAT, but the model is not equipped for explaining immediate recognition of error and its correction.

Tip-of-the-tongue behavior (Brown & McNeill, 1966) is also of this general type, except that the subject will often run through several responses similar to the correct one before actually making the correct response. As the subject runs through a series of similar responses, he has the clear feeling that he knows the correct response, has it on the tip of his tongue, and can give it in just a moment. Moreover, the subject not only knows he is in error and must reject wrong responses, but also knows the relative magnitude of the errors. For example, a subject might be asked to give the capital of the state of Illinois. He might say, "The capital of Illinois is Bloomington. No, that's wrong! Plainfield! No, that isn't it either! Summerfield! That's close! Spring-field! That's it!" The subject certainly seems to know that his first response is a relatively large error and should be summarily rejected, that the second response has smaller error and is in the general region of the correct response, that the third response is very close to being correct, and so on. Through a kind of free association, the subject runs through a repertoire of similar re-sponses until he hits the correct one or until the repertoire ex-hausts itself. How does the subject know the approximate amount of error and discern the closeness of a wrong response to the correct one? How does he know the correct response when it occurs and when to stop the association train? The conven-tional model lacks mechanisms to account for this kind of be-havior.

3. *"The feeling of knowing."* Hart (1965) has devised a clever series of experiments. Depending upon the experiment, Hart presented subjects a list of questions or verbal paired asso-ciates and then gave a recall test. After recall, he asked them to judge whether they had a *feeling* of knowing the missed items and mark an answer sheet YES or NO. A recognition test followed, in which the correct answer for an item was among four alterna-tives of a test question, and Hart found that the subjects' "feeling of knowing" had good accuracy in predicting success on the rec-ognition test. How does a subject know his capability for a cor-rect response and then prove this capability on a recognition test?

Feedback and Response Recognition at Recall

The conventional model of recall is inadequate for the phe-nomena which have just been described, and the inadequacy is an absence of a mechanism for *response recognition*. Just as stim-ulus recognition is the capability for deciding whether a stimulus has or has not been experienced before, response recognition is the capability for deciding whether a response had been made before. In passing, Chapter 2 observed that stimulus recognition has received all the attention and response recognition has been bypassed. Chapter 9 discussed the history of perception psychology, its concern with how we perceive the stimuli of our world, and how emphasis rests on recognition of the complex shapes that impinge on our dominant visual modality. Given this understandable frame of reference, there was no need for response recognition. And the emphasis of the psychology of learning came to dwell on the recall paradigm, the strength of habit connections, and whether or not they were sufficient to activate responses. Response recognition was not needed here either. Yet when we look at the three categories of failures for the conventional recall model, we see need for a mechanism whereby subjects can know about the correctness of the response and use this knowledge as a basis for action. Postman (1963, p. 47) has also recognized this need.

Response recognition will be assumed to rely on the same mechanisms as nonmediated stimulus recognition (Chapter 9). For stimulus recognition the stimulus trace of an environmental stimulus lays down a perceptual trace, called S perceptual trace, and subsequent appearance of the stimulus on the retention test activates the perceptual trace and results in identification of the stimulus. Similarly, response recognition will assume that each response occurrence has a response-produced stimulus trace which imprints a perceptual trace, hereafter called R perceptual trace. A response will be identified as having occurred before if its stimulus trace aftereffects match the perceptual trace. The R perceptual trace, a mechanism for response recognition, conforms to Mowrer's hypothesis (1960, pp. 164–175) that any stimulus, internal or external, produces a conditioned sensation, or image as he calls it. A function of the image is to act as a reference against which current behavior is compared and adjusted (Mowrer, 1960, p. 180), and Mowrer's point of view is accepted as fundamental and containing the essentials of an important idea.

The R perceptual trace provides a reference level against which to test a response. But the response must have an agent for its occurrence in the first place, and it is habit, or memory trace, which is the associative bond between stimulus and response. It is a two-factor feedback theory that is being espoused —a memory trace to fire the response whose stimulus trace is fed back and compared against another habit state, R perceptual trace. The discrepancy between a response-produced stimulus trace and R perceptual trace is the basis for accepting or rejecting the response. We know something about the empirical reinforcement conditions for the formation of memory trace, although hardly as much as we would like, but we know less about the conditions of R perceptual trace formation because response recognition has not been a topic of systematic study. If we assume the conditions of R perceptual trace formation for response recognition to be the same as S perceptual trace formation for stimulus recognition, Noble's operations for familiarity would seem to apply (e.g., Noble, 1963). The strength of the S perceptual trace, and thus familiarity and the power of recognition, is a positive function of frequency of stimulus exposure. Translated for R perceptual trace this means that occurrences of a response, with its response-produced stimuli each time, are the conditions of trace strengthening. Mere frequency may not be the sole contributor to strength of the R perceptual trace, although it would certainly seem to be a main contributor. The intensity of response-produced stimuli may be a variable for the trace's strength, as might be the number of sense modalities in the total response feedback. Another factor which affects the apparent rather than the absolute strength of the R perceptual trace is interaction among the multiple perceptual traces present from other responses in the situation. If the R perceptual traces of the several responses are similar and about equal in strength, their confusability is high and the subject may have trouble in reliably recognizing a response even though absolute strength of the R perceptual trace is high. In other words, the trace's relative strength is low because it is submerged in a background of similar traces, and its distinctiveness is obscured.

One other main assumption is that the subject can perceive the amount of discrepancy between the stimulus trace from the response and the perceptual traces against which it is compared. This awareness of error magnitude is the basis of the subject's confidence in his response as might be revealed in confidence ratings or a feeling of knowing, and this confidence reaction may be used as the basis for other responses. When the R perceptual trace for a response is strong, the response will be unequivocally accepted. But when an R perceptual trace is weak absolutely or relative to other similar traces, uncertainty arises. The subject may attempt another similar response, as in tip-of-the-tongue behavior, if he perceives the error to be small. However, if the error is large, a subject might not be impelled to try other responses because it would be risky to base further responses on it. Of course, some subjects may be willing to try further responses even though they have little confidence in the correctness of their behaving—they have a relaxed criterion and are willing to accept a measure of error. Those who would not venture a response in the presence of such doubt are the cautious among us with a strict criterion.

There is reason to believe that judgment of error magnitude occurs for stimulus recognition also, which is theoretically desirable if stimulus and response recognition are to be based on the same mechanisms. Gibson and Gibson (1955) presented meaningless shapes to their subjects and then administered a recognition test. Of particular interest were quasi-quantitative judgments that subjects verbalized in the recognition test about the differences between a new test item and a similar old one of the original set. The subjects made observations like "too thin" or "rounder" (pp. 38–39), just as an artist painting a portrait from memory will decide that the hair is too golden and should be changed. If this sort of recognition act is mediated, and the subject attaches descriptive verbal cues to the old stimulus, the perceptual traces of these earlier verbal responses are compared with current verbal responses aroused by the new item of the recognition test, and an estimate of error magnitude results. Effectively, mediated stimulus recognition reduces to the paradigm for recall and response recognition. On the other hand, if the recognition act is nonmediated, the mechanism of quantitative error judgment must lie solely in the discrepancy between stimulus traces of current stimuli and perceptual traces of previous stimuli.

Paired-associate Learning. It will be profitable to examine paired-associate learning for the feedback model with its memory and perceptual traces, rather than memory traces alone as is in the conventional model.

Response recognition is assumed to be based on the same mechanism as stimulus recognition, but an additional consideration is involved for verbal paired associates. In stimulus recognition the subject must indicate only whether he experienced the stimulus before, and theoretically this is achieved by a matching of stimulus trace and its S perceptual trace from prior experience. But in a stimulus-response situation like paired-associate learning, the subject must do more than merely recognize that the response has occurred before—he must also recognize that the response has occurred with a particular stimulus and is appropriate for it. There are undoubtedly many situations directly analogous to stimulus recognition in which the subject must say only whether or not he made the response before, and need rely only on R perceptual trace, but in paired-associate situations he must know that the response has occurred before *and* with a particular stimulus. The kind of mechanism that we are looking for requires the recognized appropriateness or inappropriateness of a response for its stimulus. It is necessary, therefore, to assume that more than the R perceptual trace of the response alone is involved, and that the R perceptual trace becomes enmeshed with the S perceptual trace to form a perceptual trace compound. It is this compound which will be called the "SR perceptual trace," and response recognition is based on it in paired-associate learning.

There are three possibilities for responses in a paired-associate list: (1) correct responses, (2) extralist errors in which responses from outside the list are given, and (3) intralist errors in which responses of the list are given to wrong stimuli. When a correct response occurs, we assume that the memory trace is strong enough to evoke the response and the SR perceptual trace is strong enough to be a good reference level for a positive verification. Extralist errors would have stored SR perceptual traces from preexperimental experiences with the same or similar stimuli, and are initially verified against relatively strong SR perceptual traces that are no longer appropriate. As the strength of the memory trace for the correct response grows through reinforcement, and the correct response occurs more frequently, the strength of the SR perceptual trace for the correct response grows also and begins to approach that of the SR perceptual trace for the wrong response that has been occurring. The SR perceptual traces have the traces of the environmental stimuli bonded to them; thus both the correct and wrong response for the same stimulus have some similarity of perceptual traces. Being somewhat similar, and with the strength difference between them lessening with practice, the subject finds it increasingly hard to accept the wrong response he has been making. Some subjects with conservative set may inhibit responses in the face of this uncertainty, and omissions rather than errors will occur, although liberally inclined subjects might continue errors for a while. Intralist errors occur for different reasons. Occurring as they do in the early trials, they would seem to arise from poor discrimination among SR perceptual traces of the list because the number of external reinforcements defining the correct responses and their SR perceptual traces has been few. The subject has the habit strength to make the response but not the SR perceptual-trace strength to determine its correctness for the stimulus. Here, too, some subjects with conservative set may inhibit responses. As trials progress, errors decrease, reinforcement increases the strength of correct responses and their SR perceptual traces, and correct responses are increasingly made, recognized, and accepted.

The dropping out of extralist errors is experimental extinction of them through nonreinforcement in the conventional model, but the feedback model implies an alternate interpretation. As the SR perceptual trace for the reinforced correct response becomes the dominant one bonded with the stimulus, the SR perceptual trace for the wrong response is overridden. As a result, a wrong response when it occurs fails in verification and is inhibited, and empirically this inhibitory effect is observed as experimental extinction. The memory trace that activates the response is not affected. The extinction is a function of the reference mechanism by which the response is tested and judged appropriate or inappropriate for the stimulus.

Closed Loop versus Open Loop.   A distinctive feature of response recognition is that it is a *feedback paradigm*. In a *closed-loop* model for an engineering system, the response of the system is fed back and compared with a *reference level* which defines the correct value for the system. If there is an error difference between the response and the reference level, the system undertakes an adjustive correction to lessen the error, compares the resultant response with the reference level again, adjusts again, and so on. The most common example is the automatic home furnace in which the reference level is the thermostat setting. For response recognition the SR perceptual trace built out of past occurrences of the response to the stimulus is the reference level, and stimulus traces of the current response are compared with it for error and a basis for further action (the action could be no response which, after all, is a response). In verbal learning the responses are discrete; therefore the continuously regulated furnace is a proper but approximate example. Contrast this feedback conception with the conventional habit family hierarchy-recall model, which is *open loop*. If there is sufficient habit strength when the stimulus occurs, the response occurs. Otherwise it does not. There is no feedback from the response for the self-regulation of ongoing behavior. An important thing about closed-loop behavior and built-in reference levels is that they represent a beginning toward understanding the continuous flow of responses, which is how behavior usually proceeds. The open-loop system abstracts a single response from among the many distributed in time and asks whether it occurs or not, but a closed-loop system accepts the feedback from a response and uses the information as a basis for the next element of the response sequence. Not all continuous adjustment comes from internal references. The Rotary Pursuit Test as a tracking task has the rotating target as an *external* reference level, and the discrepancy between the target and stylus tip is the error to be corrected by the next segment of the responding. Any tracking task will have an external reference level to define the correct response for the human operator

(Adams, 1961a, 1967), but internal reference levels from response-produced proprioceptive stimulation should be present
also to inform the subject of the correctness of his movements.
This chapter, however, primarily limits itself to verbal behavior.
Tracking research, for all its concern about feedback (Adams,
1961a), has actually had little to offer learning and recall.

Response Recognition and Failures of the Recall Model

Let us return to the failures that were listed for the recall model
for paired-associate learning and ask how response recognition
helps to explain them.

    Bypassing the obvious importance of deficient habit strength
as a variable for omission of responses, consider the case in
which responses are inhibited in a paired-associate paradigm.
We can assume that a covert response is made, the response-
produced stimulus trace seeks a match with an SR perceptual
trace and fails, and an inhibitory act follows. Uncertainty about
the correctness of a response would be expected when the perceptual trace is weak, either absolutely or relative to other similar traces, and a positive match cannot occur. In the face of such
uncertainty, the response is inhibited. The subject's self-induced
or instructional set to respond freely or conservatively would
seem a variable here, as was noted before. If his set were relaxed,
the subject would probably not inhibit the error but would say
it aloud and, upon identifying it when the response-produced
stimulus feedback was tested against the SR perceptual trace,
would reject it and perhaps try another response. An example of
this freer behavior was given before when the subject in the
paired-associates situation responded, "CAT! No! I mean CUP!"
The subject freely gives an error, rejects it, and gives another
response. Thus, omission behavior and error-rejection behavior

have essentially the same mechanisms, and were chosen to be examples of all-or-none, nongraded appraisal of the response and its correctness.

Tip-of-the-tongue and feeling-of-knowing phenomena indicate circumstances in which amount of error can be perceived and acted upon, rather than simply an all-or-none judgment about the response and its correctness. In tip-of-the-tongue behavior the subject notes that his first wrong response is close to the correct one and, on the basis of the closeness, begins to "free associate" similar responses until he makes the correct one, at which time he accepts it and stops the response sequence. Not only is closeness of the first response evaluated, but it is evaluated for each subsequent response as well. As long as error continues the subject will continue responding, at least until his repertoire of similar "free associates" is exhausted or until a response-produced stimulus trace and a perceptual trace are matched by the occurrence of a correct response.

Feeling-of-knowing behavior in Hart's experiments can be interpreted as judgment of error magnitude also. In his paired-associate experiments (Hart, in press) the stimuli were words and the responses were trigrams. The subjects were required to guess if they were unsure of a response's correctness, and for these responses they indicated a judgment of either YES or NO for feeling of knowing. Responses for which subjects were positive of correctness did not require a judgment. Suppose a response had low strength and only one letter correct. The stimulus and the response-produced stimulus from the response would find slight matching with an SR perceptual trace, error would be perceived as large, and NO would be the feeling of knowing. But suppose the trigram had substantial strength and two letters were given correctly. Here the stimulus and the response feedback would find a rather strong SR perceptual trace to match, and the error would be perceived as small. Most likely YES would be marked. A recognition test by the method of multiple stimuli followed, where the subject could be expected to read each response alternative to himself. Those items with weak SR perceptual traces should produce recognition of few of their responses, the items would be missed, and the NO judgments would predict them. Items with the stronger SR perceptual traces, on the other hand, should produce recognition of correct responses and the YES judgments would be predictive of them. The result is correlation between feeling of knowing and recognition.

Subjective Reinforcement

The conventional model of learning that was discussed earlier in this chapter said that reinforcement, as an external stimulus event, is a necessary condition for learning, and this is an accepted viewpoint among psychologists of learning. No one denies the importance of external reinforcers, but in recent years there has arisen the position that external reinforcement is necessary to start the learning process, and that learning can occur thereafter in the absence of reinforcement. This is the position of *subjective reinforcement*, and it dovetails nicely with the mechanism of response recognition that has been the emphasis of this chapter so far. If subjective reinforcement gains full theoretical status, it will greatly change our contemporary ideas of learning mechanisms.

Empirical Evidence. A paradigm that has revealed evidence in behalf of subjective reinforcement comes from experiments on one-trial learning (e.g., Estes, 1960; Postman, 1963), and it is not necessary to go into the theoretical issues that motivated these experiments. Relevant for subjective reinforcement is that the basic experimental procedure, which is called the "Estes' RTT paradigm," used the reinforcement of a verbal paired-associate item followed by nonreinforced test trials. The R stands for a presentation of the pair (reinforcement), and the T's are test trials in which the stimulus term of the pair is presented alone and the subject attempts recall. Depending upon the purposes of the experiment, there can be any number of reinforcements and any number of test trials.

Estes, Hopkins, and Crothers (1960) apparently were the first to notice suggestions of learning on nonreinforced test trials, but they made little theoretical capital of it. Jones (1962), however, documented the phenomenon in more detail and saw its theoretical implications. She gave subjects one opportunity to study a consonant-number pair, and followed it by four test trials; thus her procedure was RTTTT (Jones's Experiments II & III). As an example of her data (Experiment II), she found that 45 percent of the items were incorrect on the first test trial, and of these 29 percent shifted to the correct response on the second test trial. This could be a random oscillatory effect, but these responses tended to stay in the repertoire, with 61 percent of those correct on the second test trial being correct on the third and 77 percent of these being correct on the fourth test trial. Stable occurrence of correct responses over trials is a common manifestation of learning. Jones hypothesized that the subjects had some capability for distinguishing correct from incorrect responses, and that this recognition was the basis for learning.

Even more convincing evidence for learning in the absence of external reinforcement came from studies of verbal "extinction." These studies of verbal extinction are analogous to those in animal research in which a reinforcement is given a response during the acquisition trials and then is withdrawn during an extinction series. The animals' performance declines during extinction. The analogous verbal experiments require acquisition of a verbal list by the anticipation method, in which after each response, the subject is shown the stimulus paired with the correct response as his reinforcement, or knowledge of results. In the extinction series, the subject is given repeated test trials in which only the stimulus members of the pairs are presented, and he attempts the correct responses. There is no knowledge of results. In general outline these experiments parallel those of Estes' RTT experiments in which learning follows repeated test, except that a list is learned and often an extensive series of test (extinction) trials is given (Goss, 1965, gave 56 of them). A general finding of these studies is that there is a significant *increase* in number of correct responses on the nonreinforced test trials. There is no decline in performance when reinforcement is withdrawn, as the conventional model of verbal learning implies. Although Goss (1965) found items correct on test trials that had never been correct in acquisition, the number of correct occurrences for an item on the test trials was positively related to the number of correct occurrences in acquisition. Other studies which have shown unmistakable learning on nonreinforced test trials are Richardson and Gropper (1964), Butler and Peterson (1965), Goss, Morgan, and Golin (1959), and Goss et al. (1962). In asking why number of correct responses increases in the absence of reinforcement, one is drawn to the position of self-reinforcement, although not all are convinced. A criticism of the self-reinforcement hypothesis (Lazar and Van Laer, 1966) is that another factor like warm-up after a retention interval is a cause of the performance increase. Successive test trials gradually warm the subject up, and his performance improves. But these experiments, which have been cited above, have used a single session without a sizable retention interval between acquisition and test trials and have avoided the possibility of warm-up effects. It is possible that warm-up might be a factor in experiments of the type that use relatively long retention intervals (e.g., Richardson, 1958), but it cannot be considered an influence when the learn and test sequences are successively given and are not separated by a retention interval. Also, one should be cautious in using warm-up in explanation because it is a phenomenon of uncertain status (Adams, 1961b).

A recognized index of learning is latency of response, with a decrease in latency (increase in response speed) representing an increase in habit strength. Changes in latency have been one of the ways of inferring about subjective reinforcement and habit. Leonard and Conrad (1963) used a 10-key keyboard task and taught their subjects a code association between pairs of keys and letters of the alphabet. Original learning with knowledge of results occupied four 45-minute sessions spread over two days, and on the subsequent eight days subjects had four 5-minute test runs without knowledge of results. Errors remained stable over the eight days at about 3 percent, but speed of responding steadily increased from about 35 letters per minute on the first test day to over 70 letters per minute on the eighth day. This is impressive learning, and the authors conclude that knowledge of results is only required initially to establish the responses in the repertoire and that after that learning can proceed without it. Using verbal paired associates and a form of the Estes' RTT paradigm, Eimas and Zeaman (1963) and Eimas (1964) found the same thing. On nonreinforced test trials the speed of correct responses became steadily faster. Furthermore, Eimas (1964) found that speed increased for incorrect responses repeated over the test trials, although this finding had not appeared in the earlier study (Eimas and Zeaman, 1963). Eimas and Zeaman (1963) coined the phrase "subjective reinforcement" to explain their results, although others (Marston, 1964; Marston & Kanfer, 1963) have called essentially the same principle "self-reinforcement."

Theoretical Considerations. Subjective reinforcement is an important idea because it challenges the first principle of contemporary learning theory that reinforcement from external sources is solely the basis for learning. Subjective reinforcement does not deny the value of external reinforcement in defining the correct response for the subject and placing it in his behavioral repertoire originally, but it does say that subsequent learning is not necessarily dependent on it. At least for human beings, experimental extinction as a decrement in response strength does not always set in when reinforcement is withdrawn (motor behavior can be an exception—see Adams, 1968). Instead, increases in performance level can occur, and of the kind customarily associated with increases in habit strength. Actually we have had a need for an idea like this all along. How else, for example, can we account for covert rehearsal benefiting recall in STM experiments (Chapter 5)? There is no external knowledge of results during the silent repetition. By simply repeating the response it grows stronger. The reinforcement must be internal.

In their discussion of subjective reinforcement, Eimas and Zeaman (1963) have a computer-sounding model which uses terms like "search," "store," and "scan." They assume that the subject stores paired-associate data on reinforced trials; that is, what response goes with what stimulus. The stored traces are scanned when a response is made on a nonreinforced test trial, and if there is a match between the response and a stored trace, a subjective reinforcement occurs and an increment of habit strength takes place.

What Eimas and Zeaman (1963) call "searching for a trace and matching a response with it" is essentially what we have been calling response recognition. Response recognition, being the compatibility of a response-produced stimulus trace and a stored perceptual trace from past responses, accounted for hitherto unexplained behavior in paired-associate tasks. The subjective reinforcement position goes beyond this, however, and says that matching of stimulus and perceptual traces from responses is a condition for reinforcement, in addition to the value it might have for handling the facts of omissions, error rejection, tip-of-the-tongue behavior, etc. On the assumption that the perceptual trace for stimulus recognition is the same as for response recognition, we might suppose that the coincidence of the environmental stimulus trace and its perceptual trace from previous experience is a condition of perceptual learning also. Speculative, certainly, but theoretically plausible in the face of these other considerations.

The Eimas-Zeaman model was on the right track, but the feedback model, with response recognition and the distinction between memory and perceptual trace, would appear to have more power in accounting for the facts of behavior. Their model is designed for their data on the latency measure when the correct response is securely in the repertoire. The correct response occurs, a search of stored traces is made, and when a match occurs, a subjective reinforcement takes place and the latency of the response is faster next time. But how do we account for number of correct responses increasing on nonreinforced test trials in the verbal "extinction" experiments? Omissions and wrong responses must be set aside and replaced by correct responses. And what of the strengthening of wrong responses on nonreinforced test trials? Whether measured as latency (Eimas, 1964) or increased regularity in the occurrence of the same wrong responses (Butler & Peterson, 1965), there would appear to be circumstances in which wrong responses become strengthened. The Eimas-Zeaman model, with its focus on occurrence of the correct response and its strengthening, cannot embrace these additional facts.

Consider first the matter of explaining an increased number of correct responses on nonreinforced test trials with memory and perceptual traces as explanatory mechanisms. A typical case would be a wrong response occurring on a test trial, followed by a correct response, which tends to stay in the repertoire from then on. Theoretically this case can be seen as a discrepancy between the strengths of memory traces and perceptual traces for the correct and wrong responses. The wrong response has never been reinforced in the experimental situation, but it must have had considerable extraexperimental reinforcement because it dominates the correct response for the stimulus and must have a stronger memory trace than the correct response. However, the wrong response must have a weaker perceptual trace because no match was obtained. It was rejected and replaced by the correct response (although there is no necessity for the next response to be the correct one). The correct response would have a stronger perceptual trace. A match with it is reinforcing, and it tends to stay in the repertoire from then on. Why the wrong response might have a stronger memory trace but a weaker perceptual trace than the correct response is not clear. Yet this must be so because the wrong response had strength enough to occur (strong memory trace) but was not accepted (weak perceptual trace). Perhaps forgetting processes were stronger for one type of trace than for the other. An experimental attack on this problem should be concerned with the independent manipulation of the strength of the memory trace and perceptual trace in the verbal recall paradigm.

But not all responses are replaced by correct ones. Actually only a few are because the rate by which the number of correct responses increases on nonreinforced test trials is slow, although the effect is a clear, significant one. Mentioned before was the strengthening of wrong responses on the nonreinforced test trials that produced their regular, repetitive occurrence and a decrease in their latency. This effect is a clear dominance of the wrong response over the correct response in both the strength of the memory and the perceptual trace. The memory trace is strong enough to activate the wrong response, and the perceptual trace is strong enough for a match to be made. With the match come recognition and acceptance of the response even though it is wrong, and subjective reinforcement and strengthening of the wrong response.

As a final remark on theory, we could use additional indices of subjective reinforcement on nonreinforced test trials as habit. The argument of Lazar and Van Laer (1966) that the effects could be a warm-up phenomenon rather than habit increments from subjective reinforcement is a good form of scientific challenge, and the proponents of the habit interpretation should anticipate these attacks by tightening their position whenever they can. Increase in number of correct responses and shortening of the latency are convincing measures for the habit view, but other approaches should be sought. One possibility would be a retention paradigm that capitalizes on the well-known empirical fact that forgetting decreases with increases in habit strength for the response. If self-reinforcement on nonreinforced test trials occurs and is truly building habit, retention should be a positive function of the number of subjective reinforcements.

Implications of Response Recognition for Forgetting

Given the assumption that stimulus recognition and response recognition are based on the same kind of perceptual trace, we can assume that response-produced perceptual traces can be forgotten because we know that forgetting occurs for stimulus recognition. What are the implications for recall when the perceptual traces for responses are weakened by forgetting processes, whatever they might be? Forgetting operates on the memory trace too; thus we now have the problem of understanding forgetting for both memory and perceptual traces.

Forgetting processes operating on the memory trace have the obvious effects of lowering habit potential for the response and decreasing performance level at recall. The consequences for some forgetting of a response-produced perceptual trace are not so obvious, however. Serving a verification function as it does for response recognition, a loss in strength for the perceptual trace will affect the behavior that we have listed in the previous section of this chapter entitled "Response Recognition and Failures of the Recall Model."

The response-produced perceptual trace is hypothesized as the reference against which the subject tests his current response. If this reference is weakened by forgetting, these characteristics of omission behavior will be changed. It was conjectured that the withholding of correct responses was due to a subject's failure to find a positive match between his response-produced stimulus trace and an *SR* perceptual trace, which created a state of uncertainty and caused responses to be inhibited if the subject was a cautious type. If perceptual traces were weakened by forgetting, a subject's indecisiveness should become even greater and increase the chances of correct and incorrect responses being withheld. The result would be fewer correct responses and lowered performance at the retention test. If the subject is relaxed in his response set, however, and tends to blurt out responses even when he is not sure of his response correctness (and he would not be sure with the definition of *SR* perceptual traces decreased through forgetting), there should be a large number of responses, both correct and incorrect, with the subject tending to find them unacceptable and change them because he cannot obtain a match with the stored traces.

Tip-of-the-tongue behavior was hypothesized to rest on a judgment of amount of error between a response-produced stimulus trace and an *SR* perceptual trace, with a series of responses similar to the correct one occurring. The subject will continue responding until his repertoire of similar responses is exhausted or until he hits on the correct response. Forgetting of *SR* perceptual traces could have two effects. One would be a reduced

accuracy in estimating amount of error, with a result that the
chain of responses may never be emitted because the subject does
not perceive his closeness to the correct response. Second, if the
chain is emitted, it may result in responses that are not too similar
to the correct one because the accuracy of error judgment is low,
and there is a reduced likelihood that the correct response will be
the end product. The result is a lowered performance at recall
for both cases.

Conclusions about Response Recognition

We began with a description of the conventional model of learning for verbal recall, discussed its inadequacies, and concluded
with preliminary recommendations for a more complex feedback
model. The primary recommendation for change in the conventional model is response recognition, in which the subject assesses
the correctness of his response and adjusts his behavior accord-
ingly. Response recognition required the postulation of a perceptual trace which is built from the action of response-produced
stimulus traces. It is assumed to be the same kind of stimulus
trace that results from the action of environmental stimuli and
produces the perceptual traces for stimulus recognition. Moreover, there is a new point of view, with some interesting supporting evidence, which contends that response recognition is more
than simply recognition—it is the basis for subjective reinforcement which can produce habit increments just like external
reinforcement. If all this is true, and it will take a big empirical
and theoretical effort to prove it, perceptual traces and recognition will come to lie at the heart of the learning process and, of
course, memory.

Natural language mediation (NLM) was discussed in previous chapters as a way in which verbal paired associates are
learned. Rather than learn a pair by rote, a subject will often

transfer his past language skills to the experimental task as a way of learning it. At this early stage of theoretical development, it is hard to say how the mechanisms of response recognition and subjective reinforcement apply to NLMs. An NLM is a response, and all that has been said about the criterion response members that are acquired when a list of paired associates is learned should also apply to NLMs. An NLM only makes the response to the pair longer, and it introduces the process of decoding. These factors should not affect the operation of basic mechanisms.

THEORIES OF FORGETTING

These few concluding remarks on theories of forgetting will apply to the data and ideas that were covered in the earlier chapters and will not attempt to reconsider these data and ideas in the light of the feedback model of verbal learning that has just been discussed. Interesting though it might be to discuss the feedback model with respect to, say, the laws of interference and the interference theory of forgetting, there would be a distinct prematureness about such a discussion. The scientific merit of the feedback model would seem best decided by a research strategy that focuses on the acquisition phase of learning and asks if response recognition and subjective reinforcement are empirically verifiable in their implications. The study of forgetting should follow after some confidence has been gained in the worth of these theoretical ideas concerning the acquisition stage of learning.

Interference Theory

There is little to say in summation about the interference theory of forgetting that has not been said in earlier chapters. For all its problems, it is the best theory of forgetting that we have, and the evidence is almost solely derived from verbal behavior and recall. The significance of interference theory for nonverbal response classes and for recognition is mostly untested and vague. This is a grievous deficit because an overriding issue for memory is whether one set of lawful principles, or more than one, is required to explain forgetting. No strong resolution of this issue will take place until the laws of forgetting are tried in a multitude of situations and for a variety of response classes. With memory research so thoroughly centered in verbal behavior, we are on shaky terrain to announce that interference is *the* explanation of forgetting. There is nothing wrong with an inductive generalization from limited data to a potential universe of data, but there is a danger of premature generalization, and it can deflect a science from forceful challenge of a principle. Too often a science is lulled by the successes of a law and fails to ask if there are situations in which the law will not hold. A limited domain for a law does not make it a poor law because it may be very effective for prediction within the domain, but we must always push for the variables, laws, and theories that lie outside it and which may be very different.

Even within its domain the interference theory of forgetting is beset with uncertainties, although none that stand as disproof. The attempts (e.g., Underwood & Postman, 1960) to test the PI influences of extraexperimental language experience have failed, but as Chapter 7 said, the failure may be in the empirical approaches chosen and not a failure of the theory itself.

Natural language mediation is another problem area for verbal forgetting, primarily because of its newness. Verbal materials are not learned in a simple rote fashion, with only a hierarchy of simple associate words operating. Rather, a subject much of the time integrates a pair into the structure of his entire language behavior and may use complex associations like sentences to learn it. For memory, it is of special interest that NLMs promote high retention (e.g., Montague, Adams, & Kiess, 1966). Interference theory, retention, and verbal learning at large have a long way to go before the role of NLMs is fully grasped.

Trace Decay

Trace decay theory has always been a potential challenger of the interference theory of forgetting, but never a serious one. Trace decay postulates the effects of time per se for forgetting, like the spontaneous decay of a radioactive substance, and it is very hard to achieve a condition of pure time and experimentally rule out the confounding effects of events that can occur in time. These events take two forms in human beings. One is covert rehearsal that commonly occurs with human subjects in the retention interval, and it can be strengthening for the trace and offset any decay effects that might occur. The other is experiences that are potentially interfering. Studies in behalf of interference theory (e.g., Jenkins & Dallenbach, 1924), in which an attempt was made to control events in the retention interval by sleep, ideally could have disproved trace decay theory, but empirically they did not. If the control of interfering events had been completely successful, and *no* forgetting was observed, time per se would have had no effect and interference would have been the sole agent for forgetting. As it was, forgetting was only reduced in experiments like this, not eliminated, and it is not clear whether the control of interfering events was inadequate or whether interference and trace decay were both functioning. The use of EEG to monitor the depth of sleep and the degree of removal from external stimulation would be a valuable auxiliary measure. Rather than trying to eliminate interfering events in the hopes of revealing trace decay alone, another approach is to use a situation in which trace decay and interference theory have different predictions. Waugh and Norman (1965) were successful with this research tactic. Their findings support interference theory.

Adams and Dijkstra (1966) stepped outside the verbal field for their work on short-term motor memory, and they cautiously accepted trace decay as an explanation for their findings because there were no identifiable sources of motor interference. An alternative, which is scientifically conservative, is to take a stark empirical position and give no theoretical interpretation until the data on motor recall are in an advanced stage of maturity. No one can deny scientific conservatism as a point of view, sometimes even an important one, but it is a dull, slow way of arriving at a goal. A more stimulating approach is to use experiments for a decision about theory and the basis of new experiments to further refine the decision or challenge it. To clarify the Adams-Dijkstra experiment, a productive research tactic would be to seek sources of interference for the forgetting and challenge the trace decay explanation. Until the sources of interference are found, the experiment stands in support of trace decay. Like all empirical evidence, the Adams-Dijkstra experiment has tentativeness about it, but the data do not neatly subsume under interference theory and can stand as a threat to it.

Permanent Memory

Without evidence, but without whimsy either, Chapter 3 discussed memory as possibly permanent; forgetting is not an undoing of the trace but only an inhibitory state that denies activation of the response. It is easy to assume that forgetting is the intrinsic weakening of a trace, either by interference or decay, and that relearning after forgetting is restrengthening of the trace. But it is also reasonable (although probably less likely) that forgetting is the growth of an inhibitory barrier around the trace and relearning a dissipation of the barrier with additional reinforcement. Interference theory (Chapter 4) specifies quite a bit about the empirical operations of interference but nothing about underlying mechanisms and what happens to habits when response systems conflict. Interference can either erode the habit permanently, or it can merely inhibit the habit and leave it wholly intact. The former idea was called the erosion hypothesis in Chapter 3, and the latter the inhibition hypothesis. There is little evidence for either hypothesis, but if support could be brought to bear on the inhibition hypothesis, it would be of immense significance because it would suggest far more stored in the brain than we can recall. Eventually it may become possible to recall material that we normally consider forgotten. The proof or disproof of this hypothesis will probably lie in the study of retrieval methods for stimulating the full response potential that lies behind the inhibition barrier.

The billions of cells in the brain seem to have sufficient capacity to hold everything we have learned, so that man at least has a physiological potential to support the hypothesis. Penfield's research (Chapter 3) is evidence for the vast storage capacity of the brain and, by showing that the brain holds far more than recall reveals, is not hostile to the inhibition hypothesis. On the other hand, Penfield's work hardly proves the inhibition hypothesis for a memory trace and the recall based on it. Chapter 3 talked generally about the permanence of memory, but in Chapter 9 and in this chapter the memory trace for recall and the perceptual trace for recognition were distinguished as two different habit states. Penfield's electrical stimulation may have been arousing perceptual traces, and perhaps the memory traces related to these events were truly gone. Future investigators of the hypothesis of permanent memory must specify the kind of trace to which the hypothesis is being applied.

COMPARTMENTS OF MEMORY

The STM-LTM Distinction for Verbal Memory

Chapter 5 said that the operational meaning of compartments of memory was that different variables and laws define each compartment. Verbal retention findings make a good case for two compartments because the limited capacity of STM and its susceptibility to acoustic interference are sharply different from the very large capacity and semantic interference in LTM. The label "short-term memory" is a bit archaic now that verbal retention in STM is known not to be a function of time intervals per se, but of interfering events, just as we believe true for verbal LTM. Originally it was thought that STM might be distinguished from LTM on the basis of rapid forgetting as an intrinsic, distinctive property presumably from trace decay, but it cannot be because interference operates in both compartments, although not the same kind of interference. Thus, STM is not simply a way of saying very rapid forgetting over very brief intervals, but rather is a shorthand expression for a set of laws about interference and limited capacity that distinguish it from a related but different set of laws for LTM. This does not deny rapid forgetting in STM, but instead says that the conditions of interference often produce instances of rapid forgetting in STM. Chapter 3 also discussed physiological evidence for the STM-LTM distinction.

Compartments for Nonverbal Response Classes

Memory research is so strongly weighted toward verbal behavior that we sometimes forget how little we know about the forgetting of other response classes. Motor behavior has received some effort, but the findings mostly provoke questions, not answers, to theoretical issues. Memory for other response classes, like touch and smell, has not been investigated. And what of the forgetting of "emotional" responses? Psychotherapists have long been impressed with the stability of fears and anxieties in their patients.

An important issue for nonverbal response classes is whether they deserve their own compartments of memory, in the sense of having different laws from verbal responses. It would be tidy if memory fit a single set of laws, as some interference theorists contend. But memory could be fragmented with, say, each response class having its own domain and each domain further subdivided into STM and LTM compartments. There is little evidence that this possibility has truth in it, but nevertheless there are preliminary suggestions that an impressively austere memory governed by one set of principles may be empirically false. The STM experiments by Adams and Dijkstra (1966) and Posner and Konick (1966) suggest that motor behavior might deserve a compartment of its own. In the absence of identifiable interference, Adams and Dijkstra found forgetting of simple motor responses over seconds and suggested trace decay as an explanation. With verbal forgetting reasonably well explained by interference, the fact that motor retention might be explained by trace decay is the kind of evidence which suggests a motor compartment distinct from verbal memory, perhaps with STM and LTM subdivisions of its own. The *very* high retention of well-learned continuous motor responses in LTM, in contrast to the rather rapid forgetting of verbal responses, also hints that a motor compartment is justified. It is too early to push this line of reasoning hard, but these are examples of the data that produce hypotheses about new compartments of memory.

Perceptual Trace

Memory and the perceptual traces were defined as two different habit entities serving different functions, and this distinction is a kind of memory compartmentalization. The necessity for perceptual traces is compelling, but we know little of the laws that govern their learning and retention and how they differ from the laws for memory traces. They are at the heart of stimulus recognition, and if the first part of this chapter on response recognition is provisionally accepted, they are intimately involved with recall also.

Eidetic Imagery. In view of the theory that has been offered in Chapter 9 and this chapter on the distinction between perceptual and memory traces, there is cause to conjecture that eidetic imagery is a phenomenon linked with perceptual traces and is, therefore, germane to the general line of reasoning that has been followed and the distinction that has been made.

There was a lively interest in eidetic imagery which began after World War I with the work of Jaensch (1930) and lasted until the 1930s. Klüever (1928, 1931, 1932) has written very thorough reviews of the research literature, but Allport (1924) has the most readable of the general discussions. With the exception of a minor modern interest (Haber & Haber, 1964; Holt, 1964; Doob, 1966; Siipola & Hayden, 1965), there has been virtually no serious concern with eidetic imagery since the post-World War I period.

The distinctive, striking feature of eidetic imagery is that recall is based on a conscious mental image which the eidetiker (as one who has it is called) claims literally to "see." The experience apparently corresponds to seeing a photographic slide projected on a screen. A usual experimental method is to show the subject a picture for a few seconds and then ask him to describe its contents with his eyes closed or while staring at a blank, neutral surface. Although all of us have afterimages that can last up to a minute or so, and all of us can devise a gross verbal description of the picture, the eidetiker's image far outlasts the afterimage and has a level of detail that vastly exceeds the powers of verbal encoding. In describing this amazing detail, Allport (1924, p. 104) says that the eidetiker can describe the number of buttons on a jacket, the number of whiskers on a cat's face, or the letters in a *foreign* word. In addition to reports of exceptional detail, the eidetiker often reports that his eidetic image is in original colors rather than the complementary colors of an afterimage, and that it is not affected by eye movements as is an afterimage.

Most laymen are convinced of the existence of individuals with a "photographic memory," and presumably they mean eidetikers. To the lay world the eidetiker has no memory problems because all he need do is turn on his image of the material to be recalled, see it in all its original detail, and have perfect recall. Perhaps this ideal man exists somewhere, but in reality the typical eidetiker fails to measure up to the ideal. His images customarily are reported as imperfect and unstable, and they are not immutable over time. Eidetic images are often short-lived, although they last significantly longer than the afterimages of noneidetikers (see, for example, Siipola & Hayden, 1965, Table 1). Haber and Haber (1964) worked with eight eidetikers who reported images still present after eight months, although no attempt was made to test the quality of the images. Presumably the eidetic image is a long-term as well as short-term carrier of information.

Eidetic imagery is rare. When it occurs at all, it is almost always in children, and even here the rate of occurrence is low. Haber and Haber (1964) were able to identify only 12 eidetikers in 151 elementary school children whom they tested. Most psychologists agree that eidetic imagery is negatively correlated with age and is virtually absent in adults. As an eidetiker grows older and his verbal skills mature, he seems to rely less and less on his capabilities for eidetic imagery. From such thinking came hypotheses that special groups whose level of verbal symbolization is low would have a higher frequency of eidetic imagery than groups with normal level of verbal symbolism. Siipola and Hayden (1965) found some support for this view in their tests of brain-injured children, but Doob (1966) was unable to confirm it in field studies of eidetic imagery in primitive African cultures.

Even if an experimental psychologist takes a relaxed attitude toward introspective accounts of mental images, which is hard for him to do, he cannot easily accept the experimental methods that have been, and are still being, used. Probably all would admit that exceptional feats of memory can occur and deserve laboratory study, but few modern-day psychologists would endorse the procedures used to sift the few eidetikers from the mass of non-eidetikers. The basic problem is distinguishing the eidetic image from the afterimage and verbal encoding. The problem does not need contemporary awareness to identify it because early workers certainly knew about it (e.g., Allport, 1928). Even modern experimenters have not solved the problem. Haber and Haber (1964) and Siipola and Hayden (1964) would show their subjects a picture and then elicit a verbal report immediately. By this method both afterimages and verbal encoding could contribute to the report, along with eidetic images. Although undoubtedly some eidetikers were correctly identified, operations were lacking for unequivocally screening out those who might have had very persistent afterimages or who were unusually adroit at verbal encoding. We might surmise that the 12 eidetikers whom Haber and Haber (1964) identified out of 151 children were not all true eidetikers.

A good experimental solution to this problem is not easy to find, but two possibilities are suggested. One is to use delayed recall so that there is no question that afterimages influence the verbal report in any way. Delayed recall does not, however, escape the matter of verbal encoding. When a subject at recall says that the man in the picture has 10 buttons on his coat, how do we know that he did not count and verbally encode this information in his original study of the picture? Verbal encoding will always be present to some degree, but we would admit to its limitations, and we should expect the eidetiker to describe detail far in excess of anything possible by verbal encoding. For example, suppose that we briefly presented our subjects 10 closely written textbook pages and then a week later found a subject who could reproduce them exactly, complete with accurate punctuation, paragraphing, and hyphenation. Our sense of reasonableness would be strained to attribute this remarkable performance to verbal encoding. Neither old nor new studies get at striking, convincing proof of this kind although some of the anecdotal accounts suggest that performance of this sort might be obtained.

What theoretical speculations can we hazard for eidetic imagery? Speculations they will be, to be sure, because the data are not sound enough for systematic theorizing. The provocative work on brain stimulation by Penfield and his associates was reviewed in Chapter 3, and they obtained evidence for the central storage in the human being of complex images that are of the kind which the eidetiker can arouse for himself voluntarily. In Chapter 9 and in this chapter the behavioral construct of the S perceptual trace was developed, which is the storage of a form of the environmental stimulus whose arousal by the stimulus on a subsequent occasion is the basis for its recognition. There is a scientific distance between Penfield's findings and the S perceptual trace, but they both point to the storage of sensory-perceptual data of the kind which the eidetiker uses. Is it fair to assume that the eidetiker has an internal cue mechanism which allows him to activate these stored data, in contrast, say, to Penfield's electrode or a stimulus recognition situation in which the environmental stimulus is required as a cue? Is this rare talent a genetic gift to a few? Can it possibly be acquired with the proper training conditions, even among those who would otherwise be noneidetikers? Can it be maintained among those who are eidetikers as youths but lose it in our intensely verbal culture? Questions like these are farfetched now, but someday they may become meaningful as our programs of memory research give more attention to the storage and retrieval of sensory-perceptual inputs.

IN SUMMATION

The laws of memory must appear flimsy to the reader who is on intimate terms with more mature sciences, but there is no need to apologize for their frailty. Psychology is a young science whose laws are low-order when they exist at all and whose variables in many realms are yet to be discovered and conceptualized. Youth is not a fault, only a gauche state to be passed through, and the vigor of modern psychology as an experimenting science leaves little doubt that middle-aged maturity will soon be upon us. It cannot be said that memory research has given us a catalog of sophisticated, empirically proved laws with which to predict retention, although our powers of prediction are not weak by any means, but it has given us a sensitive feeling for directions of investigation that should lead to tough, secure laws and theory. It is poor policy to urge and press basic scientists because the strength of science is in the freedom of ideas which investigators bring to the scientific marketplace and offer on the block for acceptance. Risking poor policy, nevertheless, memory needs a focus on big themes such as mechanisms of forgetting, whether memory has compartments and how many, and whether memory is permanent. We need workers whose labors bind the elements of a grand plan, but more than workers we need dreamers, theoreticians, and idea men who continually inquire of the master plan and ask if it is truly masterful or if it should be cast anew. The psychology of today is enmeshed in empiricism, in which one fact is often taken to be as good as another, and facts are gathered for their own sake. Empirical facts have a sanctity in science, and rightly so, but unsystematic empirical minutiae can remain just that, forever. Without the formalism of theory that embraces the facts with a few elegant principles, we shall never really understand the separate facts that give us the laws of that thing we call memory, and we shall never have the power to predict new facts and laws before they are found.

REFERENCES

Adams, J. A. Human tracking behavior. *Psychol. Bull.*, 1961, **58**, 55–79. (a)

Adams, J. A. The second facet of forgetting: A review of warm-up decrement. *Psychol. Bull.*, 1961, **58**, 257–273. (b)

Adams, J. A. Motor skills. *Annu. Rev. Psychol.*, 1964, **15**, 181–202.

Adams, J. A. Engineering psychology. In H. Helson & W. Bevan (Eds.), *Contemporary approaches to psychology*. Princeton: Van Nostrand, 1967. Pp. 345–383.

Adams, J. A. Acquisition of motor responses. In M. R. Marx (Ed.), *Learning: Processes*. New York: Macmillan, 1968, in press.

Adams, J. A., & Dijkstra, S. Short-term memory for motor responses. *J. exp. Psychol.*, 1966, **71**, 314–318.

Allport, G. W. Eidetic imagery. *Brit. J. Psychol.*, 1924, **15**, 99–120.

Allport, G. W. The eidetic image and the after-image. *Amer. J. Psychol.*, 1928, **40**, 418–425.

Bilodeau, Ina McD. Information feedback. In E. A. Bilodeau (Ed.), *Acquisition of skill*. New York: Academic, 1966. Pp. 255–296.

Brown, R., & McNeill, D. The "tip of the tongue" phenomenon. *J. verbal Learn. verbal Behav.*, 1966, **5**, 325–337.

Butler, D. C., & Peterson, D. E. Learning during "extinction" with paired associates. *J. verbal Learn. verbal Behav.*, 1965, **4**, 103–106.

Doob, L. W. Eidetic imagery: A cross-cultural will-o'-the-wisp? *J. Psychol.*, 1966, **63**, 13–34.

Eimas, P. D. Subjective reinforcement in the paired-associate learning of retarded and normal children. *Canad. J. Psychol.*, 1964, **18**, 183–196.

Eimas, P. D., & Zeaman, D. Response speed changes in an Estes' paired-associate "miniature" experiment. *J. verbal Learn. verbal Behav.*, 1963, **1**, 384–388.

Estes, W. K. Learning theory and the new "mental chemistry." *Psychol. Rev.*, 1960, **67**, 207–223.

Estes, W. K., Hopkins, B. L., & Crothers, E. J. All-or-none and conservation effects in the learning and retention of paired associates. *J. exp. Psychol.*, 1960, **60**, 329–339.

Gibson, J. J., & Gibson, Eleanor J. Perceptual learning–differentiation or enrichment? *Psychol. Rev.*, 1955, **62**, 32–41.

Goss, A. E. Manifest strengthening of correct responses of paired-associates under postcriterion zero percent occurrence of response members. *J. gen. Psychol.*, 1965, **72**, 135–144.

Goss, A. E., Morgan, C. H., & Golin, S. J. Paired-associates learning as a function of percentage of occurrence of response members. *J. exp. Psychol.*, 1959, **57**, 96–104.

Goss, A. E., Nodine, C. F., Gregory, B. N., Taub, H. A., & Kennedy, K. E. Stimulus characteristics and percentage occurrence of response members in paired-associate learning. *Psychol. Monogr.*, 1962, **76** (Whole No. 531).

Groninger, L. D. Natural language mediation and covert rehearsal in short-term memory. *Psychon. Sci.*, 1966, **5**, 135–136.

Haber, R. N., & Haber, Ruth B. Eidetic imagery: I. Frequency. *Percept. mot. Skills*, 1964, **19**, 131–138.

Hart, J. T. Memory and the feeling-of-knowing experience. *J. educ. Psychol.*, 1965, **56**, 208–216.

Hart, J. T. Memory and the memory-monitoring process, in press.

Holt, R. R. Imagery: The return of the ostracized. *Amer. Psychologist*, 1964, **19**, 254–264.

Jaensch, E. R. *Eidetic imagery and typological methods of investigation.* (Trans. by Oeser from 2d ed.) New York: Harcourt, Brace, 1930.

Jenkins, J. G., & Dallenbach, K. M. Obliviscence during sleep and waking. *Amer. J. Psychol.*, 1924, **35**, 605–612.

Jones, Joan E. All-or-none versus incremental learning. *Psychol. Rev.*, 1962, **69**, 156–160.

Kimble, G. A. *Conditioning and learning.* New York: Appleton-Century-Crofts, 1961.

Klüever, H. Studies on the eidetic type and eidetic imagery. *Psychol. Bull.*, 1928, **25**, 69–104.

Klüever, H. The eidetic child. In C. Murchison (Ed.), *A handbook of child psychology.* Worcester, Mass.: Clark Univer. Press, 1931. Pp. 643–668.

Klüever, H. Eidetic phenomena. *Psychol. Bull.*, 1932, **29**, 181–203.

Lazar, G., & Van Laer, J. Successive recall as a warm-up task for paired adjectives. *Psychon. Sci.*, 1966, **5**, 137–138.

Leonard, J. A., & Conrad, R. Maintenance of high accuracy without augmented feedback. *Nature*, 1963, **199**, 512–513.

Marston, A. R. Response strength and self-reinforcement. *J. exp. Psychol.*, 1964, **68**, 537–540.

Marston, A. R., & Kanfer, F. H. Human reinforcement: Experimenter and subject controlled. *J. exp. Psychol.*, 1963, **66**, 91–94.

Montague, W. E., Adams, J. A., & Kiess, H. O. Forgetting and natural language mediation. *J. exp. Psychol.*, 1966, **72**, 829–833.

Mowrer, O. H. *Learning theory and the symbolic processes.* New York: Wiley, 1960.

Noble, C. E. Meaningfulness and familiarity. In C. N. Cofer & Barbara S. Musgrave (Eds.), *Verbal behavior and learning.* New York: McGraw-Hill, 1963. Pp. 76–119.

Posner, M. I., & Konick, A. F. Short-term retention of visual and kinesthetic information. *Organiz. Behav. and hum. Perf.*, 1966, **1**, 71–86.

Postman, L. The history and present status of the law of effect. *Psychol. Bull.*, 1947, **44**, 489–563.

Postman, L. Does interference theory predict too much forgetting? *J. verbal Learn. verbal Behav.*, 1963, **2**, 40–48.

Richardson, J. The relationship of stimulus similarity and number of responses. *J. exp. Psychol.*, 1958, **56**, 478–484.

Richardson, J., and Gropper, Mitzi S. Learning during recall trials. *Psychol. Rep.*, 1964, **15**, 551–560.

Siipola, Elsa M., and Hayden, S. D. Exploring eidetic imagery among the retarded. *Percept. mot. Skills*, 1965, **21**, 275–286.

Spence, K. W. Theoretical interpretations of learning. In S. S. Stevens (Ed.), *Handbook of experimental psychology.* New York: Wiley, 1951. Pp. 690–729.

Spence, K. W. *Behavior theory and conditioning.* New Haven: Yale Univer. Press, 1956.

Thorndike, E. L. *Human Learning.* New York: Century, 1931.

Underwood, B. J., & Postman, L. Extraexperimental sources of interference in forgetting. *Psychol. Rev.*, 1960, **67**, 73–95.

Waugh, Nancy C., & Norman, D. A. Primary memory. *Psychol. Rev.*, 1965, **72**, 89–104.

Index

Achilles, Edith M., 252, 271
Adams, J. A., 12, 18, 19, 82, 88–91,
   93, 97, 99, 125, 126, 129, 138,
   148, 197–201, 204, 207, 210,
   218, 221–223, 225, 227–230,
   233, 235–237, 239–241, 282,
   293, 297, 299, 306–308, 311,
   317, 319
Adams, Pauline A., 170, 177
Allen, C. K., 115, 149
Allen, J., 234, 240
Allport, G. W., 312, 314, 317
Ammons, Carol H., 240
Ammons, R. B., 230, 235, 236, 240,
   241
Andrew, G., 201, 209
Angevine, J. B., 47
Apprehension, span of, 39
Arnoult, M. D., 247, 250, 251, 269,
   271
Attention, span of, 39
Averbach, E., 39, 45, 130, 146

Baddeley, A. D., 40, 45, 118–120,
   146
Bahrick, H. P., 248, 256, 263, 264,
   267, 271, 272
Bahrick, Phyllis O., 248, 256, 267,
   272
Ballard, P. B., 252, 272
Barnes, Jean M., 62, 63, 65, 66, 74,
   84, 94, 97
Bartlett, F. C., 26, 45, 266, 272
Battig, W. F., 82, 85, 97, 140, 146,
   230, 240
Bell, H. M., 230, 240
Bilodeau, Ina McD., 54, 71, 98, 282,
   317
Binder, A., 11, 19
Björgen, I. A., 88, 98
Blankenship, A. B., 130, 146
Block, E., 240
Born, D. G., 115, 149
Bousfield, W. A., 153–155, 157, 160–
   162, 164, 167, 173, 175, 176
Bower, G. H., 5, 6
Braun, H. W., 84, 98
Briggs, G. E., 63–66, 74, 75, 98, 138,
   146, 215, 222, 241
Broadbent, D. E., 24, 45
Brogden, W. F., 230, 240

Brown, J., 13, 15, 19, 24, 45, 107,
   110, 111, 114, 146, 265, 272
Brown, R., 284, 317
Bruce, D., 252, 256, 267, 272
Bugelski, B. R., 77, 81–85, 87, 98,
   138, 146
Burns, B. D., 12, 19
Butler, D. C., 297, 300, 317

Cadwallader, T. C., 77, 81–85, 98
Chang, J., 246, 258, 261, 262, 274
Chunk, in free recall, 170–172, 174–
   175
   in short-term memory, 130–136
Clark, H. J., 246, 247, 266, 269,
   272
Clark, L. L., 87, 98
Clark, W. H., 132, 133, 147
Clustering, associative, 153–154, 160–
   167
   category, 153–160
Cofer, C. N., 78, 98, 99, 153, 164–
   167, 173, 176, 252, 256, 267,
   272
Cohen, B. H., 155, 175, 176
Concepts, retention of, 201–206
Conrad, R., 24, 40, 45, 86, 98, 117–
   119, 124, 146, 147, 298, 319
Context stimuli, 54–55, 69–71
Cowan, T. M., 157, 164, 176
Cronbach, L. J., 271, 272
Cross, K., 238, 242
Crossman, E. R. F. W., 124, 147
Crothers, E. J., 296, 318

Dale, H. C. A., 40, 45, 118, 119,
   146
Dallenbach, K. M., 87, 98, 182–186,
   189, 207–210, 307, 318
Dallett, K. M., 79, 80, 98
Davis, R., 248, 256, 262, 267, 272
Dean, S. J., 88, 96, 100
Deese, J., 156, 160, 162–164, 176,
   246, 269, 272
Dey, M., 240
Dijkstra, S., 225, 227–229, 233, 240,
   307, 308, 311, 317
Dollard, J., 269, 273
Doob, L. W., 312, 313, 317
Duncan, C. P., 224, 235, 240

Earhard, B., 95, 98
Ebbinghaus, H., 3, 6, 107, 109, 147, 203, 204, 209, 252, 272
Egan, J. P., 246, 272
Ehrenfreund, D., 234, 240
Eidetic imagery, 312–315
Eimas, P. D., 298, 299, 300, 317
Ekstrand, B. R., 194, 209
Ellis, H. C., 246, 268, 272
Erskine, J. M., 99
Estes, W. K., 86, 98, 109, 147, 270, 272, 295–298, 317, 318
Evans, C. R., 12, 19
Eysenck, S. B. G., 238, 240

Familiarity, 249–251, 265, 287
Farr, R. G., 240
Feeling of knowing, 285, 294–295
Feldman, S. E., 11, 19
Fields, P. E., 201, 209
Fisher, C. M., 47
Fitch, F. B., 20, 99
Fleishman, E. A., 230–232, 240
Foord, E. N., 27, 45
Forgetting, definition of, 9–10
Freeman, P. R., 40, 45, 86, 98
Freud, S., 4, 6, 30, 37, 45

Gagne, R. M., 234, 240
Gainer, C. A., 230, 235, 241
Garskof, B. E., 78, 98, 99
Garvin, E. A., 268, 275
Gibson, Eleanor J., 288, 318
Gibson, J. J., 258, 272, 288, 318
Gladis, M., 84, 98
Glanzer, M., 132, 133, 147
Goggin, J., 63, 99
Golin, S. J., 297
Gomulicki, B. R., 3, 6, 23, 45, 265, 272
Gorman, A. M., 250, 251, 273
Goss, A. E., 269, 273, 297, 318
Greenberg, Ruth, 69, 70, 99, 114, 147, 257, 258, 273
Greenhouse, P., 148
Greenspoon, J., 54, 71, 99
Gregory, B. N., 318
Grissom, R. J., 182, 184, 209
Groninger, L. D., 125–129, 133, 138, 144, 147, 200, 209, 318
Gropper, Mitzi S., 297, 319

Haagen, C. H., 78, 79, 99
Haber, R. N., 312–314, 318
Haber, Ruth B., 312–314, 318
Hall, J. F., 5, 6, 156, 176
Hall, M., 20, 99
Harlow, H. F., 201, 209
Hart, J. T., 285, 294, 318
Hayden, S. D., 312–314, 319
Hebb, D. O., 27, 45, 112, 147
Hellyer, S., 111, 112, 116, 137, 138, 145, 147, 225, 227–229, 240
Heyer, A. W., Jr., 15, 19
Hilgard, E. R., 5, 6
Hille, B. A., 24, 45
Holt, R. R., 266, 273, 312, 318
Hopkins, B. L., 296, 318
Houston, J. P., 63, 78, 98, 99
Hovland, C. I., 20, 99
Hufford, L. E., 236, 240
Hull, A. J., 40, 45, 86, 98, 117, 147
Hull, C. L., 12–18, 20, 31, 37, 45, 46, 86, 99
Hunt, E. B., 201, 209
Hunter, W. S., 181, 186, 209, 210

Images, 32–37, 265–266, 312–315
Inhibition (see Proactive inhibition; Retroactive inhibition)
Interference, in concept formation, 205
    erosion hypothesis of, 27, 309
    extinction hypothesis of, 57–67, 76
    independence hypothesis of, 61–62, 65
    inhibition hypothesis of, 27–28, 309
    in long-term memory, 39–41, 309–310
    for motor behavior, 220–225
    and natural language mediation, 86–97
    paradigms of, 52–57
    and recognition, 257–262
    in short-term memory, 39–41, 113–123, 126, 309–310
    similarity of verbal materials, 76–86
        acoustic effects, 85–86, 116–120, 137
        definitions, 77–78
        semantic effects, 86, 118–120, 137

Interference, unlearning hypothesis of, 62–63
  versus trace decay, 23, 120–123, 227–230, 307–308
Interference theory of forgetting, 27–28, 50–52, 77, 93–94, 181–196, 305–306
Irion, A. L., 61, 99
Irwin, J. M., 61, 62, 73, 100

Jackson, J. H., 32, 33
Jaensch, E. R., 312, 318
Jahnke, J. C., 124, 147
James, W., 29–30, 37, 46
Jasper, H., 32, 47
Jenkins, J. G., 182–185, 189, 207–209, 307, 318
Jenkins, J. J., 87, 95, 99, 154, 161–163, 176, 177
Jenkins, W. O., 246, 252, 263–265, 274
Jensen, A. R., 195, 204, 209
Jones, Joan E., 296, 318
Judd, B. R., 248, 256, 262, 267, 272

Kanfer, F. H., 298, 319
Kennedy, K. E., 318
Kent, G. H., 161, 176
Keppel, G., 86, 101, 109, 113–115, 126, 136, 139, 142–144, 147, 149, 181, 192–195, 209, 211, 228, 229, 238, 241
Kernoff, Phyllis, 15, 16, 20
Kiess, H. O., 96, 100, 125, 129, 138, 148, 197–201, 204, 207, 210, 306, 319
Kimble, G. A., 5, 6, 13, 15, 20, 31, 46, 57, 99, 282, 318
King, D. J., 169, 176
Klemmer, E. T., 135, 147
Klüever, H., 312, 318, 319
Knowing, feeling of, 285, 294–295
Koffka, K., 26, 46
Köhler, W., 26, 46
Konick, A. F., 225, 227–229, 242, 311
Konorski, J., 12, 20
Krueger, W. C. F., 109, 147, 193, 209, 210

Lansford, T. G., 87, 98

Lashley, K. S., 4, 6
Law, S., 148
Lazar, G., 297, 302, 318
Learning, definition of, 31
Learning-performance distinction, 13–14, 19
Leonard, J. A., 298, 318
Lewis, D., 220–223, 241
Lindley, R. H., 128, 129, 148, 149
Lloyd, K. E., 201, 204, 210
Lockhart, A., 238, 242
Loess, H., 115, 136, 143–145, 148, 228, 229, 241
Lorente De Nó, R., 12, 20
Lorge, I., 119, 149, 154, 167, 171, 177, 190, 211, 250, 275
Luh, C. W., 252–255, 273

McAllister, Dorothy E., 221–223, 241, 269, 273
McBurney, Judith, 145, 148
MacDougall, R., 252, 273
McGeoch, J. A., 18–20, 24, 25, 46, 61, 62, 65, 68, 72, 73, 99
McGovern, Jean B., 63, 99
McKinney, F., 259–261, 273
McNeill, D., 284, 317
McNulty, J. A., 127, 148, 172, 175, 176
Madden, Marian S., 82, 99
Mancall, E. L., 47
Mandler, G., 95, 98
Marion, R., 240
Marshall, G. R., 78, 99, 164–166, 173
Marston, A. R., 298, 319
Martin, E., 85, 99
Martin, R. B., 88, 96, 100
Mediation, chaining paradigms, 95–96
  natural language, 86–97, 125–128, 131–133, 157, 196–201, 204, 207–208, 304–305
  training of, 134–136
Melton, A. W., 5, 6, 38, 39, 46, 61, 62, 73, 100, 112, 133, 148, 221, 230, 238, 241
Memory, brain locus of, 4, 32–37
  compartments of, 37–44, 309–315
  definition of, 9–10
  dual conception of, 38–44
  long-term, capacity of, 39, 137
    definition of, 38

Memory, long-term, inhibition, proactive, effects of, 187–196
retroactive, effects of, 182–
186
interference, effects of, 181–196,
205
mediation, effects of, 196–201,
204, 207–208
methodological problems of,
208, 237–239
for motor responses, 230–237
practice, effects of, 38, 39, 192–
194
motivational influences, 14–17
permanency of, 28–37, 308–309
short-term, capacity of, 39, 130–
136, 137
chunk as unit of, 130–136
definition of, 38, 136–138
inhibition, proactive, effects of,
113–116, 126–127, 143–144
retroactive, effects of, 113,
121–123
interference, effects of, 39–41,
113–123, 126
mediation, effects of, 125–128,
130–136
methodological problems of,
139–145, 237–239
for motor responses, 225–230,
307–308, 311
physiological evidence, 41–44
practice, effects of, 38, 39, 109–
112
retention-interval effects, 107–
109
span of, 130
viewpoints of learning theory, 30
work inhibition influences, 17–18
Memory trace, definition of, 10, 11–
12
Memory trace hypothesis, 264–265,
267–271, 309
Mengelkoch, R. F., 230, 235, 241
Miller, A., 127
Miller, G. A., 39, 46, 131, 134–136,
148, 158, 167–172, 175–177
Miller, N. E., 269, 273
Milner, B., 41, 43, 46, 105, 137,
148
Minami, H., 186, 210
Mink, W. D., 154, 162, 163, 176
Modified free recall (MFR), 63, 65,
74, 90
modification of (MMFR), 65, 74

Montague, W. E., 88–91, 93, 96, 97,
100, 125, 126, 129, 138, 148,
197–201, 204, 207, 210, 306,
319
Morgan, C. H., 297
Morgan, R. L., 78, 79, 100
Morrison, M., 15, 16, 20
Mowrer, O. H., 266, 273, 286, 287,
319
Muller, D. G., 246, 268, 272
Murdock, B. B., Jr., 109, 112, 133,
148, 246, 273
Myers, G. C., 252, 273

Nagel, E., 25, 46, 230, 240
Naylor, J. C., 215, 241
Nedler, S. E., 128, 148
Neimark, Edith, 113, 127, 148
Neumann, Eva, 235, 236, 240, 241
Newman, E. B., 183, 210
Noble, C. E., 78, 100, 197, 210, 249–
251, 265, 273, 287, 319
Noble, M., 236, 238, 242
Nodine, C. F., 318
Norman, D. A., 121, 122, 136, 149,
307, 319
Noyd, D. E., 99

O'Kelly, L. I., 15, 19
Oseas, L., 201, 210
Osgood, C. E., 5, 6, 24, 25, 40, 46,
77, 80–85, 100, 201, 210

Parker, J. F., Jr., 230–232, 240
Patkau, J. E., 171, 172, 175, 177
Pavlov, I. P., 12, 20
Peixotto, Helen E., 257, 258, 262,
274
Penfield, W., 32–37, 41, 46, 47, 309
Perceptual trace, 11–12
Perceptual trace hypothesis, 265–
271, 309, 311–315
Perkins, D. T., 20, 99
Peterson, D. E., 297, 300, 317
Peterson, L. R., 47, 105, 107, 108,
109, 111, 113–116, 127, 136,
144, 148, 187, 210
Peterson, Margaret J., 47, 105, 107–
109, 111, 113–116, 127, 136,
144, 148, 187, 210
Phillips, L. W., 175, 177, 250, 274
Pillsbury, W. B., 105, 148
Platt, J. R., 121, 148

Pollack, I., 112, 149
Posner, M. I., 225, 227–229, 242, 311, 319
Postman, Dorothy L., 246, 252, 263–265, 274
Postman, L., 11, 20, 63, 68, 72–74, 93, 100, 109, 149, 170, 175, 177, 188–193, 195, 196, 207, 210, 211, 234, 242, 246, 249, 252–255, 259–265, 270, 274, 282, 286, 295, 306, 319
Proactive inhibition, amount of practice, effects of, 68–72
context stimuli, effects of, 54–55, 69–71
definition of, 27, 52–57
in motor behavior, 224–225
in paired-associate learning, 68–70
in prose passages, 71–72
in recognition, 257–258
semantic similarity, effects of, 78–80
in serial learning, 68
in short-term memory, 113–116
Psychoanalysis, 30–31
Puff, C. R., 157, 176
Purdy, B. J., 238, 242

Ranyard, R., 54, 71, 99
Rau, Lucy, 246, 252–255, 264, 274
Recall, definition of, 10
free recall, clustering, effects of, 153–167
definition of, 105–107, 153
vis-à-vis recognition, 251–257, 309
serial recall, definition of, 105–106
verbal model of, 280–285
revised, 285–295
Recognition, definition of, 10, 245
and familiarity, 249–251
methods of, 245–246
perceptual trace hypothesis of, 265–271
and recall compared, 251–257, 309
of responses, 11, 285–305
feedback paradigm, 291–293
of stimuli, 11, 247–251, 286–287
theories of, 263–271
Reed, H. B., 87, 100, 197, 201–204, 210
Reed, W. G., 215, 241
Reinforcement, empirical, 280–282
subjective, 295–302

Retroactive inhibition, amount of practice, effects of, 72–76
definition of, 27, 55–57
in motor behavior, 220–223
in paired-associate learning, 73–75
in prose passages, 75–76
in recognition, 258–262
semantic similarity, effects of, 80–85
in serial learning, 72–73
in short-term memory, 113, 121–123
Reynolds, B., 18, 19
Richardson, J., 205, 206, 210, 297, 319
Richardson, Patricia, 170, 177
Rickwood, J., 138, 146
Riley, D. A., 68, 72, 73, 100, 250, 274
Roberts, L., 32, 47
Robertson, A. D. J., 12, 19
Rohwer, W. D., Jr., 195, 204, 209
Rosanoff, A. J., 161, 176
Ross, R. T., 20, 99
Russell, R. W., 182, 186, 210
Russell, W. A., 154, 161–163, 176, 177
Ryan, E. D., 238, 242

Saltz, E., 63, 101
Sanders, A. F., 111, 112, 144, 149
Schaub, G. R., 128, 129, 149
Schlosberg, H., 54, 71, 98, 130, 149
Schulz, R. W., 87, 101, 192, 250, 274
Scott, T. H., 183, 211
Selfridge, J. A., 167–172, 177
Sharp, H. C., 170, 177
Sheffield, F. D., 266, 267, 274
Shepard, A. H., 221, 241
Shepard, R. N., 246–248, 250, 251, 257, 258, 260–262, 274
Siipola, Elsa M., 312–314, 319
Similarity, acoustic, 39–41, 116–120
for motor responses, 220–221
semantic, 39–41, 78–80, 80–85, 118–120
Slamecka, N. J., 71, 72, 75, 76, 101
Smith, S., 134, 135
Spence, K. W., 12, 15, 20, 96, 101, 319
Spence, Shirley A., 82, 99, 282
Sperling, G., 116, 130, 131, 149

Spight, J. B., 183, 211
Stark, Karen, 63, 100
Steward, J. R., 164, 176
Stimulus trace, 12
Strong, E. K., Jr., 105, 149, 246, 248, 249, 275
Suedfeld, P., 182, 184, 209
Sutherland, N. S., 248, 256, 262, 267, 272
Swets, J. A., 246, 275
Sylvester, A., 105, 148

Taub, H. A., 318
Taylor, J., 32, 33, 47
Teghtsoonian, Martha, 260, 274
Teghtsoonian, R., 247, 258, 266, 275
Thompson, R., 4, 6
Thorndike, E. L., 24, 47, 119, 149, 154, 167, 171, 177, 190, 211, 250, 275, 281, 319
Thune, L. E., 73, 101
Thysell, R., 250, 274
Tip-of-the-tongue behavior, 284–285, 294, 303–304
Tolman, E. C., 24, 47
Trace decay, definition of, 23–25
  versus interference, 23, 120–123, 227–230, 307–308
Trace transformation, 26–27
Transfer and retroaction surface, 80–85
Trumbo, D., 236–238, 242
Tulving, E., 157, 171, 172, 175, 177

Ulrich, L., 236, 238, 242

Underwood, B. J., 5, 6, 47, 52, 54, 56, 62, 63, 65, 66, 68–70, 72–74, 76, 78, 79, 84, 86–88, 94, 97, 99–101, 109, 113–115, 126, 136, 139, 142–144, 147, 149, 158–160, 173, 177, 181, 187, 188, 189–196, 201, 204, 207–209, 211, 224, 228–230, 234, 235, 238, 240–242, 254, 255, 257, 258, 273, 275, 306, 319

Vanderplas, J. M., 268, 275
Van Laer, J., 297, 302, 318
Van Ormer, E. B., 183, 211
Vernon, J. A., 182, 184, 209, 211
Victor, M., 41, 47
Voss, J. F., 170, 177, 230, 240

Walker, A. E., 41, 47
Walker, E. L., 15, 16, 20
Waugh, Nancy C., 121, 122, 136, 149, 307, 319
Weiner, B., 14, 15, 16, 20
Weinheimer, S., 148
Weiskrantz, L., 43, 47
Wheaton, J. L., 184, 211
Whitmarsh, G. A., 155, 176
Wickelgren, W. A., 40, 48, 86, 101, 117–119, 149
Wickens, D. D., 115, 149
Wimer, R., 52, 102
Woods, Elizabeth L., 265, 275
Woodworth, R. S., 39, 48, 130, 149

Zeaman, D., 298–300, 317